DINING ETHNIC AROUND PUGET SOUND

By Steve & Mary Taylor

POVERTY BAY PUBLISHING

"I look upon it, that he who does not mind his belly will hardly mind anything else."

Samuel Johnson

• •

To Mel Matteson and Greg Walters, for their boundless enthusiasm, support and good humor, our special thanks.

Published by: *Poverty Bay Publishing Co.*
                     529 S.W. 294th Street
                     Federal Way, WA 98023

Cover Design by: *Greg Walters Design*
                     (206) 362-1310

Printed in the United States of America
First Edition, 1993

ISBN # 0-936528-02-8

Contents

Southern Europe

Dining Ethnic Around Puget Sound   v

Africa, the Middle East and India

The Americas

Appendix

Introduction

It sounded simple enough. "Why don't we do an ethnic cookbook, and get the recipes from the best ethnic restaurants around Seattle?" my wife, Mary, suggested. Prior book projects we'd done had dealt with restaurants, too, but more as guidebooks. This would clearly be primarily a cookbook, but with recognition of the contributing restaurants, and a brief description of each.

But there was more to the idea. "What if," she continued, "we made this a win-win situation, by earmarking a share of the proceeds for Northwest Harvest?" Feeding the hungry was, we knew, a continuing problem of huge proportions, but in addition, there was something - well, *right* - for a book about enjoyable eating to benefit people for whom just getting *enough* to eat was a daily challenge. A meeting with Northwest Harvest was held, they liked the idea and an agreement was reached.

Now, how to choose the restaurants? Our own experience would give us a start, but we needed to cover far more territory than one couple reasonably could. Thus the aid of friends was secured, opinions of others were sought and recent reviews were read in an effort to find the best restaurants in each of the ethnic cuisines. Once found, they needed to be contacted. A letter was drafted and mailed to the restaurants we'd chosen, and we waited expectantly for the anticipated flood of return mail.

The flood turned out to be a trickle. The restaurants that did respond promptly sent beautiful recipes and were very positive about the project, but the lack of response from so many puzzled and worried us. After all, we reasoned, there's no cost of any kind, and to be chosen to be included in a really first-class book, and even to support a good cause - why *wouldn't* a restaurant respond to our letter?

Many reasons, it turned out. First and most obvious, most restaurants - like the rest of us - get tons of junk mail. If they don't recognize the name of the sender, they assume it's just more junk mail, and out it goes.

Another reason was the fact that for many ethnic restauranteurs, English is their second language. Translating our letter was, for some, a real challenge.

There was one more important reason: the restaurant business is a totally crazy business. Every day brings some new emergency that has to be dealt with *right now:* the head waiter calls in sick, the freezer goes on the blink, the expected delivery of lamb doesn't arrive (and it's your daily special). We began to get an insider's view of the business, and came to realize that the challenges and obstacles restauranteurs overcome routinely every day would drive most of us nuts. So, for many restaurants, the problem was in finding the time to craft a couple of recipes, rather than any reluctance to do so.

It should be pointed out here that cooking in a restaurant is vastly different from cooking at home. First, of course, is the matter of scale. While you and we may make up dishes for four or six people, restaurants routinely make them for ten times that number. Added to the difficulties of downsizing complex recipes is the difference in techniques; good restaurant chefs frequently cook to taste, intuitively and from long experience, with no precise measurements other than "a handful of this" and "two handfuls of that." Even though the recipes herein are frequently not from the restaurants' regular menus, they are representative of each restaurant's style, and translating them into home-sized recipes was no small feat.

The restaurants you'll find in this book are, we believe, the cream of the ethnic crop: the best you'll find in the Puget Sound region. At that, they are also a diverse group, ranging from tiny, small town cafes to slick, bustling night spots in the big city. The common denominator is a reputation for quality dining. Each restaurant contributed at least one recipe. We initially asked for two, with the idea that we would choose one from the two submitted. That didn't work; we found each of the recipes interesting, and choosing too difficult. Thus, in most cases, if the restaurant provided us with the requested two recipes, we included both. Some recipes are "classics" - dishes you might expect to find at any quality restaurant, but with a special technique or ingredient that makes the recipe unique to the restaurant that submitted it. Other recipes were developed and perfected by the submitting restaurant. In either case, we believe that all the recipes are original, as submitted by each of the restaurants; however, since they were not developed by us, we cannot guarantee their originality.

You will find that a few recipes are for the same dish. For example, there are three for the uniquely Italian dish called polenta, and three for the dessert tiramisu. On closer examination, however, you'll find that each recipe is quite different, each is interesting in its own right and worthy of a try at home. Some of the recipes are quite simple, while others are complex. They are pretty much as they were submitted to us, although we've edited for clarity and consistency to present them in a simple, uniform format, with ingredients shown in the order you'll use them and instructions in a concise, step-by-step chronology.

Ingredients for some ethnic dishes can be hard to find, so we've included a Sources section that will provide you with some good places to look for special ingredients. Many of these sources were suggested by the restaurants themselves, and in a few cases *are* the restaurants, when they import specialized ingredients not commercially available elsewhere.

We've also provided a detailed Glossary to help you decipher words that may be unfamiliar or confusing. Here, too, the restaurants helped with definitions. Many others were found in our own files, source books in libraries, and in conversations with specialty importers.

Lastly, we should discuss briefly what ethnic meant to us, and how we came to organize the restaurants and recipes into the order in which you'll find them. To us, ethnic cuisine means any non-mainstream American cuisine. Cajun and Creole, for example, can be considered just as ethnic as Vietnamese and Thai. Some of the cuisines we've included, such as Italian, Mexican and Chinese, may seem too "common" to be singled out as ethnic. However, there is a vast difference between, for example, the offerings of the Italian restaurants included here and the standard "spaghetti and meat balls" some people still think of when they think Italian. We set out to choose restaurants that serve special food, and that meant that Americanized versions of dishes with ethnic origins in their distant past were not part of the program.

Classifying the restaurants and their cuisines was perhaps the trickiest decision of all. Many restaurants today practice a style of cooking that ignores borders, and sometimes traditional rules as well. Thus we have eclectic styles of cooking such as "Euro-Asian" that borrow aspects of several cuisines. Is this truly ethnic? Some may quibble, but we thought so.

Other restaurants offer two or more very distinct styles of cuisine. In itself, this is nothing new. Chinese restaurants, particularly neighborhood ones, have offered American food for as long as most of us can remember. Some of the new pairings, however, are very different; Cajun and Chinese, as but one example. There is also the problem of one word meaning different things to different people. For instance, the term "Mediterranean" in some cases really means the north shore of the Mediterranean, especially Italy, but in other cases has more of a Middle Eastern connotation.

We finally concluded that no system for classification could be perfect, and rather than having many tight, narrowly-defined classifications (and where do we draw the lines? Should all Italian restaurants be classified together, or should we separate them into northern and southern regions?), we came up with the five sections you'll find here, in a kind of geographical order that starts in northern Europe and moves generally eastward.

There you have it. We hope you will enjoy our book for years to come and in several different ways. First, as a kind of introduction to some wonderful restaurants for those times when only dining "out" will do. Second, as a cookbook that we hope will broaden your culinary horizons a bit and provide you with some interesting new ideas to try at home. Last, as another way of supporting Northwest Harvest in their efforts to feed the hungry, a cause we can all support.

Steve and Mary Taylor

Northern
Europe

Cafe 196

Hotel International, 5621 - 196th Street S.W., Lynnwood. Phone 771-1777. Open for breakfast Monday through Friday, 6:30 to 10:30 A.M.; Saturday, 7:30 to 11:30 A.M.; Sunday brunch, 7:30 A.M. to 1:00 P.M.; open for lunch Monday through Friday, 11:00 A.M. to 2:00 P.M.; open for dinner Monday through Thursday, 5:00 to 10:00 P.M.; Friday and Saturday, 5:00 to 11:00 P.M.; Sunday, 5:00 to 9:00 P.M.

Traditional labels fail us when traditions are broken, or at least dismantled and re-assembled in new and unique ways. Cafe 196 calls its cuisine Euro-Asian, and indeed there are obvious elements of these two diverse culinary schools; the sauces are along the lines of nouvelle cuisine, but the presentation is more Oriental, and the ingredients are primarily Northwest. Whatever it should be called, the result is pleasing to the eye and the palate, prepared under the supervision of executive chef Thomas Buccarelli.

• •

Pollo del Pesto Fettucine

4 8-ounce boneless chicken breasts
1/2 cup plus 1/2 cup Pesto Sauce (recipe follows)
Olive oil for seasoning the grill or barbecue
2 tablespoons pure olive oil
4 tablespoons chopped garlic
3 tablespoons chopped basil
2 tablespoons chopped Italian parsley
1 cup white wine
1-1/2 cups whipping cream
1/2 cup plus 3 tablespoons Parmigiano Reggiano cheese
1 pound cooked fettucine

Brush chicken breasts with 1/2 cup Pesto Sauce. Let stand 10 minutes. Brush grill preheated to medium with olive oil. Place chicken breasts on grill, skin side down. Cook about 5 minutes. Turn chicken over. Complete cooking until just done. Chicken should have a light crust. Remove and place in a warmed oven.

Heat a heavy skillet to medium heat. Add 2 tablespoons olive oil, garlic, basil and Italian parsley. Pan roast herbs just until golden brown. Add wine. Reduce by two-thirds. Add cream and reduce by half. Add remaining 1/2 cup of Pesto Sauce. Blend in 1/2 cup cheese. Turn to low heat. Let sauce thicken, about 3 minutes. Toss fettucine in pan. Coat fully with sauce.

Remove chicken from oven. Slice into strips.

Place pasta on 4 plates, reserving some sauce. Top with chicken and remaining sauce. Garnish with remaining cheese.

Chef Thomas recommends a full white wine, such as Montevina Chardonnay, with this pasta dish. Serves 4.

PESTO SAUCE:
1 cup chopped basil
1/2 cup fresh grated
    Parmigiano Reggiano
1/4 cup chopped, roasted pine
    nuts
1/4 cup chopped garlic
1/2 cup pure olive oil

Combine basil, cheese, pine nuts and garlic. Cover with layer of olive oil. Refrigerate.

• •

Sautéed Soft Shell Crab Salad

1 cup all-purpose flour
1 teaspoon cayenne pepper
1 teaspoon salt
1 teaspoon fresh oregano
1 teaspoon paprika
1 teaspoon garlic powder
1 teaspoon onion powder
1 teaspoon fresh thyme
4 soft shell crabs, about 4 inches
    across in width
1/2 cup pure olive oil
3 tablespoons salted butter
3 tablespoons chopped garlic
3 tablespoons chopped fresh
    basil
1 tablespoon chopped fresh
    Italian parsley
1 cup white wine
Juice of 1 lemon
1 tablespoon capers
1/2 pound cooked linguini
1/4 pound wild mixed greens
1 cup Parmigiano Reggiano
Homemade garlic croutons
8 lemon wedges

Mix flour with cayenne, salt, oregano, paprika, garlic, onion and thyme. Set aside.

Cut each crab into 6 pieces using a very sharp knife. Coat crab thoroughly with flour mixture.

Place oil in large, heavy skillet over high heat. Add crab. Sauté until crab is golden brown and crisp, being careful not to burn. Remove pan from heat. Drain off excess oil, leaving the seasoning residue in the pan. Add butter. Return to medium heat. Add garlic, basil and parsley. Roast until golden, all the while turning the crab. Add the wine. Simmer 2 minutes. Add lemon juice. Simmer 1 minute. Add capers. Let sauce thicken on low heat about 2-3 minutes. Toss pasta into pan. Coat well with sauce.

Rim 4 large plates with wild mixed greens. Portion pasta evenly in the center of each plate. Spoon crab and sauce over pasta and greens. Top with cheese and croutons. Place 2 lemon wedges on each salad plate.

A fruity red, such as a Columbia Merlot, is recommended by chef Thomas to accompany this salad.

Serves 4.

• •

du jour

1919 First Avenue, Seattle. Phone 441-3354. Open Monday through Friday, 7:00 A.M. to 6:00 P.M.; Saturday, 8:00 A.M. to 5:00 P.M; closed Sunday.

Step off First Avenue into a bright and cheery restaurant with white table linens and a spectacular view of Elliot Bay and the Olympics. The service is cafeteria style, but the food is assuredly not. You'll find a contemporary European, and highly varied menu, changing daily; pastas, poultry, hearty soups, salads, desserts, and a nice surprise: imported and local truffles. And by the way: "du jour" is never capitalized...at least, not here!

• •

Pacific Salmon with Pinot Noir/Currant Sauce

2 cups Oregon Pinot Noir
1/4 cup chopped shallots
1/4 cup fresh or dried currants
1/4 pound sweet butter, cut into
    1/2 inch cubes
4 6-ounce salmon filets,
    trimmed and boned
Drawn butter
Salt and pepper, to taste
Currant sprigs
Lemon zest

Prepare the sauce. Combine Pinot Noir and shallots in a small stainless steel or glass sauce pan. Bring to a boil. Reduce liquid to 1/2 cup. Remove from heat. Add currants. Allow to sit for 15 minutes. Over a low heat, whisk in butter, one piece at a time, until incorporated.

Prepare the salmon. Preheat oven to 400°. In a medium size skillet, heat butter over high temperature. Crack fresh pepper onto one side of salmon filets and sprinkle with salt. Place filets, peppered side down, in heated skillet. Sauté 1 minute. Remove to a baking dish lined with parchment paper. Bake 8-10 minutes, or until just firm.

To serve, divide the sauce among 4 warm plates. Top each with salmon filet. Garnish with sprig of fresh currant and lemon zest.

Owner Gretchen Smyth recommends an Oregon or Washington Pinot Noir with this presentation.

Serves 4.

• •

Moroccan Eggplant Salad

3 cloves of garlic, peeled
1/2 teaspoon salt
1/4 teaspoon cayenne pepper
2 teaspoons cumin
1/2 teaspoon ground ginger
2 tablespoons red wine vinegar
1/2 cup olive oil
2 large eggplants, diced and cut
    into 1 inch cubes
1 tablespoon kosher salt
1/2 cup olive oil
1 cup Kalamata olives, rinsed
4 tomatoes, seeded, diced into
    1/2 inch cubes
1/2 cup chopped green onions
1/4 cup coarsely chopped
    parsley
1/4 cup chopped cilantro

Prepare the dressing by grinding the garlic and salt in a food processor. Add the cayenne pepper, cumin, ginger, vinegar and oil. Pulse lightly until blended. Set aside while preparing salad.

Toss eggplant with salt. Set aside and allow to drain for 30 minutes. Blot dry. Lightly toss with oil. Place on a baking sheet in a single layer. Roast in 400° oven 30-40 minutes, or until lightly browned. Allow to cool 30 minutes.

In a large mixing bowl, combine the olives, tomatoes, green onions, parsley and cilantro with the cooled eggplant. Mix lightly with hands. Pour dressing over the salad. Toss again with hands until all pieces are evenly coated.

This dish is a perfect summer side dish for grilled lamb chops or pork roast, du jour suggests.

Serves 4-6.

Labuznik

1924 First Avenue, Seattle. Phone 441-8899. Open Tuesday through Saturday, 4:30 P.M. to midnight; closed Sunday and Monday.

Consistently included at or very near the top of everyone's list of Seattle's finest restaurants - ethnic or otherwise - Labuznik serves up a tantalizing array of delectables drawn from the culinary traditions of Czechoslovakia. The cuisine is unique, but borrows enough from those of neighboring countries so that it isn't wholly unfamiliar. Under owner Peter Cipra's watchful eye, Labuznik has developed a reputation for consistency and attention to even the smallest details; the food is outstanding.

• •

Pork Tenderloin, Prague Style

1 pork tenderloin
Garlic
Dijon mustard
Salt and pepper, to taste
1 slice of ham, julienne cut
2-3 mushrooms, sliced
2 green onions, sliced
1 teaspoon sour cream
1 teaspoon lemon juice
1 dill pickle

Rub tenderloin with garlic and mustard. Season with salt and pepper. Roast at 375-400° for 12-15 minutes. Don't roast too long or the meat will be dry.

Sauté ham, mushrooms and green onions. Add 1 teaspoon mustard, sour cream and lemon juice.

Slice roasted tenderloin. Top with sautéed ingredients. Garnish with pickle. Serve with potatoes, rice, pasta or dumplings, but that is another recipe!

Serves 3-4.

• •

Sauerkraut Soup

1 onion, coarsely diced
1/4 pound beef chuck roast, cut
    into 1/3 inch cubes
1 teaspoon caraway seeds
Pepper flakes
Salt and pepper, to taste
1 link, about 1/4 pound, farmer
    or Polish sausage, cut into
    1/4 inch rounds, then
    quartered
3 tablespoons Hungarian
    paprika
4 medium potatoes, diced
2 carrots, julienne cut
2 14-1/2 ounce cans beef
    bouillon or home stock, if
    available
1-1/2 to 2 cups sauerkraut,
    chopped if pieces are longer
    than 2 to 2-1/2 inches
1/2 teaspoon marjoram
1 tablespoon vinegar
Sour cream

Sauté onion until light brown. Add beef, caraway seeds, pepper flakes, salt and pepper. Cook until meat is lightly brown. Add sausage. Sauté approximately 5 minutes. Turn off heat. Add paprika. Very important: Do not burn paprika or a bitter taste will result. Turn heat on. Simmer, stirring 2 minutes. Add potatoes and carrots, stirring ingredients together. Add stock, as much as 2 cans, depending on personal choice of consistency. Add sauerkraut when ingredients are tender. Bring to boil. Simmer 5 minutes. Add marjoram and vinegar. Stir. Serve garnished with a dollop of sour cream.

Serves 2-4.

Rover's

2808 E. Madison Street, Seattle. Phone 325-7442. Open Tuesday through Saturday, 5:30 to 9:30 P.M. (last seating); closed Sunday and Monday.

In six years, owner/chef Thierry Rautureau has firmly established Rover's at the very highest level of restaurants anywhere in the Northwest. A native of the Muscadet region of France, Rautureau brings the rich traditions of classic French cuisine into a loving marriage with the finest local ingredients, in combinations that at times may seem unorthodox but are always flawlessly executed. A nominee for the 1993 James Beard Award as well as "Chef of the Year" by Chefs in America, Rautureau has earned uniformly excellent reviews from numerous publications. Rover's is housed in a converted older home in the Madison Valley area, but the interior is sophisticated, intimate, and romantic, and the food is sensational.

• •

King Salmon Tournedos with Puget Sound Sea Urchin Sauce

24 ounce king salmon filet
2 tablespoons extra virgin olive
    oil
8 ounces Noilly Prat dry
    vermouth
3 shallots, peeled
3 ounces veal stock
10 ounces unsalted butter
Salt and pepper, to taste
3 ounces sea urchin roe

Shape salmon side into a loin. Tie, spaced 1 inch apart.

Put the olive oil in a hot sauté pan. Sear the tournedos on both sides. Finish cooking in a 375° oven about 3-4 minutes.

In a sauce pan, bring vermouth and shallots to boil. Reduce by two-thirds. Add veal stock. Reduce again by two-thirds. Slowly whisk in butter, little by little. Season with salt and pepper. Strain through a sieve into a blender. Add sea urchin. Blend fast until sauce becomes smooth. Serve sauce warm around salmon.

Serves 2-4.

• •

Puget Sound Seafood Bisque

1/2 cup diced onions
1/4 cup diced celery
1/4 cup diced leeks
1 tablespoon butter
1 bay leaf
1 teaspoon fresh thyme
4 black peppercorns
1/2 teaspoon fennel seed
1 teaspoon tarragon
3/4 cup dry vermouth
12 Penn Cove mussels
1 cup mussel juice (from
   cooking the mussels)
4 cups fish stock
1 cup heavy cream
4 ounces butter
Salt and pepper, to taste
6 sea urchin roe
6 Dungeness crab legs
6 Olympia oysters, diced small
Fresh chervil, chopped

Sweat onions, celery and leeks in melted butter until onions are soft. Add herbs and continue to sweat. Deglaze with vermouth. Reduce by two-thirds. Add mussels. Cook until shells open. Put mussels on the side. Add fish stock to remaining liquid. Reduce by one-third. Finish the bisque by adding cream, butter, salt and pepper. Pass through a sieve. Blend sea urchin roe in the bisque. Serve hot in a bowl with mussels, crab meat, oysters, and chervil.

Serves 6.

Charles at Smugglers Cove

8340 - 53rd Avenue West, Mukilteo. Phone 347-2700. Open Tuesday through Sunday for lunch, 11:30 A.M. to 2:00 P.M., and for dinner, 5:30 to 10:00 P.M.

An historic old manor house is now the unique and charming home of a fine restaurant. And the old mansion has a past; there are exciting tales of bootlegging and smuggling in the 1930's, which owners Claude Faure and Janet Kingman often share with guests. The excitement today lies primarily in the traditional French cuisine, which is consistently excellent, and the ambience, which is delightfully romantic.

• •

Poulet aux Crevettes

2 boneless, skinless chicken breasts
Salt and pepper, to taste
1 teaspoon flour
1 tablespoon butter
1 shallot, minced
1 clove of garlic, minced
1/4 cup diced tomatoes
6 prawns
1/4 cup dry white wine
1/4 cup heavy cream
Parsley

Lightly season chicken breasts with salt and pepper. Sprinkle with flour on both sides. Sauté in a casserole with butter over fairly high heat until the chicken is golden on both sides. Drain the casserole of all fat. Add shallot, garlic, tomatoes, prawns, wine and cream. Season with salt and pepper. Place in 375° oven 10 minutes. Sprinkle with parsley. Serve very hot.
Serves 2.

• •

Chocolate Mousse

16 ounces sweet cooking chocolate
1/2 cup cream
1/2 teaspoon vanilla
1/2 teaspoon coffee extract
1/2 teaspoon Kahlua
1-1/2 cups heavy cream, whipped

Melt the chocolate in the cream. Add vanilla and coffee extract. At serving time, beat in Kahlua and whipped cream.
Serves 4-6.

• •

Janot's Bistro

419 Commercial Avenue, Anacortes. Phone 299-9163. Open daily for lunch, 11:30 A.M. to 2:30 P.M.; open daily for dinner, 5:30 to 9:30 P.M.

Lest you imagine that classic French cuisine might be unavailable in Anacortes, Janot's stands ready to convince you otherwise. As you would expect, the entrées incorporate the plentiful and varied fresh seafoods, meat and produce available locally and are served in simple but elegant fashion.

• •

Grilled Salmon in Sorrel Sauce

1 bunch of sorrel, cleaned,
   stemmed and chopped
1/2 teaspoon minced shallots
1 ounce butter
2 ounces white wine
1 cup whipping cream
Pinch of salt
Pinch of white pepper
2 salmon steaks or filets

   Cook sorrel and shallots in a sauce pan with butter, mashing the sorrel with a whip or spoon.

Add white wine and reduce by half. Add the cream and reduce by half again, or until sauce consistency. Strain sauce through a fine sieve, pressing as much of the pulp through as possible. Season with salt and pepper.
   Grill salmon. Place sauce on the plate and salmon on top. Serve with fresh seasonal vegetables of your choice.
   Serves 2.

• •

Steamer Clams with Curry and Basil

1 pound Manila clams, small,
   washed and cleaned well
1 teaspoon chopped shallots
1 teaspoon chopped garlic
1 teaspoon curry powder
1 teaspoon fresh basil, fine
   julienne cut
1/4 ounce leek, fine julienne cut
1/4 ounce carrot, fine julienne cut

1/4 ounce celery, fine julienne cut
1 cup white wine
Salt and pepper, to taste

   Place all ingredients in a sauce pot with a lid. Bring to a boil and simmer until clams open. Place in bowl and serve immediately.
   Serves 2.

• •

Gerard's Relais de Lyon

17121 Bothell Way N.E., Bothell. Phone 486-9227. Open Tuesday through Saturday, 5:00 to 9:00 P.M.; closed Sunday and Monday.

Gerard's Relais de Lyon is located on a wooded acre in the Seattle suburbs, but it feels like a lot further away; the hustle and bustle of the city quickly become distant memories. The lovely old home which houses the restaurant is comfortable, and the small, intimate dining rooms are elegant and beautifully romantic. The cuisine is classic French, prepared under the watchful eye of the gracious owner, Gerard Parrat, and is among the best you will find anywhere. The service, as you might expect, is impeccable.

• •

Salmon with Basil Sauce

4 tablespoons minced shallots
1 tablespoon butter
4 tablespoons chopped basil
3 ounces dry white wine
1 ounce Pernod
1/2 cup fish stock
1/2 cup heavy cream
1 tablespoon beurre manie
Salt and pepper, to taste
3 salmon filets, baked

Sauté the shallots in butter until soft. Add basil, white wine and Pernod; reduce by half. Add fish stock and reduce by half again. Add the cream and reduce by two-thirds. Add beurre manie and allow to thicken briefly. Season with salt and pepper. Serve sauce over salmon filets.
Serves 3.

• •

Soupe de Poisson
(Fish Soup)

2 medium carrots
2 stalks of celery
1 medium onion
2 tablespoons olive oil
Pinch of saffron
1/2 cup white wine
1 quart fish stock
1 medium potato
1 clove of garlic
Salt and pepper, to taste
2 teaspoons chervil or chives
Croutons rubbed with garlic

Chop carrots, celery and onion in food processor.

Sauté vegetables in olive oil. Add saffron and continue to sauté. Add wine and cook about 3 minutes. Add fish stock and boil until vegetables are tender.

Boil potato in separate pan until cooked. Process with garlic clove to form a paste.

Mix paste slowly into soup, season with salt and pepper, and bring to a boil. Pour into soup tureen. Sprinkle chervil or chives and croutons on top.

Serves 4.

Kasteel Franssen

5861 State Route 20, Oak Harbor (Whidbey Island). Phone 675-0724. Open during winter Monday through Saturday, 5:00 P.M. to closing. Open during summer every day, 5:00 P.M. to closing.

Kasteel Franssen has become a Whidbey Island landmark. Standing at the entrance to Oak Harbor, this unique restaurant is designed after castles in the south of Holland. The food is Continental, leaning toward the French, but the menu wouldn't be complete without a Dutch entrée, for which co-owner and chef Scott Fraser has graciously provided the recipe.

• •

Kasteel Franssen Dutch Biefstuk

2-1/4 pounds trimmed beef
    tenderloin, cut into
    12 3-ounce portions
2 teaspoons salt
1 teaspoon black pepper
2 tablespoons butter
1 tablespoon oil
1/3 cup brandy
2 tablespoons Dijon mustard
1 cup cream

Season beef with salt and pepper. Heat large sauté pan. Add butter and oil. Cook filets until done. Transfer to serving dish and keep warm.

Pour off excess fat and return pan to heat. Add brandy and flame off alcohol. Add mustard and cream, and whisk while reducing to desired consistency. Season to taste. Pour sauce over meat pieces.

Serves 6.

• •

Grilled Swordfish with Whidbey Island Loganberry Liqueur Sauce

6 ounces liquid honey
1 cup white wine vinegar
1 cup fresh or frozen
    loganberries (blackberries
    or raspberries may be
    substituted)
1/2 cup Whidbey's Liqueur
1 cup unsalted butter, cubed
6 8-ounce swordfish filets

Prepare sauce. In a heavy sauce pan, bring honey to a boil. Reduce until it becomes a hazelnut color. Add vinegar and berries. Reduce by one-third. Add liqueur and reduce until 1 cup of liquid remains. Whisk in cold butter cubes, a little at a time, over medium heat, until incorporated. Keep warm on very low heat, stirring occasionally.

Grill fish and present with sauce underneath or on the side.

Chef Fraser notes that this sauce goes well with many other types of fish and game birds.

Serves 6.

Crêpe de Paris

1333 - 5th Avenue (Rainier Square), Seattle. Phone 623-4111. Open Monday through Wednesday, 11:00 A.M. to 9:00 P.M.; Thursday through Saturday, 11:00 A.M. to 10:00 P.M.; closed Sunday (except for private parties).

The Crêpe de Paris is perennially one of Seattle's favorite places, serving fine food with a French flair, and dinner theatre performances that have been the talk of the town (one recent show, 'Waiter, there's a slug in my latté', was a spoof of Seattle's foibles and - in addition to fine reviews - was great fun). Yes, there are crêpes, and any number of other good things to eat, some more French than others, but all presented with style. Owner Annie Agostini (a native of southern France) is such a warm and gracious hostess, it is hard to imagine any customer leaving dissatisfied.

• •

Gratin of Apricots with Rum

6 ounces white bread, about 5
  slices
1 pint milk
6 ounces sugar
4 eggs
8 cooked apricots, puréed
1 cup raisins
5 teaspoons rum
3 teaspoons vanilla
5 ounces butter, softened
Fresh fruits
Chocolate sauce

Cut bread into small pieces. Allow to soak overnight in the milk and sugar.

Whip the eggs. Add bread mixture, apricots, raisins, rum, vanilla and butter. Pour into a buttered mold. Bake in 450° oven 30 minutes. Let cool 1 hour. Unmold on serving dish. Decorate with fresh fruits and chocolate sauce.

Serves 6.

• •

Roast Duck with Honey and Kumquats

5-6 pound roasting duck
2 teaspoons honey
1/4 cup water
1 tablespoon brandy
1 teaspoon salt
1/2 teaspoon fresh ground
    pepper
1/2 pound kumquats
1/4 cup olive oil
2 tablespoons chopped shallots
2 tablespoons sugar
1/4 cup red wine vinegar
1/2 cup red wine
2 cups brown chicken stock
4 tablespoons butter

Prepare the duck the day before by removing the neck, giblet and any excess fat in the cavity. Rinse thoroughly, inside and out, under cold, running water. Combine the honey, water, brandy, salt and pepper in a small bowl. Brush evenly over duck. Set duck in refrigerator and leave, uncovered, until the next day. Roast in a 400° oven 45 minutes, or until the skin is crisp and meat is medium rare.

Prepare the sauce by blanching the kumquats in boiling water 5 minutes. Heat oil in small sauce pan. Add kumquats, shallots and sugar. Cook a few minutes. Add the remaining ingredients at once. Reduce heat to low. Cook about 10-15 minutes, or until kumquats are tender. Transfer to a food processor and blend until smooth. Finish with butter, salt and pepper to taste.

Carve duck and arrange over the sauce on serving plates. Bon appetit!

Serves 4.

Chez Shea

94 Pike Street, Suite 34, Seattle. Phone 467-9990. Open Tuesday through Sunday, 5:30 to 10:00 P.M.; closed Monday.

A hideaway in the Pike Place Market, Chez Shea looks out over the rooftops of the market at Elliott Bay, and you may need directions to find it. Strictly speaking, Chez Shea is not exactly French; it is more like an eclectic mix of Northwest cuisine with a French influence, along with several other ethnicities for good measure, cooked with originality and flair. The combination works; owner Sandy Shea has created a popular and intriguing restaurant, with something to appeal to any taste.

• •

Blackberry Mousse

1-1/4 pounds fresh blackberries,
    about 5 cups, or
    unsweetened frozen
    berries, thawed
1/2 cup plus 2 tablespoons sugar
2 teaspoons unflavored gelatin
2 tablespoons water
1 egg yolk
1 cup chilled heavy cream
Whipped cream
Mint sprigs
Fresh blackberries

Cook berries and 1/2 cup sugar in heavy, large sauce pan over medium heat until mixture is juicy, stirring occasionally, about 15 minutes. Transfer to processor or blender and purée. Strain to remove seeds.

Meanwhile, sprinkle gelatin over 2 tablespoons water in heavy, small sauce pan. Let stand until softened, about 10 minutes. Stir over low heat just until melted. Whisk gelatin mixture into hot blackberry purée. Refrigerate until cold but not set, stirring occasionally, about 45 minutes.

Whisk egg yolk and remaining sugar in small bowl until thick and pale. Fold into berry mixture. Whip cream in large bowl until soft peaks form. Carefully fold whipped cream into berry mixture. Divide mixture among balloon goblets. Chill until set, about 3 hours (can be prepared 1 day ahead; cover and refrigerate).

Garnish with additional whipped cream, mint sprigs and fresh blackberries, if available.

Serves 6.

• •

Tenderloin of Beef with Gorgonzola Sauce

2 tablespoons peanut oil
6 6 to 8-ounce beef tenderloin
    steaks, each sliced thickly
    and wrapped with a slice of
    bacon
1/4 cup brandy
Caramelized Onions (recipe
    follows)
Gorgonzola Sauce (recipe
    follows)

Heat oil in large cast iron skillet over high heat. Add steaks. Sauté 3-6 minutes on each side, according to desired degree of doneness.

To serve, remove from pan. Drain off fat. Deglaze pan with brandy and add Caramelized Onions. Top each filet with Caramelized Onions and then Gorgonzola Sauce.

Serves 6.

CARAMELIZED ONIONS:
4 tablespoons unsalted butter
2 large Walla Walla sweet
    onions, thinly sliced
4 tablespoons brown sugar

Melt butter in sauce pan over medium heat. Reduce heat. Add onions and brown sugar. Sauté about 25 minutes, until onions become golden brown and caramelized. Set aside.

GORGONZOLA SAUCE:
5 shallots, minced
3 cloves of garlic, minced
3 tablespoons unsalted butter
1 cup Cabernet, Merlot or
    Zinfandel
1 cup beef stock
2 cups crème fraîche
8 ounces Gorgonzola cheese,
    crumbled
Fresh ground black pepper

Sauté shallots and garlic in butter until translucent. Add wine and stock. Cook until reduced by half. Add crème fraîche. Reduce again by half. Lower heat. Add cheese, whisking until cheese is melted and sauce is very smooth. Transfer to food processor or blender and pulse. Return to medium heat. Simmer gently until desired thickness. Add pepper. Keep warm or reheat when ready to serve.

Le Gourmand Restaurant

425 N.W. Market Street, Seattle. Phone 784-3463. Open Thursday through Saturday, 5:30 to 10:00 P.M. (last seating); closed Sunday through Wednesday.

This lovely and intimate French restaurant has been the site of many a memorable meal. Owner Bruce Naftaly is also the chef, and the limited hours the restaurant is open were chosen in part to allow him to devote extreme attention to quality and detail. The results are imaginative and superb. For those looking to improve their own culinary skills, Bruce also conducts cooking classes at the restaurant.

• •

Nettle Soup

1/4 pound yellow Finn potatoes, peeled, cut into small pieces
3 cups chicken stock
1/2 pound stinging nettles
1/2 cup whipping cream
Salt and fresh ground white pepper, to taste
Fresh ground nutmeg
Sprigs of chervil

In non-aluminum soup pot, cook potatoes in stock about 10 minutes, until soft. Add nettles. Gently boil about 5 minutes, until tender. Strain. Purée nettles and potatoes. Return to soup pot with stock. Add cream to proper consistency. Gently simmer 5 minutes. Season to taste with salt, pepper and nutmeg. Serve hot or chilled, garnished with chervil. Serves 4.

• •

Rack of Lamb with Chestnut and Pear Sauce

3 cups dark brown lamb stock
1 pound Seckel pears (may substitute Bosc, Anjou or Bartlett), peeled, cored, cut into small pieces
1/2 cup peeled, chopped chestnuts
1/2 cup whipping cream
3 French-cut racks of lamb
Peanut oil
24 whole chestnuts, peeled
24 Seckel pears, peeled, halved and cored
2 tablespoons poire (eau-de-vie)
Salt and fresh ground black pepper, to taste

Bring stock to simmer in heavy, non-aluminum sauce pan. Add pears and chopped chestnuts. Simmer very gently about 40 minutes, or until chestnuts are soft and liquid has reduced by half. Purée in food processor. Sieve through fine strainer into heavy, non-aluminum sauce pan. Add cream and reduce until sauce-like consistency. Set aside.

Brown lamb racks well on all sides in hot peanut oil. Roast in preheated 500° oven 5 minutes. Add whole chestnuts and halved pears to roasting pan. Continue roasting about 15 minutes, or until an internal temperature of about 125° is reached for medium rare.

Remove lamb, chestnuts and pears from pan. Pour off fat. Set pan over high heat. Deglaze with poire. Strain into sauce. Finish sauce, seasoning with salt and pepper.

Carve racks into chops. Spoon sauce onto plates. Arrange 4 chops on each in pinwheel pattern. Garnish with roasted chestnuts and pears.

Serves 6.

Le Tastevin

19 West Harrison, Seattle. Note: at press time, word came that Le Tastevin had closed.

Farewell, old friend. For many years, Le Tastevin had been among the most respected and well-liked classic French restaurants in the Seattle area. As such, they were invited to - and did - submit recipes for this book. Sadly, word came shortly before publication that Le Tastevin had closed its doors, perhaps forever. While one hopes for a resurrection, either way, we raise our glass in toast to the many fine meals and memorable evenings Le Tastevin provided over the years.

• •

Halibut in Walnut Coating with Vegetable Relish

2 zucchini, cut into 1/4 inch
    pieces
1 Belgian endive, sliced into
    strips
1 red bell pepper, diced
1 medium onion, Walla Walla if
    available, diced
1/2 head of radicchio, sliced
    into strips
1 teaspoon finely chopped fresh
    thyme
2 tablespoons chopped Italian
    parsley
1 tablespoon soy sauce
1 tablespoon balsamic vinegar
2 tablespoons olive oil
Salt and pepper, to taste
6 halibut filets
1/2 cup finely chopped walnuts
1 teaspoon cooking oil
Dab of butter

Toss zucchini, endive, bell pepper, onion, radicchio, thyme and parsley in a bowl with soy sauce, vinegar and oil. Cook on baking sheet in preheated 400° oven, stirring often, just until warmed through, or grill on barbecue. Reserve.

Lightly salt and pepper halibut. Dredge in walnuts.

Heat cooking oil and butter in sauté pan until very hot. Sear one side of halibut about 1 minute, turn and place in oven about 5 minutes, or until fish becomes firm. Halibut will overcook easily, so remove from oven a little early, as the fish will continue cooking while it is hot.

Serve over the vegetable relish.

Serves 6.

• •

Baked Scallops with Roast Apple and Garlic Sauce

Butter
1 Granny Smith apple, seeded,
  peeled and chopped
8 cloves of garlic, chopped
2 shallots, chopped
1 cup white wine
2 cups veal stock
Pinch of salt
16-20 large scallops
Seasoned flour: paprika, thyme,
  cayenne pepper
Splash of brandy
Sautéed apple slices
Sprig of parsley

In a sauté pan, melt 1 tablespoon butter. Add apples, garlic, and shallots. Cook over medium heat, tossing regularly, until apples are golden brown and soft. Add wine and reduce to one-quarter volume. Add stock and reduce by one-half.

Purée in blender until smooth. If sauce is too thick, add a little water. If it is too thin, return to pan and reduce a little more. Finish sauce with salt and 1 teaspoon butter. Keep warm.

Dredge scallops in flour. In a sauté pan, melt a little butter over high heat. Sear scallops, on one side only, until brown. Turn and place in preheated 400° oven 3-4 minutes. Remove from oven, drain off excess oil and flambé with brandy.

Ladle sauce on plates. Arrange 4-5 scallops around sauce. Garnish with apple slices and parsley.

Serves 4 as an appetizer.

Maximilien In The Market

81A Pike Street (Pike Place Market), Seattle. Phone 682-7270. Open Monday through Saturday, 7:30 A.M. to 10:00 P.M.; Sunday, 9:30 A.M. to 4:00 P.M.

A real French market restaurant-cafe, Maximilien offers a changing parade of old favorites and imaginative "plats du jour" created from the abundant fresh fish, meat and produce from the surrounding market. Owner Francois Kissel - a Culinary Olympics gold medalist - and his wife, Julia, have carefully chosen a small but select wine list to accompany the varied menu and offer full bar service, specialty coffees, pastries and homemade desserts as well. There is another element to accompany the meals: a spectacular view of the busy Elliot Bay harbor, the Olympic Mountains in the distance, and lovely sunsets.

• •

Cold Melon Soup

2 cups diced, ripe melon
    (cantaloupe is best)
1 cup beef bouillon
3 cups chicken stock
2 ounces cream sherry
Salt and pepper, to taste
1/2 cup thinly sliced melon
    (different kind for contrast
    of color)
2-3 mint leaves, lightly crushed

In a blender, purée diced melon with beef bouillon. Add chicken broth, sherry and seasonings. Chill.

Serve with thinly sliced melon and mint leaves.

Serves 2-4.

• •

Souffléed Sole Stuffed with Crab and Spinach

3 tablespoons chopped shallots
4 tablespoons unsalted butter,
    divided
1 cup cooked, drained, chopped
    spinach (frozen will do)
1 cup crab meat
1/2 cup fresh grated Parmesan
    cheese
3 eggs
Salt and pepper, to taste
12 large sole filets
1 cup white wine
1/2 cup whipping cream

Sauté shallots in 1 tablespoon butter until golden.

Combine the shallots, spinach, crab meat, cheese, eggs, salt and pepper in a bowl.

Butter a baking dish with 1 tablespoon butter. Lay 6 filets in bottom of dish. Apportion the crab mixture equally in the center of each. Turn up the ends of the filets to prevent the stuffing from running.

Slit the remaining 6 filets through the middle, making a lengthwise opening about 2-1/2 inches long. Cover each filet in the baking dish with one that is slit, keeping the slits open so that the crab mixture shows. They should look like feline eyes!

Pour wine and cream gently over the fish. Cover with foil. Bake 10-12 minutes in preheated 450° oven. When cooked, quickly transfer the fish onto serving dishes or platter. Keep warm.

Pour stock into a sauce pan. Reduce to two-thirds on high heat. Remove from heat. Whisk in the 2 remaining tablespoons of butter. Season to taste and pour over fish. Serve immediately.

Accompany this dish with rice (plain or with chopped nuts), new potatoes, or even buttered noodles suggests owner Kissel.

Serves 6.

Madrona Bistro

1416 - 34th Avenue, Seattle. Phone 328-2987. Open Tuesday through Thursday, 5:30 to 9:30 P.M.; Friday and Saturday, 5:30 to 10:00 P.M.

A handsome old, turn of the century house in Seattle's historic Madrona neighborhood has found an exciting new life as the home of a fine dinner establishment: the Madrona Bistro. Owner Lysle Wilhelmi, together with chef Kris Pearson and sous chef Jean Szeles, feature a cuisine that is southern European, with an emphasis on fresh, seasonal ingredients and homemade pastas, sausages, breads, soups and desserts. Daily fresh fish specials and vegetarian plates are offered. In addition to four private dining rooms, outdoor deck seating is available on those lovely summer evenings when the weather cooperates. The extensive beer and wine list includes Wilridge Cabernet Sauvignon, made in the on-premises winery.

• •

Grilled Ellensburg Lamb Chops with Sun-dried Tomatoes, Kalamata Olives, and Mint Vinaigrette

2 ounces lime juice
2 ounces lemon juice
2 cloves of garlic, chopped
1 teaspoon mint, chopped
12 ounces olive oil
3 ounces sun-dried tomatoes, julienne cut
2 ounces Kalamata olives, julienne cut
16-24 Ellensburg lamb chops
Salt and pepper, to taste
Olive oil
Sprig of mint

Combine the lime and lemon juices with the garlic and mint. Slowly whisk in oil. Add tomatoes and olives. Season to taste. Set aside.

Season chops with salt and pepper. Rub with olive oil. Grill a 3/4 inch thick chop for 3 minutes on each side (or until an internal temperature of 130° is obtained - medium rare).

Serve chops on vinaigrette with roasted new potatoes and seasonal vegetables; garnish with a sprig of mint.

Serves 8.

• •

Roasted Cornish Game Hens
Stuffed with Grape Leaf "Pesto"

16 ounces grape leaves -
   drained, rinsed twice,
   drained again and stems
   removed
2 cups walnuts - blanched 30
   seconds in boiling water to
   remove bitterness; toasted at
   375° for 15-20 minutes
Juice of 2 oranges
2 cloves of garlic, chopped
2 tablespoons fresh chopped
   oregano
1/4 cup feta cheese, drained
1/2 cup olive oil
1/2 cup walnut oil
Salt and pepper, to taste
6 whole Cornish game hens,
   rinsed, seasoned with salt
   and pepper over the skin
   and inside the cavity
Walnut oil
Whole grape leaves, fried

Prepare the pesto. Purée the first 6 ingredients in a food processor, then slowly add the olive and walnut oils to yield a smooth paste. Season to taste with salt and pepper (grape leaves and feta are fairly salty, so start with just a pinch of salt). Set aside.

Loosen skin from hen breast, and, using a spoon or pastry bag, stuff 1-2 tablespoons of pesto under the skin on each side of the hen.

Roast hens 30-40 minutes at 425°, or until juices run clear.

To present, cut hens in half, drizzle with walnut oil and garnish with fried whole grape leaves. Accompany with orzo or cracked wheat and sautéed zucchini.

Serves 6.

Campagne

86 Pine Street, Seattle. Phone 728-2800. Open for lunch Monday through Saturday, 11:30 A.M. to 2:00 P.M.; open for dinner daily, 5:30 to 10:00 P.M.; late night menu available in lounge until midnight.

Intimate and sophisticated, Campagne overlooks the produce stands and flower stalls of Seattle's beloved Pike Place Market from the courtyard of the Inn at the Market. Owner Peter Lewis says his restaurant draws its inspiration from the sun-drenched cuisine of Provence, just the thing for those occasional damp and dreary winter days. Campagne and its chef, Tamara Murphy, have earned critical acclaim and several awards, including the DiRona Award for two consecutive years.

• •

Spot Prawns and Scallops with Citrus

16 large spot prawns, shelled
16 large sea scallops
2 tablespoons olive oil
1/2 cup chopped red or Walla
   Walla onions
1 cup dry white wine
20 peeled grapefruit sections
20 peeled lime sections
20 peeled Satsuma orange or
   tangerine sections
1 cup fresh basil, julienne cut
2 tablespoons butter
Salt and pepper, to taste

In a hot pan, sauté the prawns and scallops in oil about 3 minutes, or until cooked through. Remove to a warm plate.

Add onions to pan for 2-3 minutes, or until translucent. Add wine. Reduce briefly. Add grapefruit, lime and orange sections. Warm through.

Return seafood to pan with basil, butter, salt and pepper. Serves 4.

• •

Provencal Fish Soup with Rouille

FOR THE FUMET:
2 pounds white fish bones
1 onion
1 leek, white part only
1 celery rib
2-1/2 ounces fennel bulb
7 ounces white wine

6 coriander seeds
5 black peppercorns
Sprig of fresh thyme

Rinse fish bones under cold, running water until clear. Chop into small, manageable pieces.

Peel or trim onion, leek, celery and fennel. Chop in a small dice. In a large sauce pan, combine vegetables, wine, spices and thyme. Bring to a simmer. Cover and let "sweat" 8-10 minutes. Add fish bones and just enough cold water to cover bones. Bring to a boil. Reduce heat and simmer 20 minutes. Be sure to skim off any impurities which rise to the surface. Strain through a fine sieve. Strain again through cheesecloth to obtain a clear stock.

FOR THE BROTH:
1 leek, white part only
1 ounce fennel
Assorted vegetables such as asparagus, small new potatoes, peas, turnips, etc.

Prepare leeks, fennel and choice of vegetable in a careful manner to enhance final presentation.

Blanch vegetables until al dente. Set aside.

FOR THE ROUILLE:
1 egg
1 teaspoon mustard
1 teaspoon lemon juice
1 tablespoon red pepper purée (Roast red pepper on top of grill or gas burner until skin blisters. Cool, remove skin and seeds. Purée.)
1/4 cup good olive oil
Salt and pepper, to taste

Add egg, mustard, lemon juice and red pepper purée to food processor. Purée. Very slowly add just enough olive oil to make a nice mayonnaise. Season with salt and pepper.

FOR THE PRESENTATION:
7-8 ounces seafood per person, any combination of shellfish, white fish and salmon. The key to success with this dish is in the selection of seafood. Only the freshest will do!
Pinch of saffron
1 tablespoon fresh lemon juice
1 tablespoon fresh chopped parsley
1 tablespoon butter
Salt and pepper, to taste
Croutons

Bring fumet to boil. Add seafood that has been prepared in small, attractive pieces. Add blanched vegetables. Poach until fish is just pink. Remove from pot and arrange in large soup bowls. Finish broth with saffron, lemon juice, parsley, butter, salt and pepper. Garnish with warm crouton topped with rouille.

Serves 4-6.

· ·

The European Connektion

717 S.W. 148th Street, Burien. Phone 243-0229. Open for lunch Monday through Saturday, 11:00 A.M. to 2:00 P.M.; open for dinner Monday through Thursday, 5:00 to 10:00 P.M.; Friday and Saturday, 5:00 to 11:00 P.M.; closed Sunday.

Although primarily German in its cuisine, the European Connektion also offers other European as well as American entrées, all served up in a European setting. A trademark of owner Denny Humphrey's approach is the complimentary cheese fondue that accompanies every dinner. Desserts also delight: mostly French, with only the finest quality chocolate used. However, no German restaurant would be complete without offering strudel, and their version melts in your mouth!

• •

Jager Schnitzel
(Hunters Pork)

Approximately 1/2 pound pork tenderloin, cut into 2-4 thin slices
2 eggs, whipped with dash of milk
Seasoned bread crumbs
4 tablespoons butter, divided
2 strips of bacon, chopped
1 small carrot, chopped
3 mushrooms, quartered
1/8 cup chopped onion
3 tablespoons flour
White wine
1 tablespoon heavy cream
1/4 cup beef consommé

Dip pork in egg mixture. Coat with bread crumbs. Heat 2 tablespoons butter and bacon in skillet. Add pork and cook until golden brown on both sides. Remove meat and set aside.

Add carrot, mushrooms, onion and remaining butter to pan. Cook until vegetables soften and mixture is bubbly. Add flour and mix well. Simmer 5-7 minutes. Add wine, cream and consommé. Simmer 5 minutes.

Present meat with 3-4 tablespoons of mixed veggies and sauce on top.

Serves 2-4.

• •

Bavarian Pork Roast

Salt, to taste
2-1/2 pounds pork roast (skin
   on shoulder)
1-1/2 cups water
15-25 cloves
1 large onion, diced
1-2 bay leaves
1/4 cup chopped parsley
5 black peppercorns
1 clove of garlic, halved
Salt water
Cornstarch
Pepper, to taste

Rub salt into meat. Place pork in a roasting pan, skin side down. Add water. Roast in a 425° oven 15 minutes. Turn over and, using a sharp knife, make a crisscross design on the meat. Insert cloves into the intersections. Roast 45 minutes, basting frequently. Add onion, bay leaves, parsley, peppercorns and garlic. Roast 10 minutes, basting with salt water. Bind stock with cornstarch. Season with pepper.

The European Connektion recommends that if you wish to keep with the Bavarian traditional style, serve with dumplings and a generous mug of beer.

Serves 4.

Manfred Vierthaler Winery Restaurant

17136 Hwy. 410E, Sumner. Phone 863-1633. Open daily, 11:00 A.M. to 10:00 P.M.

Large windows allow diners at the Vierthaler Winery Restaurant to gaze out on the beautiful Puyallup River valley while they dine on traditional German and American dishes. Sauerbraten, weiner schnitzel and bratwurst are here, of course, but so are a variety of game dishes, such as venison, bear roast, wild boar and hasenpfeffer. Wines from the on-premises winery are offered, as are German beers and other libations.

· ·

Rindsrouladen (Filled Rolled Beef)

Top round beef, thin sliced (1/4 inch) to about a piece 4 inches x 10 inches
Medium hot mustard
2 ounces of a diced mixture of onions, pickles and bacon
Salt and pepper, to taste
Water
Beef base
Flour
Red wine

Lay beef flat. Spread with mustard. Top with diced mixture, spreading to about 1 inch from edges. Sprinkle with salt and pepper. Roll up tight. Secure with toothpicks.

Brown beef roll on all sides in skillet. Add water to half way up beef roll. Add some beef base. Cook about 1-1/2 hours at 350°.

When tender, transfer to heated plate. Remove toothpicks. Thicken gravy with a little flour.

Add red wine to taste. Pour sauce over beef to serve.

Serves 4.

· ·

Rotkraut (Red Cabbage)

Water
3 medium red cabbages, sliced 1/8 inch thick
1 medium onion, diced
1/4 cup oil
8 ounces applesauce
3 cloves
2 bay leaves
Pinch of salt and pepper
1 cup dry red wine
2 tablespoons vinegar

Place 1 inch of water in a large pot. Add all ingredients. Add additional water to fill pot to half the level of the cabbage. Boil until tender. Serves 8-12.

· ·

Tannhauser

1135 East Front, Port Angeles. Phone 452-5977. Open for breakfast and lunch Tuesday through Sunday, 7:00 A.M. to 2:00 P.M.; open for dinner Tuesday through Saturday, 5:00 to 9:00 P.M.; Sunday to 8:00 P.M.; closed Monday.

First-rate German cuisine is not easy to find even in the Northwest's largest cities, but good restaurants are where you find them, and Horst Thanheiser has put together such a place in Port Angeles. American food is also served, but the emphasis here is on the German, and the preparation is thoughtful and authentic.

• •

Wiener Schnitzel

4 8-ounce veal cutlets
Salt and pepper, to taste
1 tablespoon flour
1 egg, beaten slightly
1/2 cup bread crumbs
1/2 cup butter
Lemon slices

Pound meat until very thin. Sprinkle with salt and pepper. Dip into flour, turn in beaten egg, and dip into bread crumbs.

Heat butter in skillet. Sauté cutlets until light brown on each side.

Garnish with lemon slices. Accompany with German hot potato salad and sauerkraut.

Serves 4.

• •

Gulasch

2 tablespoons oil
4 large onions, diced
Cloves of garlic, minced
3 pounds stewing beef, cubed
2 cups hot water
Salt and pepper, to taste
2 teaspoons cornstarch,
   dissolved in 1 tablespoon
   water

Heat oil in large pot or frying pan. Add onions and garlic. Sauté until brown and tender.

Add beef cubes and brown on all sides. Add water, salt and pepper. Bring to a boil; reduce heat. Simmer until meat is tender, about 1 to 1-1/2 hours. Stir in cornstarch mixture to thicken. Cook several more minutes.

Serve with, or over, hot spätzle with red cabbage as a vegetable.

Serves 6.

• •

The Kaleenka

1933 First Avenue, Seattle. Phone 728-1278. Open Monday through Thursday, 11:00 A.M. to 9:00 P.M.; Friday and Saturday, 11:00 A.M. to 10:00 P.M.; closed Sunday.

For fifteen years, the Kaleenka has brought the unique cooking traditions of the Russian people to those of the Northwest. Many of the dishes are regional, from Georgia, Ukraine and Uzbekistan as well as Russia itself. All are tasty and hearty fare, different and exotic to our tastes but always enjoyable. Chefs here were trained by renowned Russian chefs, and the food is authentic and high quality. By the way, the Kaleenka derives its name from a ubiquitous shrub that grows all across Russia, which has been revered since ancient times as a symbol of the land and culture.

• •

Borshch

1 onion, chopped
2 beets, grated
3 carrots, grated
1 potato, cubed
2 tablespoons oil
4 cups water
1 head of cabbage, chopped
1/2 green pepper, chopped
3 stalks of celery, chopped
1/4 teaspoon salt
1/2 teaspoon pepper
1 cup tomato juice
1/2 cup sour cream
Dill

Brown onions, beets, carrots and potato separately in 1/2 tablespoon oil.

Bring water to boil. Add cabbage, green pepper and celery. Bring back to boil. Add browned vegetables, salt and pepper. Cook until vegetables are soft but not mushy. Add tomato juice.

Serve hot, topped with sour cream and a sprinkle of dill.

There are many variants of the soup called "borshch," according to the Kaleenka. This one is a vegetarian recipe.

What's the secret of a good borshch? Brown the vegetables separately.

How do you pronounce "borshch?" Like the "sh ch" in "fresh cheese." In Russian it is indicated by a single letter.

Serves 4.

• •

Piroshky

1 onion, chopped
2 pounds lean ground beef
1 clove of garlic, finely chopped
1/2 teaspoon salt
1/2 teaspoon pepper
2 packages yeast
4-5 cups flour
2 tablespoons sugar
1 teaspoon salt
1 egg
3 tablespoons oil
1/4 cup warm water
1-1/2 cups milk
1 pound mild cheddar cheese,
    cut into 1 inch squares, 1/2
    inch thick

Brown chopped onion. Set aside.

In a separate pan, brown the ground beef. While still hot, mix in the reserved onion, garlic, salt and pepper. Chill to 40 degrees and pick out solid fat. Set aside.

Dissolve yeast in warm water. Let stand 11 minutes.

Place 4 cups flour, sugar, salt, egg, oil, warm water and milk in a large bowl. Combine and mix, adding flour as needed to make a dough that is soft but not sticky. Knead about 10 minutes. Let rise 1/2-1 hour. Punch down.

Pinch off a piece of dough about the size of an egg. Roll out to 1/8 inch thick. Place a piece of cheese and 2 tablespoons of meat filling in the center. Lift up the edges of the dough and pinch together to completely enclose the filling. Pinch tightly so that dough knits together. Place on a tray, seam side down. Microwave, allowing 10 seconds each, and allow to rise 10 minutes.

Heat oven to 350°. Bake until golden brown. Or, deep fry at 300°.

The Kaleenka notes that "piroshky" is derived from a Russian word pronounced "peer," which means "feast." Many different fillings are common, including chicken, fish, and fruits, but this beef and cheese filling is the favorite.

Serves 4-6.

Matzoh Momma Delicatessen & Restaurant

509 - 15th Avenue East, Seattle. Phone 324-6262. Open daily, 9:00 A.M. to 9:00 P.M.

This small deli and restaurant is unique in the Puget Sound area and is a delight. The deli section is full of homemade salads, pickles, knishes, meats and cheeses, and you can also order anything off the menu 'to go'. Or, step into the old world charm of the dining room. Light and cheery, the walls are lined with a combination of very old photographs of the owners' great great grandparents, along with contemporary watercolors of Seattle. Either way, the food is wonderful, and, of course, strictly kosher. If you've been longing for that matzoh ball soup like your grandmother used to make, this is the place!

• •

Chocolate Cream Cheese Fudge Brownies

1 cup plus 2 tablespoons soft margarine
3 eggs, beaten
1 tablespoon salad oil
1/2 cup cocoa powder
1 cup broken walnuts

Mix until wet and well blended. Add:

2 cups white sugar
3 cups flour
1/2 teaspoon baking powder

Mix well. Lay out in bottom of 9 inch x 13 inch pan.

1 pound softened cream cheese
1/2 pound margarine
1 cup white sugar

1/4 cup flour
3 eggs
1 teaspoon vanilla

Blend in food processor until creamy and smooth. Pour evenly over brownie layer. Bake 45 minutes in 350° oven. Cool.

3/4 pound soft cream cheese
1/4 pound soft margarine
4 cups powdered sugar
1/4 cup cocoa powder

Mix well with a wooden spoon. Spread over baked brownies. Cut into small pieces - they're very rich!
Makes 9 inch x 13 inch pan.

• •

Potato Latkes

**6 large baking potatoes, grated
in food processor or by hand**
**1 large yellow onion, grated
and juice drained off**
3 eggs, beaten
1/2 cup matzoh meal
2 tablespoons schmaltz
1 tablespoon kosher salt
2 teaspoons black pepper
2 tablespoons oil
Sour cream
Applesauce

Mix potatoes, onion, eggs, matzoh meal, schmaltz, salt and pepper together by hand.

In a cast iron skillet, heat oil until very hot. Drop latkes in with a large spoon. Flatten the tops. Brown over medium heat on both sides. Drain on paper towels. Serve with sour cream and applesauce.

Serves 6.

Southern
Europe

Ponti Seafood Grill

3014 Third Avenue North, Seattle. Phone 284-3000. Open for lunch Monday through Saturday, 11:30 A.M. to 2:30 P.M.; open for brunch Sunday, 10:00 A.M. to 2:30 P.M.; open for dinner Sunday through Thursday, 5:30 to 10:00 P.M.; Friday and Saturday, 5:30 to 11:00 P.M. Extensive menu available in lounge at other times.

Attaching labels to some restaurants is tricky, and that is especially true of Ponti. The name implies Italian, and yes, they offer some Italian dishes. Also Mediterranean, Asian and South American, to name a few, in innovative, very original combinations that sometimes surprise but always satisfy. Surely one of the most unique restaurants in Seattle, it is one of the very finest as well. Owner Jim Malevitsis - who also owns the Adriatica - knows what it takes: the food, service, ambience and waterside location are all simply outstanding.

• •

Brazilian-Thai Lobster Stew

Stew Base (recipe follows)
1/2 cooked lobster, claws
   cracked
3-4 mussels
Scoop of rice
1 tablespoon Cilantro Pesto
   (recipe follows)
Crushed peanuts

1/2 cup sliced onion
Pinch of dried red chilies
Olive oil
16-ounce can pear tomatoes in
   juice, chopped coarsely
2 8-ounce cans coconut milk
1 teaspoon salt
1/2 teaspoon black pepper

Bring 1-1/2 cups of Stew Base to a simmer. Add lobster and mussels. Cover and simmer until mussels open. Pour stew into a bowl which has a scoop of rice in it. Top with Cilantro Pesto. Sprinkle with peanuts.
   Serves 1.

STEW BASE:
1 tablespoon julienne cut ginger
   root
1 small jalapeño pepper, minced

Sauté ginger root, jalapeño, onion and chilies in olive oil until onions are soft. Add tomatoes, coconut milk, salt and pepper. Bring to simmer. Simmer 10-15 minutes.

CILANTRO PESTO:
1/2 bunch of cilantro, chopped
4 green onions
2 teaspoons chopped garlic
2 teaspoons chopped ginger root

1/2 small jalapeño pepper
1 teaspoon salt
Pinch of dried red chilies
1/2 cup olive oil
Juice of 1/2 lime

Blend cilantro, green onions, garlic, ginger root, jalapeño, salt, and chilies thoroughly in food processor. Drizzle in oil and lime juice while processor is running.

• •

Chilean Sea Bass Braised in Smoked Grape Leaves

Grape Leaves (recipe follows)
Pine-Nut Herb Butter (recipe
    follows)
8 ounce filet of sea bass, no
    thicker than 1/2 inch
Dry white wine and water, in
    equal portions

On work surface, arrange 3-5 leaves, depending upon size, so that they overlap by 1 inch. You should end up with about a 12 inch round. Place a heaping tablespoon of the Pine-Nut Herb Butter in center. Place filet over butter. Wrap grape leaves around filet to make a tight package.

In a skillet, add wine and water to a depth of 1/4 inch. Bring to a simmer. Place fish in pan, butter side down. Cover and simmer 2-3 minutes. Turn over. Continue cooking 3-4 minutes, or until done.

Remove to serving dish, opening to expose filet. Pour braising liquid over the top.
    Serves 1.

GRAPE LEAVES:
Fresh or canned grape leaves
Apple or alder wood chips,
    preferably cut fine
Olive oil

If using fresh leaves, blanch in boiling, salted water.

In a foil lined wok, spread a couple of handfuls of wood chips. Set over high heat.

Coat grape leaves lightly with oil. Spread evenly in a single layer on the wok rack. Cover tightly. Smoke hot for about 10 minutes. Set aside to cool.

PINE-NUT HERB BUTTER:
Juice and zest of 1 lemon
1/2 cup toasted pine nuts
1/2 pound butter, softened
1 tablespoon chopped chives
1 tablespoon chopped shallots
1 tablespoon chopped parsley
Salt and pepper, to taste

Blend all ingredients well.

• •

Cafe Luna

3rd and Railroad, Shelton. Phone 427-8709. Open Thursday through Saturday only, 5:00 to 9:00 P.M.

Every so often, one discovers a really good restaurant in an unexpected place. Cafe Luna is like that. The meals are primarily Mediterranean, with occasional forays into other cuisines, in what owner Victoria Benenate describes as "elegant peasant - simple, fresh, quality food." Fresh is right: the produce is all organic (much of which Victoria grows herself), and all desserts - including ice creams - are made daily at the restaurant. Little surprise, then, that Cafe Luna has earned outstanding reviews and an avowedly loyal and admiring clientele.

• •

Luna Ice Cream

2 bananas
Juice of 2 oranges
Juice of 2 lemons
2 cups sugar
2 cups cream
2 cups milk

Process the bananas, juices and sugar in a blender until smooth. Stir in cream and milk. Freeze in an ice cream maker following manufacturer's directions.
Serves 4.

• •

Polenta

1-1/3 cups polenta
4-2/3 cups cold water
1/2 cup butter
2/3 cup fresh grated Romano
   cheese
2 heads of garlic, roasted,
   peeled and coarsely chopped
Salt and pepper, to taste
Olive oil

Slowly stir polenta into the water. Place over medium low heat and, stirring constantly, cook until mixture has thickened, and there is no bite left to the polenta, about 20-30 minutes. Remove from heat. Stir in butter, cheese, garlic, salt and pepper until well blended.

Pour into a pan or baking dish, approximately 8 inches by 12 inches. Cool. Cut into serving pieces. Sauté in a small amount of olive oil.

Cafe Luna suggests serving this over a number of different dishes: sautéed wild and field mushrooms with fresh herbs; a ragout of fresh tomatoes, onions and Kalamata olives laced with balsamic vinegar; a mixture of grilled eggplant, grilled onions, golden raisins, currants and green olives.

Serves 4.

Tulio

Hotel Vintage Park, 1100 Fifth Avenue, Seattle. Phone 624-5500. Open for breakfast Monday through Friday, 7:00 to 10:00 A.M.; Saturday and Sunday, 8:00 to 11:00 A.M.; open for lunch Monday through Friday, 11:30 A.M. to 2:30 P.M.; Saturday and Sunday, noon to 2:30 P.M. (dinner menu in effect); open for dinner Sunday through Thursday, 5:00 to 10:00 P.M.; Friday and Saturday, 5:00 to 11:00 P.M.

Tulio is not for the faint of heart in culinary matters. It is a restaurant of bold, assertive Italian flavors, wide selection and elegance. Executive chef Walter Pisano - already well-known and respected among Seattle diners - has built a classic Italian bistro and a skilled staff (including pastry chef Peggy Elliott), that knows and cares about its product. Tulio can be crowded and busy, but the atmosphere is warm and friendly, and the food is terrific.

· ·

Roasted Chicken with Caramelized Garlic and Sage

16 cloves of garlic, peeled
3 cups sugar
2 tablespoons unsalted butter
8-10 sage leaves
4 fresh chicken breasts with
   wing bone, skin on
2 teaspoons salt
1 teaspoon black pepper
2 ounces olive oil

Caramelize garlic. Peel and slice garlic paper thin. Blanch in water 10-12 minutes, or until garlic is soft. Heat sugar in heavy pan over low heat until sugar starts to turn brown. Remove from heat or sugar will continue to cook and may burn. Add blanched garlic and butter. Mix well. Set aside to cool.

Remove fresh sage from stem and chop. Take chicken breast and carefully lift skin. Slip caramelized garlic and fresh sage under skin, keeping skin attached on side of bird. Salt and pepper chicken.

Heat oil in pan. Add chicken breast. Brown skin side. Turn over. Place in 375° oven approximately 15 minutes. Remove chicken from oven. Let rest 5 minutes.

Chef Pisano suggests accompanying the chicken breasts with roasted rosemary potatoes or sautéed spinach with pancetta.

Serves 4.

· ·

Tiramisu

SPONGE CAKE:
8 eggs, separated
2 ounces sugar
2 ounces cake flour
1-1/2 ounces cornstarch
3 ounces sugar

Have eggs at room temperature. Beat yolks and sugar until thick and triple in volume. Sift cake flour and cornstarch over yolks and gently fold in. Beat whites and 3 ounces sugar until stiff and glossy. Fold into yolk mixture. Spread evenly into 3 9-inch cake pans with parchment paper and vegetable spray. Bake at 350° until light brown and springy to the touch, about 20 minutes.

FILLING:
2 cups heavy cream
24 ounces mascarpone cheese
5 ounces powdered sugar
1-1/2 ounces Meyers dark rum
1 tablespoon vanilla

Beat cream to soft peaks. Beat mascarpone with paddle until smooth, only a few minutes. Add sugar, rum and vanilla. Whip in lightly. Add whipped cream. Fold in by turning machine on and off and scraping in-between. Turn machine on high for a minute. Whip until just combined. The mixture should be stiff. Do not go beyond this point because the mixture can break down.

PAINT:
2 cups sugar
1-1/2 cups water
3 ounces instant espresso
2-1/2 cups Meyers dark rum
1/4 cup brandy

Bring sugar and water to boil. Off heat. Whisk in espresso, rum and brandy. Refrigerate until cool.

FINISH:
12 ounces mascarpone
2 ounces powdered sugar
1 teaspoon vanilla
1 cup half and half
1-1/2 ounces Meyers dark rum

Put mascarpone into mixing bowl. Beat with whisk attachment until broken up. Add sugar and vanilla and blend. While machine is running, slowly add half and half to incorporate. Add rum. Mixture should be fairly thin. This is used as a sauce. If there are any lumps, use a whisk and whisk them out. If too thin, add more sugar.

ASSEMBLY:
1 teaspoon fresh ground
    espresso
1 teaspoon grated sweet
    chocolate
1 tablespoon grated chocolate

(recipe continued on next page)

Tiramisu (continued)

Place 1 cake layer in a 9 inch springform pan. Put paint into squirt bottle. Squirt paint onto sponge until completely saturated. Take one-third of the filling and spread evenly over cake. Sprinkle with 1/2 teaspoon freshly ground espresso and 1/2 teaspoon grated chocolate. Place second cake layer on top. Saturate as above.

Repeat all processes. Sprinkle top with 1 tablespoon grated chocolate only (no espresso).

Refrigerate cake at least 1 hour. Can be made up to 3 days ahead. Cut into 8-10 slices. Ladle 1 ounce of finish over each serving. Sprinkle with grated chocolate.

Serves 8-10.

• •

Trattoria Carmine

3130 East Madison Street, Seattle. Phone 323-7990. Open Monday through Thursday, 11:30 A.M. to 10:00 P.M.; Friday, 11:30 A.M. to 11:00 P.M.; Saturday, 5:00 to 11:00 P.M.; Sunday, 5:00 to 10:00 P.M.

Traditional Italian cooking methods devised to preserve the qualities of the ingredients and properly marry them; these are the techniques used at Trattoria Carmine. Of course, the ingredients themselves receive equal attention: superior Northwest meats, fish and shellfish from both coasts, homemade pastas, fine olive oils and fresh stock. The antipasto misto is a specialty of the house and will remind any Italian traveller of home.

• •

Calamari in Umido (Squid in Broth)

1 teaspoon chopped garlic
1 tablespoon chopped Italian parsley
2 Kalamata olives, pitted and halved
14 capers, rinsed
1 teaspoon kosher or fine sea salt
1/2 teaspoon fresh ground black pepper
Pinch of chili flakes
2 ounces good olive oil
1/2 pound cleaned calamari
Juice of 1/2 lemon
1 lemon wedge
2 ounces chopped, peeled tomatoes with juice

In order to prepare this dish properly, all ingredients must be ready before you begin. It takes 2 minutes to make once the oil is hot.

In a small bowl, combine garlic, parsley, olives, capers, salt, pepper and chili flakes. Set aside.

Heat oil in pan until smoking. Add garlic mixture. Bloom aroma. Add calamari and all other ingredients at once. Simmer 45 seconds. Serve at once.

Serves 1.

• •

Adriatica

1107 Dexter Avenue North, Seattle.   Phone 285-5000.   Open Sunday through Thursday, 5:30 to 10:00 P.M.; Friday and Saturday, 5:30 to 11:00 P.M.

To lovers of Mediterranean food, Adriatica is a special place. Owner Jim Malevitsis has carved out a large and enthusiastic following here (as he has with his newer restaurant, Ponti Seafood Grill) by providing impeccable service and a rich and varied menu, with something for every taste. Better still, the food lives up to the menu's promise.

- -

Grilled Pork Tenderloin with Port and Dried Cranberries

1 cup olive oil
1/4 cup dry vermouth
2 tablespoons fresh thyme or 2
   teaspoons dried thyme
2 teaspoons ground black
   pepper
1 teaspoon salt
1 tablespoon minced garlic
6 pork tenderloins, about 7
   ounces each, trimmed well
1 fifth Port
1 pint whipping cream
2 teaspoons black pepper
1 tablespoon fresh thyme or 1
   teaspoon dried thyme
1/2 cup dried cranberries

Combine oil, vermouth, thyme, pepper, salt and garlic. Add pork. Marinate overnight.

In a large sauce pan, reduce Port down to 1 cup over high heat. Add cream, pepper, and 1 tablespoon fresh thyme. Reduce until sauce thickens, being careful that the cream doesn't overflow. Add cranberries. Simmer 2-3 minutes. Set aside.

When ready to prepare pork, allow it to reach room temperature for 1 hour before grilling. Charcoal grill the pork over hot coals, turning on all sides, about 10 minutes, until juicy and still a little pink. Slice on the bias. Pour Port sauce over slices.

Serves 6.

- -

Prawns Constantina

1/2 cup butter, divided
1/2 cup minced green onions
2 teaspoons minced garlic
3/4 teaspoon salt
1/4 teaspoon thyme
1/2 teaspoon cayenne pepper
1/4 teaspoon white pepper
1/4 teaspoon black pepper
1/4 teaspoon basil
Pinch of oregano
Pinch of cumin
1/2 cup diced red bell pepper
1/2 pound mushrooms,
    quartered
1 pound prawns, shelled and
    deveined
1/4 cup shrimp stock or dry
    white wine
1-2 tablespoons fresh lemon
    juice
1/4 cup minced parsley

In large sauté pan, melt 1/4 cup butter. Add green onions, garlic, salt, thyme, peppers, basil, oregano and cumin. Stir well. Add red bell pepper, mushrooms and prawns. Stir well. Sauté about 1 minute. Add stock or wine and lemon juice. Swirl in remaining 1/4 cup butter. Add parsley. Serve immediately. Great over pasta or rice.

Serves 2-4.

Serafina

2043 Eastlake Avenue East, Seattle. Phone 323-0807. Open for lunch Monday through Friday, 11:30 A.M. to 2:30 P.M.; open for dinner Sunday through Thursday, 5:00 to 10:00 P.M.; Friday and Saturday, 5:00 to 11:00 P.M.

Just a few minutes away from the hustle and bustle of downtown Seattle, there is a stylish neighborhood bistro that draws guests from all over the map. That place is called Serafina, a darkly romantic restaurant that offers an imaginative bill of memorable Italian fare some describe as rustic. Others describe it variously as innovative, imaginative and delicious, judgments that owner Susan Kaufman works hard to earn.

• •

Pasta Con Rucola

1 tablespoon olive oil
2 cloves of garlic, smashed
1 ounce prosciutto, julienne cut
1-1/2 tablespoons chopped
    parsley
1/2 tablespoon chopped basil
2 ounces white wine
6 ounces chicken stock
Salt and pepper, to taste
3 cups mixed torn greens (equal
    portions of spinach, arugula,
    and field greens)
1 tablespoon butter
1/2 cup sorrel
Lemon
8 ounces linguini, cooked al
    dente

Heat oil and lightly brown garlic. Add prosciutto, parsley, and basil. Sauté briefly. Add white wine to deglaze, and then add chicken stock. Season with salt and pepper. Simmer 3 minutes. Add greens and cook only long enough to wilt. Swirl butter into sauce. Add sorrel and a squeeze of lemon. Toss with linguini.

    Serves 2.

• •

Salsiccia All'uva

1 tablespoon olive oil
3-4 ounces Cascioppo sausage
4 cups green seedless grapes
(picked off stems and
washed)
1/2 cup Roasted Balsamic and
Honey Red Onions
(recipe follows)
1 tablespoon fresh rosemary
1 tablespoon balsamic vinegar
2-1/2 cups Polenta (recipe
follows)

Heat oil in skillet. Brown
sausage. Add grapes and toss to
coat in oil. Reduce to a low heat
and add onion mixture. Cook
slowly 8-10 minutes. When
thoroughly cooked, add rosemary
and balsamic vinegar. Grapes
should be soft but should not lose
their shape. Serve over polenta.
Serves 2.

ROASTED BALSAMIC AND
HONEY RED ONIONS:
2-1/2 cups thinly sliced red onion
1/4 cup balsamic vinegar
1/2 cup honey
1 tablespoon olive oil

Mix all ingredients thoroughly
and roast 1 hour in 350° oven, or
until vinegar and honey have
reduced. Makes 1 cup.

POLENTA:
1/4 cup milk
1-1/2 cups chicken stock
1 cup polenta (coarse style)
Salt and pepper, to taste

In a 2 quart sauce pan, heat
milk and chicken stock until
boiling. While stirring, add
polenta in a slow, even stream.
Continue stirring polenta until it
is thick and starts to pull away
from the sides of the pan, about
15 minutes. Add milk. Polenta
should be smooth and creamy.

Trattoria Sostanza

1927 - 43rd Avenue East, Seattle. Phone 324-9701. Open for lunch Monday through Friday, 11:00 A.M. to 2:30 P.M.; open for dinner Sunday through Thursday, 5:30 to 9:30 P.M.; Friday and Saturday, 5:30 to 10:00 P.M.

Consistently rated among the very finest of Seattle restaurants, Trattoria Sostanza specializes in authentic regional Italian cuisine, with an emphasis on Tuscany. The atmosphere is that of a warm country inn, and the food is simply marvelous, with daily specials chosen to take advantage of seasonal ingredients. Located in Madison Park, Sostanza has legions of loyal customers from all over Seattle; reservations are recommended. Owner/chef Erin Rosella's personal touch is evident everywhere you look.

• •

Gnocchi

2 pounds ricotta cheese, whole milk only
2-3/4 cups flour, plus extra for rolling
1/4 cup Parmigiano cheese, Italian brands suggested
Pinch of fresh grated nutmeg
Pinch of salt

In a large bowl, mix all ingredients together by hand. Add more flour if mixture is too sticky. Roll into a ball. Place on floured board. Cut into 8 pieces. Roll pieces into long rolls about 1 inch in diameter. Cut strips into 1/2 inch pieces. Place on sheet pan, being careful that pieces do not touch. Freeze until hard.

Add gnocchi to well salted boiling water until they float. Remove quickly. Toss with favorite tomato-basil sauce.

Pasta chef Mimi Martin proudly notes that this recipe was handed down by her great grandmother, thus carrying on a proud Italian tradition.

Serves 4.

• •

Rigatoni Alle Cime Di Rape
(Rigatoni with Italian Broccoli)

1 pound broccoli rabe
2 yellow or red bell peppers
1/2 cup extra virgin olive oil
2 cloves of garlic, chopped
Large pinch of hot pepper
    flakes
1/2 cup whipping cream
1 pound rigatoni pasta (use
    Italian brands only)
Parmigiano cheese

Cook broccoli in large sauce pan with salted boiling water about 45 minutes, or until very soft.

Meanwhile, roast peppers in 500° oven until they begin to blister. Remove from oven, place in brown paper bag, close bag tightly, and wait about 6-10 minutes, or until peppers are cooled. Remove from bag, peel skins, remove core and seeds, and slice thin.

Drain broccoli.

Clean the same sauce pan. Heat oil, garlic, and hot pepper flakes on medium heat about 3 minutes, being careful not to brown garlic. Add sliced peppers, cream and broccoli. Let simmer about 8-10 minutes.

Cook pasta according to directions on package. Serve pasta tossed with sauce and plenty of cheese.

Serves 2-4.

La Buca Ristorante Italiano

102 Cherry Street, Seattle.   Phone 343-9517.   Open for lunch Monday through Saturday, 11:30 A.M. to 2:30 P.M.; open for dinner Monday through Thursday, 5:30 to 11:00 P.M.; Friday and Saturday, 5:30 P.M. to midnight; Sunday, 4:00 to 10:00 P.M.

This charming cellar restaurant just north of Pioneer Square is a romantic hideaway, with lots of atmosphere, splendid service, and southern Italian cuisine the equal of any you will find.   Owner Luigi Da Nunzio is a gracious host as well as showman, and the dining experience here is consistently first rate.

• •

Spaghetti with Speck

1 box dry spaghetti, preferably
   Barilla brand
4 tablespoons olive oil
1/2 onion, thinly sliced and
   minced
2 ounces speck
1 ounce grappa
4 ounces heavy cream
Salt and pepper, to taste
Parsley
Parmesan cheese

In salted water, boil spaghetti, adding a bit of olive oil to prevent sticking. Cook pasta al dente, approximately 7 minutes.

In a large sauté pan, add oil, onion and speck. Flame with grappa. Let evaporate. Add cream, salt, pepper and parsley. Reduce the cream. Add spaghetti and toss vigorously. Dust with Parmesan. Serve hot.

Serves 4.

• •

Fazfalle Orto-Maze
(Bow Tie Pasta Garden-Sea)

1 box dry spaghetti, preferably
   Barilla brand
10 tablespoons olive oil (first or
   second press)
32 Manila clams, thoroughly
   washed
2 cloves of garlic, thinly sliced
2 zucchini, sliced paper thin
2 tablespoons fresh sage,
   minced or whole
2 tablespoons fresh basil,
   minced or whole
4 tablespoons olive oil
Salt and pepper, to taste

Cook pasta in abundant water with salt and olive oil al dente.

Sauté clams in olive oil and garlic until clams open.

Brown zucchini in olive oil. Season with sage and basil.

Place remaining 4 tablespoons of oil in a large sauté pan. Add a little garlic. Transfer the clams with their juices. Add the zucchini and pasta. On high heat, toss all together. Adjust with salt and pepper. Serve hot - and, Luigi says - "please, no cheers!"

Serves 4.

Saleh al Lago

6804 E. Green Lake Way North, Seattle. Phone 524-4044. Open for lunch Monday through Friday, 11:30 A.M. to 1:45 P.M.; open for dinner Monday through Saturday, 5:30 to 9:30 P.M; closed Sunday.

Perennially a favorite of critics and restaurant goers alike, the elegant Saleh al Lago has been serving up wonderful central Italian fare for over a decade, and in the process has drawn national attention. It was the first in the Pacific Northwest to receive the prestigious Restaurant Hall of Fame Award and has received numerous other honors as well. Never content to rest on their laurels, co-owners Saleh Joudeh and Dorothy Frisch bring an almost religious commitment to quality in every aspect of the operation, down to the smallest detail. A lovely view of Green Lake from its northeast corner and the open kitchen provide entertainment for guests awaiting delivery of the first course; after that, the food takes center stage.

• •

Filetto con Aceto Balsamico

Olive oil
4 6-ounce beef tenderloins or 1
    whole 24-ounce filet
1/4 cup red wine
1 cup beef stock
4 tablespoons balsamic vinegar
12 cloves of garlic, roasted
1 teaspoon green peppercorns
1 tablespoon butter
Salt and pepper, to taste

Heat oil in large sauté pan. Brown filet(s) on all sides. Remove from heat. Place in preheated 375° oven to cook to desired temperature.

Deglaze pan with red wine and reduce. Add stock, vinegar, garlic and peppercorns. Reduce to one-third. Lower heat and stir in butter. Season with salt and pepper. Remove from heat, but keep warm.

Slice tenderloin. Arrange on warm plate. Spoon sauce over all. Serves 4.

• •

Risotto Verde

4 ounces butter, divided
1 medium yellow onion, minced
2 cups arborio rice
1/4 cup dry white wine
4 cups chicken stock, heated
1/2 cup heavy cream
1 cup fresh spinach, washed,
    drained and chopped fine
1/2 cup grated Parmesan
    cheese, divided
Salt and pepper, to taste
Grated nutmeg, optional

Melt 2 ounces butter in large sauce pan. Sauté onion until transparent. Add rice. Stir until coated with butter. Add wine. Cook until all liquid is absorbed. Add heated stock, one cup at a time, stirring constantly, until each successive cup is absorbed. Just after adding fourth cup of stock, stir in cream and spinach. Continue stirring until mixture is creamy. Add 1/4 cup Parmesan cheese and remaining butter. Stir well. Adjust seasonings with salt, pepper and nutmeg. Divide among 4 warmed soup plates. Top with remaining Parmesan cheese.

Saleh al Lago notes that the cooking time will be about 20-25 minutes over medium heat. The rice should be tender but not overcooked.

Serves 4.

Al Boccalino

One Yesler Way, Seattle. Phone 622-7688. Open Monday through Thursday, 5:00 to 10:00 P.M.; Friday and Saturday, 5:00 to 10:30 P.M.; Sunday, 4:30 to 9:00 P.M.

Chef Timothy Roth points out that good food transcends ethnic classification. Al Boccalino, he says, "serves wonderful food that happens to be Italian." And so they do; obvious dedication to only the freshest and finest ingredients, combined with talent and hard work, have made Al Boccalino a local favorite.

• •

Vermicelli with Crab

**4 tomatoes, ripe, medium size
 or 8-ounce can whole
 plum tomatoes**
**4 tablespoons extra virgin olive
 oil**
6 cloves of garlic, chopped fine
1/2 teaspoon crushed red chilies
**12 fresh basil leaves, thinly
 sliced**
**3 tablespoons chopped Italian
 parsley**
**1 pound high quality Italian
 vermicelli**
**1 pound fresh Dungeness crab
 meat**
**Salt and fresh ground
 black pepper, to taste**

Blanch fresh tomatoes in boiling water 1 minute. Cool under cold water. Remove skin and chop into small pieces. Or, chop canned tomatoes. Set aside.

Heat oil in large skillet. Gently sauté garlic, chilies, basil and parsley 4 minutes. Add chopped tomato. Sauté 2 minutes.

Boil pasta in large quantity of salted water until just al dente. Drain.

Add crab to sauce. Heat through 1-2 minutes. Add pasta to sauce in the skillet along with salt and pepper. Toss thoroughly. Serve in pasta bowls.

Serves 4 as an entrée, or 8 as a first course.

• •

Tiramisu

8 egg yolks
1/2 cup sugar
1/2 cup dry Marsala
12 ounces mascarpone

Whisk egg yolks, sugar and Marsala vigorously in a stainless steel bowl set over a pot of boiling water until thick and fluffy, about 4 minutes. Take off the heat. Whisk in the mascarpone. Chill overnight.

1 cup heavy whipping cream

Beat until stiff. Fold into the chilled mascarpone custard. Set aside in refrigerator.

1 cup very strong espresso
1/4 cup sugar
1/2 cup brandy or Cognac
7-ounce package of
**   commercially made**
**   ladyfingers**
2 ounces semi-sweet chocolate,
**   grated**

Mix the espresso with the sugar while the espresso is still hot. Cool, then add the brandy. Mix thoroughly.

To assemble, use a ceramic casserole 8 inches x 8 inches or 8 inches x 10 inches with at least 2 inch sides. Put about one-half of the chilled custard mixture in the bottom of the casserole. Spread evenly. This will be a thin layer. Very quickly, dip the ladyfingers in and out of the espresso mixture, just 4-5 at a time. Make a single layer of dipped ladyfingers on bottom of casserole, laying them side by side and cutting them as necessary to fit the casserole.

Spread one-half of the remaining custard over the ladyfingers, then sprinkle with one-half of the grated chocolate. Reserve the remaining chocolate for later.

Make another layer of dipped ladyfingers, then the other half of the custard. Cover with plastic wrap. Chill overnight.

1 cup whipping cream

Whisk the cream until stiff but still a little soft.

To finish, unwrap and either pipe the cream or spread it, or put large dollops of it on top of the custard. Sprinkle with reserved grated chocolate.

Serve by scooping from top to bottom, so as to get some of all the layers in each portion.

Serves 6-8.

Il Terrazzo Carmine

411 First Avenue South, Seattle. Phone 467-7797. Open for lunch Monday through Friday, 11:30 A.M. to 2:30 P.M.; open for dinner Monday through Thursday, 5:30 to 10:00 P.M.; Friday and Saturday, 5:30 to 11:00 P.M; closed Sunday.

Carmine Smeraldo has developed a solid following among lovers of Italian food. His restaurant, Il Terrazo Carmine, is near the Kingdome, so it's a convenient place to dine before an event. Allow yourself some time, though; it's a shame to rush through a meal, when the Tuscany style decor, attentive service, and delicious smells from the kitchen bid you to relax and linger a while.

• •

Bucatini Delicati

3 ounces olive oil
3 cloves of garlic
4 ounces pancetta, diced
28-ounce can peeled Italian tomatoes, pulsed in food processor
Salt and pepper, to taste
1 gallon (or more) salted water
Oil
1 pound bucatini pasta or spaghetti noodles (preferably De Ceceo brand)
2 fresh mozzarella balls (approximately 6 ounces total), cubed
Fresh basil, julienne cut
2 ounces fresh grated Parmesan cheese
Fresh ground pepper, to taste

Heat oil in large skillet and brown garlic. Remove garlic from pan and set aside.

Add pancetta and cook on medium heat until translucent but not crisp. Add reserved garlic and tomatoes. Reduce heat to medium low. Cook sauce 30 minutes. Season with salt and pepper.

Bring water to a fast boil. Add salt and a few drops of oil. Cook bucatini about 8 minutes, or spaghetti about 7 minutes. Drain well. Keep warm while finishing sauce.

Add mozzarella and basil to sauce. Toss pasta with sauce, mixing well. Sprinkle with Parmesan and pepper.

Serves 4.

• •

Pollo Contadino

2 medium whole chickens,
approximately 2-1/2 to 3
pounds each
1 large red bell pepper
1 large green bell pepper
1 large Spanish onion
1/2 pound champignon
4 ounces olive oil
4 cloves of garlic, minced
2 tablespoons black olives (with
pits preferred)
1 tablespoon capers
8 ounces puréed Italian
tomatoes
Salt and pepper, to taste

Cut chicken into 8 pieces. Remove skin and wash in cold water. Set aside.

Cut peppers, onions and mushrooms into julienne strips. Heat oil in oven proof pan. Add vegetables and sauté 5 minutes.

Add garlic to vegetable mixture and stir. Add olives, capers, tomatoes, salt and pepper. Bring to a slow simmer. Add chicken.

Cover pan with aluminum foil, poking several holes in it to allow some steam to escape. Transfer pan to preheated 375° oven. Cook for 1 hour. Present with potatoes or rice as a side dish.

Serves 4.

Ristorante Machiavelli

1215 Pine Street, Seattle. Phone 621-7941 or 324-5439. Open Monday through Thursday, 5:00 to 10:00 P.M.; Saturday, 5:00 to 11:00 P.M; closed Sunday.

This congenial neighborhood trattoria is a stimulating, lively place; the tables are close together, and it can be busy, especially on weekends. The foods are from northern Italy, with light sauces and handmade ravioli and gnocchi, and are presented with authenticity and style.

• •

Roast Chicken with Garlic and Rosemary

2-3 sprigs of rosemary
3-1/2 to 4 pound chicken
2 heads of garlic, cloves peeled
1/2 cup white wine
2 cups chicken stock
Salt and pepper, to taste
3 tablespoons butter

Place rosemary inside cavity of chicken. Close cavity with toothpick. Roast in 400° oven, adding a few tablespoons of stock or wine after the first 15 minutes and basting occasionally thereafter.

When chicken is half done and juices have accumulated in pan, add the garlic and roast along with the chicken. Don't allow the pan to get dry or garlic will burn. Add wine or stock if necessary.

Roast approximately 1 hour. Skin should be golden, and juices should run clear when thickest part of thigh is pierced. Remove chicken from pan. Let rest while making the sauce.

Skim as much grease as possible from pan juices. Add white wine to the pan. Scrape up pan drippings. Let boil down briefly. Add chicken stock, salt and pepper. Reduce sauce by almost half, until it begins to thicken a bit. Add salt and pepper. Remove from heat. Swirl in butter.

Cut chicken into serving pieces and pass sauce.
Serves 2-4.

• •

Fettucine Carbonara

1 pound fettucine noodles
4 eggs
1 cup Parmesan cheese
Fresh ground black pepper
8 slices thick cut bacon
1 tablespoon chopped garlic
1/2 teaspoon crushed red chilies
1/4 cup white wine
2 tablespoons butter

Bring a large pot of salted water to boil. Drop in noodles. Cook 10 minutes, or until al dente. Drain, reserving 1/2 cup of pasta cooking water.

In a bowl large enough to accommodate all the cooked noodles, crack the eggs. Add the cheese and a generous quantity of pepper. Mix well with a fork. Set aside.

In a sauté pan, brown the bacon until three-quarters done.

Remove bacon and set aside. Discard fat and clean pan. Add bacon back to pan. Cook until as done as you like. Add garlic and chilies. Stir quickly so as not to let garlic burn. Add wine and butter. Let reduce a bit. Remove pan from heat.

Place hot noodles and bacon mixture into bowl with eggs, tossing quickly so that the eggs don't coagulate. Add 1/4 cup of the reserved pasta water.

Noodles should have a creamy consistency with just the right amount of sauce clinging to them. There should not be a pool of sauce in the bowl. If noodles look too dry, add more of the reserved pasta water, a bit at a time.

Serves 4.

Mamma Melina Ristorante Italiano

4759 Roosevelt Way N.E., Seattle. Phone 632-2271. Open for lunch Monday through Friday, 11:30 A.M. to 2:00 P.M.; open for dinner daily, 5:00 to 9:30 P.M.

When you walk into Mamma Melina's, you feel as though you have been magically transported to Italy. The original Pasquale Varchetta artwork, the decor, and - often - live opera, all contribute to this impression. The food is Italian home style and as authentic as you will find. And yes, there is a Mamma Melina (moved here from Naples three years ago), and she will likely have cooked your meal. As Melina's son, Leo, promises: "always guaranteed to taste just like you would find in Naples!"

• •

Penne al Salmone

4 ounces olive oil
4 ounces white onions, chopped
   small
1/4 pound smoked lox
2 cups heavy cream
8 sprigs of Italian parsley
Salt and black pepper, to taste
1 pound dry penne pasta
Fresh parsley
Lemon peel

Heat oil in heavy gauge pan. Sauté onions and lox about 3 minutes. Add cream, parsley, salt and pepper. Reduce 3-5 minutes over low heat.
   Cook pasta in salted water while reducing the cream. Drain. Toss with sauce. Decorate with parsley and lemon peel.
   Serves 4.

• •

Calamari Saltati

2 cloves of garlic
1/3 cup olive oil
1-1/2 Roma tomatoes, diced
1/3 pound calamari, cleaned
   and cut into rings
3 sprigs of Italian parsley
Salt and black pepper, to taste
1/4 cup lightly salted water or
   fish broth, more if preferred

Sauté garlic in oil until brown. Add tomatoes. Cook 2 minutes on high heat. Add calamari, parsley, salt and pepper. Cover and simmer approximately 3 minutes. Add water or broth. Present in a hot bowl.
   Serves 2 as an appetizer.

• •

Portobello at the Marina

1728 W. Marine View Drive, Everett. Phone 258-6254. Open for lunch Monday through Friday, 11:00 A.M. to 3:00 P.M.; open for brunch Saturday and Sunday, 9:00 A.M. to 2:00 P.M.; open for dinner daily, 4:00 to 10:00 P.M.

Times change, and Everett - once thought of primarily as a forest products town - is changing with them. Portobello is one symbol of that change; a first-rate Mediterranean restaurant, capable of satisfying sophisticated tastes with Italian as well as French and Spanish entrées. A lovely waterfront view, a varied menu (weighted toward the abundant local seafood), and a good wine selection should satisfy even the most jaded city dwellers.

• •

Gamberoni (Prawns)

1 ounce olive oil
1/2 teaspoon garlic
6 ounces fresh tomato
3 ounces mushrooms
1 ounce wine
1/2 ounce brandy
4 prawns, 16-20 size
Salt and pepper, to taste

Heat oil. Sauté garlic. Add tomatoes and mushrooms, cooking until wilted. Add wine and brandy. Add the prawns. Season with salt and pepper.
Serves 1-2.

• •

Veal Portobello

1 ounce butter
12 ounces veal scaloppine
3 ounces mushrooms
2 ounces onions
1 ounce brandy
1 ounce white wine
1/2 teaspoon tarragon
1/2 ounce cream
1/4 teaspoon Dijon mustard
Salt and pepper, to taste

Heat butter in frying pan. Add veal, cooking until golden brown. Remove veal from pan.
Sauté mushrooms and onions. Add brandy, wine, tarragon, cream, mustard, salt and pepper. When the sauce has thickened, return veal to pan for 5 minutes.
Serves 2.

• •

Cafe Tosca

9924 S.W. Bank Road, Vashon Island.   Phone 463-2125.   Open Sunday through Thursday, 4:30 to 9:00 P.M.; Friday and Saturday, 4:30 to 10:00 P.M.

With Cafe Tosca, chef Rick Tada has provided Vashon residents and visitors with a first-rate Italian restaurant to call their very own. The menu is surprisingly varied for a relatively small island restaurant, and there are plenty of intriguing entrées to pique your interest and appetite.

• •

Roasted Garlic Linguini

2 5-ounce servings of good
   quality linguini
Oil
20 whole garlic cloves, peeled
   and trimmed
1/2 cup chopped parsley
2 pinches of kosher salt
2 pinches of fresh ground black
   pepper
2 ounces white wine
1 tablespoon fresh lemon juice
2 ounces sweet butter
Asiago or any other good dry
   cheese(s)

Cook, drain, rinse and chill pasta. Oil when cool. Refrigerate and cover what you don't use. You can bag and use for several more days.

Oil garlic. Cover and oven roast at 425° until tender, about 30 minutes. Try l0 minutes in the microwave. Cool and reserve.

Heat medium fry pan. Brown garlic. Add parsley, salt and pepper. Sauté 30 seconds. Add wine and lemon juice. Bring back to heat.

Dip al dente pasta in hot water for l minute. Drain and put in pasta bowl.

Add butter to garlic pan. Add a touch more wine if it has cooked away. Swirl butter et al around quickly. Add to cooked pasta. Toss and top with cheese(s). Best served with toasted Italian bread.

Serves 2.

• •

Chicken Marsala

Oil
2 split, boneless, skinless
  chicken breasts
Seasoned flour
1 sweet onion, thinly sliced
2 shallots, minced
10 button mushrooms,
  quartered
1 teaspoon fresh thyme
Salt and pepper, to taste
1 ounce Marsala
2 artichoke hearts, quartered
1 cup chicken stock
1/2 cup whipping cream
2 ounces sweet butter
Italian parsley
Lemon wedges

Heat oil in skillet. Dredge chicken in seasoned flour. Brown one side. Turn chicken. Add onion, shallots, mushrooms, thyme, salt and pepper. Sauté 3 minutes. Add Marsala, artichoke hearts, and chicken stock. Reduce sauce by one-half. Add cream. Reduce by one-half. Add butter and remove from heat. Adjust flavors. Garnish with Italian parsley and lemon wedges.

Serves 2.

Perche No Ristorante Italiano

621-1/2 Queen Anne Avenue North, Seattle.   Phone 298-0230.   Open for lunch Monday through Saturday, 11:30 A.M. to 2:30 P.M.; for brunch Sunday 10:30 A.M. to 2:30 P.M.; for dinner Sunday through Thursday, 5:00 to 10:00 P.M., Friday and Saturday, 5:00 to 11:00 P.M.

In Italian, "Perche No?" means "Why not?" The name seems more than appropriate for an avowedly Italian restaurant with a Chinese chef/owner. But David Kong, originally from Malaysia, developed an interest in Italian cuisine, and "the rest is history." The cooking is light and authentic, the prosciutto is homemade, and the Black Linguini with Smoked Salmon has become the house favorite. David goes to considerable trouble and expense to import many of his ingredients direct from Italy, including fresh mozzarella cheese, which, he tells us, comes from water buffalo!

• •

Scampi with Saffron

20 scampi (large prawns)
2 tablespoons flour
2 tablespoons olive oil
5 cloves of garlic, minced
5 shallots, minced
1/2 cup white wine, such as
   Chablis
1/4 teaspoon saffron threads
Juice of 1 medium lemon
1/4 cup whipping cream
1/2 teaspoon unsalted butter
1 tablespoon chopped
   Italian parsley
Salt and pepper, to taste

Peel and devein scampi; leave whole or butterfly. Dust lightly with flour. Shake off excess.

Heat oil in skillet. Sauté scampi 1 minute on each side. Add garlic and shallots. Sauté until lightly colored. Add wine, saffron threads and lemon juice. Add cream, cooking about 2 minutes. Swirl in butter. Sprinkle with parsley. Season with salt and pepper. Serve immediately with arborio rice.

Serves 4.

• •

Tortellini with Gorgonzola di Noci (with Walnuts)

Water
1 teaspoon salt
1 tablespoon olive oil
8 ounces fresh cheese tortellini (Parmesan/ricotta)
1/2 cup whipping cream
1/4 teaspoon white pepper
1/4 teaspoon ground nutmeg
Pinch of salt
4 tablespoons Gorgonzola cheese, crumbled
1 teaspoon finely chopped Italian parsley
1-2 tablespoons walnut halves
1 tablespoon fresh grated Parmesan cheese

Bring a large pot of water containing salt and olive oil to boil. Add the tortellini. Cook for about 3 minutes. Drain well.

Meanwhile, in a skillet, combine the cream with all the remaining ingredients except the Parmesan cheese. Cook 2-3 minutes, or until the sauce is reduced and slightly creamy. Add tortellini. Cook about 1 minute to heat through. Stir in Parmesan cheese. Serve immediately with extra Parmesan on the side.

Serves 2.

Prego

Stouffer Madison Hotel, 515 Madison Street, Seattle. Phone 583-0300. Open for lunch Monday through Friday, 11:00 A.M. to 2:00 P.M.; open for dinner Sunday through Thursday, 5:30 to 10:00 P.M.; Friday and Saturday, 5:30 to 11:00 P.M.

Prego has earned a place among the very best Italian restaurants in the Seattle area. This is no surprise when one considers that it is a part of the Stouffer Madison, one of Seattle's finest hotels. Still, few hotels carry off an ethnic restaurant concept as well as this one. The cuisine is northern Italian, with scrupulously fresh Northwest seafood often constituting the featured ingredient, and the presentations are unfailingly elegant.

• •

Seafood with Tomato and Saffron Broth

1 tablespoon olive oil
1 tablespoon chopped onion
1 tablespoon finely diced red
    pepper
2 medium size sea scallops,
    cleaned, muscle removed
2 prawns, 16-20 size, peeled and
    deveined
3 butter clams, cleaned
3 Penn Cove mussels, cleaned
    and de-bearded
2 ounces salmon, diced into 1
    inch pieces
2 cloves of garlic, sliced, not
    chopped
1 medium tomato, diced large
1 tablespoon of herbs (a
    combination of chopped
    basil, oregano and parsley)
5 threads of saffron
6 ounces fish stock or fumet

Place the oil in a small sauce pan. When very hot, add onions and pepper. Sauté until onions become clear. Add slightly seasoned seafood and toss with oil. Add garlic, tomato, herbs and saffron. Toss gently. Add fish stock and season. Simmer 4-5 minutes, or until clams and mussels open.

Prego recommends accompanying this dish with a nice Italian Prosicco.

Serves 1.

• •

Calamari Provencal

4 ounces best quality olive oil
12 ounces calamari, cleaned
and drained
Salt and pepper, to taste
2 tablespoons chopped garlic
4 tomatoes, diced in good size
chunks, seeds removed
8-10 green onions, chopped
1-2 tablespoons of herbs (a
combination of chopped
basil, oregano and parsley)

Heat oil in a large skillet until it just begins to smoke. Add calamari. Season with salt and pepper. Toss repeatedly to release steam. Add garlic and toss. Add remaining ingredients, continuing to toss. Serve immediately with lots of crusty bread for sopping up the sauce.

Prego's Jennifer Rogers reports this is their most popular appetizer!

Serves 4 as an appetizer.

Umberto's Ristorante

100 S. King Street, Seattle. Phone 621-0575. Open for lunch Monday through Friday, 11:00 A.M. to 2:30 P.M.; open for dinner Monday through Thursday, 5:00 to 10:00 P.M.; Friday and Saturday, 5:00 to 11:00 P.M.; Sunday, 4:30 to 9:00 P.M.

Umberto's is no secret to Seattle-area cognoscenti. Located just south of Pioneer Square, Umberto's is as popular for leisurely dinners as it is for a quick bite before an event at the adjacent Kingdome. Umberto's pasta has been voted "Seattle's Besta," and its menu runs the gamut from pastas and pizzas to tantalizing veal and seafood items.

• •

Tiramisu

20 ounces mascarpone cheese
6 tablespoons sugar
4 egg yolks
1/2 cup espresso
1 cup coffee
1/2 cup Kahlua
2 ounces rum
1/2 teaspoon nutmeg
12 ladyfingers
Chocolate shavings

Beat cheese, sugar and egg yolks together until well blended.

In a sauce pan, heat espresso, coffee, Kahlua, rum and nutmeg until warm. Soak ladyfingers in this coffee mixture.

Place soaked ladyfingers in individual serving glasses. Top with cheese mixture. Repeat to create layering. Garnish with chocolate shavings.

Serves 6.

• •

Radiatore Pepperoncini

8 ounces olive oil
4 ounces garlic, minced
4 ounces mushrooms, sliced
8 ounces tomato, peeled,
   seeded and diced
4 ounces pepperoncini, sliced
8 ounces chicken, poached and
   diced
12 ounces demi glaze
8 ounces heavy cream
1-1/2 teaspoons salt
1-1/2 teaspoons black pepper
8 teaspoons chopped parsley
12 ounces radiatore pasta
   (dried or fresh), cooked
4 ounces Parmesan cheese,
   grated

Sauté olive oil, garlic and mushrooms until garlic is fragrant, about 2-3 minutes. Add tomato, pepperoncini and chicken. Sauté an additional 2-3 minutes.

Deglaze pan with demi glaze. Add cream, salt, pepper and parsley. Cook 1 minute.

Add drained pasta and toss together. Garnish with cheese.

Serves 4.

Il Bistro

93A Pike Street, Seattle.   Phone 682-3049.   Open for lunch Tuesday through Saturday, noon to 3:00 P.M.; open for dinner Sunday through Thursday, 5:30 to 10:00 P.M.; Friday and Saturday to 11:00 P.M.; late bar menu daily, 10:00 P.M. to 12:30 A.M.

Italy is known for romance, so it seems only fitting that this lovely Italian restaurant would offer a romantic ambience for its guests.   The food is equal to the atmosphere; seafoods and produce are bought fresh daily at the adjacent Pike Place Market.   Rack of lamb, cioppino and Caesar salads are popular here, as is the select wine list; Il Bistro also features extensive collections of single malt Scotch whiskeys, fine Cognacs and vintage Ports.

• •

Fettucine Primavera

2 tablespoons olive oil
2 cloves of garlic, chopped
2 tablespoons coarsely chopped
   basil
1 teaspoon oregano
8 spears of asparagus
1 tomato, thinly sliced
1 zucchini, thinly sliced
1 small, yellow squash, thinly
   sliced
Salt and pepper, to taste
1/4 cup white wine
2 cups heavy cream
1 cup half and half
1/2 pound fresh fettucine
Boiling water
2 tablespoons butter
3 tablespoons Romano cheese
1/4 cup grated Parmesan cheese

Heat oil and lightly sauté the garlic, basil, oregano, asparagus, tomato, zucchini and squash. Season with salt and pepper. Add wine and cook, reducing slightly. Add cream along with half and half. Reduce on low heat 3-5 minutes, or until thick.

Cook pasta 5 minutes in boiling water. Drain and combine with the vegetable-cream sauce. Blend in butter and Romano cheese. Top with Parmesan cheese.

Serves 2.

• •

Cioppino

8 large Roma tomatoes
1/8 cup olive oil
1 small onion, chopped
1 clove of garlic, minced
1 small green bell pepper,
  chopped
1 small red bell pepper,
  chopped
4 crab legs
6 clams
6 mussels
4 ounces snapper
2 cups fumet
4 prawns
2 ounces squid
1/2 lemon, sliced
1 bunch of basil, chopped
1 bunch of oregano, chopped
Lemon wedges
Sprig of parsley

Roast tomatoes in oven until brown. Peel, smash and set aside.

Heat oil in skillet. Sauté onions, garlic and peppers until onions are translucent. Add crab, clams, mussels and snapper. Sauté 5 minutes. Add reserved tomatoes and fumet. Simmer about 10 minutes. Add prawns, squid, lemon slices, basil and oregano. Let simmer 10 minutes.

Present in bowls garnished with lemon wedges and parsley.

Serves 2.

Caffe Minnie's

101 Denny Way, Seattle. Phone 448-6263. Open 24 hours, daily.

Mention a round-the-clock restaurant, and most people immediately downgrade their culinary expectations. However, it isn't necessarily so. Case in point: Caffe Minnie's, which serves an eclectic mix of breakfasts, pastas, steaks and seafoods, many of them with an Italian flair. And eclectic it should be, to match its clientele: by day, the Denny Regrade area hosts advertising, sports and creative types, while at night it's a mix of musicians, actors, artists, restaurant and bar employees just getting off work, and people on their way to or from an event or performance at Seattle Center.

• •

Dutch Baby

8 eggs
1 cup half and half
1/2 cup flour
1/4 cup sugar
1/4 teaspoon salt
1/2 teaspoon vanilla
1/4 teaspoon lemon juice
2-8 tablespoons oil
Powdered sugar
Butter
Maple syrup

Thoroughly mix the first 7 ingredients together, making sure flour is totally incorporated in the mixture.

Heat a 7 inch or 8 inch Silverstone or Teflon coated skillet to medium high on the range top. Add 2 tablespoons oil to pan. Pour about 8 ounces of the well beaten egg mixture into center of pan, filling to 3/4 full.

Place pan in preheated 375° oven 25-35 minutes (15-20 minutes in convection oven), or until puffed and golden brown.

Remove and serve immediately on plate as the "baby" will start to sink and flatten. Dust with powdered sugar. Add butter and maple syrup.

Caffe Minnie's suggests that you use fresh fruit for toppings, or your favorite fruit compotes or jams, or a scoop of ricotta cheese with a dash of cinnamon.

Makes 8-10 "babies."

• •

Fettucine con Salmone

1/2 cup hazelnuts or filberts,
  peeled
5-6 ounces lox-style smoked
  salmon
2 ounces Frangelico
1-1/2 cups heavy cream
12 ounces fresh cut fettucine
1 tablespoon butter
Parmesan cheese
Fresh chopped parsley

In a large skillet or sauté pan, toast hazelnuts on medium high heat, being careful not to burn them, by rolling frequently in pan. When toasted to golden brown, add salmon. Immediately afterward, add Frangelico to deglaze pan. Be careful when adding Frangelico, especially over gas burners, as it will ignite momentarily. When liqueur is reduced by half, add cream. Cook until reduced by half.

Put fettucine in rapidly boiling water. Cook until al dente. Remove and drain in strainer.

When cream is reduced by half, add butter. Cook 1 minute, mixing butter into cream. Add cooked pasta. Mix to coat pasta. Put on large platter. Add Parmesan cheese on top. Garnish with chopped parsley.

Serves 2.

Balsano's

127 - 15th Street Southeast, Puyallup. Phone 845-4222. Open Monday through Thursday, 11:00 A.M. to 9:00 P.M.; Friday, 11:00 A.M. to 10:00 P.M.; Saturday, 4:00 to 10:00 P.M.; Sunday, 4:00 to 9:00 P.M.

Puyallup might not be the first place you would look for a really good Italian restaurant, but locals have known - and flocked to - Balsano's for years. Owned and operated by Tom Pantley and his family, the emphasis is on seafood pasta dishes, wonderful sautéed vegetables, and veal and chicken dishes, each with its own unique style. Balsano's also offers periodic cooking classes to the public.

• •

Fettucine and Fresh Mussels

12 mussels
1/2 cup white wine
2 tablespoons olive oil
1/4 cup sliced onion
1/4 cup diced celery
1 tablespoon chopped parsley
Salt and pepper, to taste
Red pepper flakes
Powdered garlic
1/4 cup thick tomato purée
1/4 cup diced tomatoes
1/8 cup sliced green onions
Cooked fettucine

Combine the first 10 ingredients in a sauce pan. Cover tightly and boil until the mussels begin to open. Remove the mussels and set aside.

Pour the remaining contents from the sauce pan into a hot sauté pan. With the pan on high heat, add the diced tomatoes and green onions. Continue cooking until sauce thickens.

To present, place mussels on top of hot fettucine and pour sauce over both.

Serves 2-3.

• •

Pasta Primavera

1/4 cup sliced carrots
2 tablespoons olive oil
1/2 cup broccoli
1/8 cup sliced onions
1/4 cup white wine
Garlic
1/2 pint heavy cream
1/2 teaspoon basil
Salt and pepper, to taste
1/8 cup diced tomatoes
2 tablespoons Parmesan cheese
Cooked fettucine

Sauté carrots in olive oil. When they begin to soften, add broccoli and onions, and brown. Pour in wine and add the garlic. As the wine is cooking off, add cream, basil, salt and pepper. Cook on high heat, stirring more frequently as the sauce thickens. Add tomatoes and cheese. Toss with hot fettucine.

Serves 1-2.

Italia

1010 Western Avenue, Seattle. Phone 623-1917. Open Monday through Friday, 7:00 A.M. to 9:00 P.M.; Saturday, 7:00 A.M. to 10:30 P.M.; closed Sunday.

A stone's throw from Seattle's busy waterfront and an easy stroll from the Pike Place Market, Italia serves downtown workers and business people as well as tourists visiting the city. It's also a destination for people from all over the area who come for the food, which is always fresh and seasonal. Especially noteworthy is the wide array of appetizers and antipasti, ideal - as manager Bernadette Scheller puts it - for tasting and menu grazing.

• •

Polenta with Vegetables

5 cups water
Salt, to taste
2-1/2 cups coarse grained
cornmeal
1 pound diced mixed vegetables,
such as carrots, celery,
yellow onions, broccoli
1/3 cup extra virgin olive oil

In a deep sauce pan, bring the water and salt to a boil. Slowly add the cornmeal in a thin, steady steam, stirring constantly. Add the vegetables. Cook over low heat about 40 minutes, stirring constantly.

The polenta is ready when it starts pulling away easily from the sides of the pan.

Dampen the inside of a deep bowl with water. Pour in the polenta and smooth the surface with a knife (wet knife is advised). Cover and let stand 10 minutes. Invert the bowl to release the polenta. Cut into wedges. Drizzle with olive oil. Serve hot or at room temperature.

Serves 6.

• •

Spaghetti con Gamberi
(Pasta with Zucchini and Shrimp)

2 small zucchini, about 10
    ounces, cut into 1/8 inch
    slices
1/2 pound small prawns or
    shrimp, unshelled
Coarse grained salt
1 lemon
4 tablespoons olive oil
1 large clove of garlic, peeled
    and coarsely chopped
4 tablespoons minced garlic
Salt and fresh ground black
    pepper, to taste
1 cup very warm chicken or
    vegetable broth prepared
    with a large pinch of ground
    saffron
1 very large ripe tomato, diced
Water
1-1/2 pounds pasta (cooked
    weight)
15 sprigs of Italian parsley,
    chopped

Grill (sear) the zucchini slices briefly and set aside.

Place shrimp in a bowl of cold water with coarse salt. Add the lemon, cut in half and squeezed. Mix and allow to soak for 30 minutes. Drain the shrimp. Shell and devein, if needed. Set aside.

Place a skillet with oil over low heat. When oil is warm, add the garlic and sauté 2 minutes. Add the zucchini to the skillet and sauté 30 seconds. Raise the heat to high. Season the zucchini with salt and pepper and add the broth. Cover the skillet and cook 2 minutes, stirring every so often with a wooden spoon. Add the shrimp and tomato to the skillet mixture. Mix well and cook 2 minutes.

Bring water to a boil. Add salt to taste. Add pasta and cook 1-3 minutes, depending on the dryness. Drain and add to the skillet. Sprinkle the parsley on top of the pasta mixture and mix gently.

Serves 6.

Cafe Lago

2305 - 24th Avenue East, Seattle. Phone 329-8005. Open for lunch Tuesday through Friday, 11:00 A.M. to 2:00 P.M.; open for dinner Tuesday through Sunday, 5:00 to 10:00 P.M.; closed Monday.

Cafe Lago is among the top-rated - and best loved - Italian restaurants in the Seattle area. It's an authentic trattoria, and Jordi Viradas says that the handmade pasta and pizza from the wood-fired oven are among the many touches that keep people coming back to this fine restaurant.

• •

Fettucine con Melanzana

1 large eggplant
Olive oil
Red wine vinegar
Salt and pepper, to taste
Handful of fresh basil leaves, chopped
2 cloves of garlic, chopped
3 salt-packed anchovies, rinsed and chopped
Fettucine, cooked in boiling water
Black pepper
2 handfuls of young arugula leaves, washed and dried

Cut eggplant in half lengthwise, then into 1/4 inch slices. Fry in very hot olive oil until browned on both sides. Remove and drain on thick layer of paper towels. When all are fried, cut the slices in halves or thirds. Place on a platter and sprinkle with vinegar. Season with salt and pepper. Mix with the chopped basil. Set aside to marinate 1 hour or so.

Heat garlic and anchovies very gently in a few tablespoons of oil. Add the eggplant. Add the cooked pasta to the pan. Season with black pepper. At the last minute, add the arugula, toss and serve immediately.

For a variation, Jordi suggests that you substitute whole basil leaves for the arugula.

Serves 4.

• , •

Ravioli di Barbabietole
(Casumzei Ampezzani)

1 pound, 2 ounces fresh beets,
   baked in oven at high heat
   (450°) about 2 hours
4 tablespoons unsalted butter
1/3 cup ricotta cheese
4 large egg yolks
1/2 cup Parmigiano cheese
1 cup fresh white bread crumbs
Salt and pepper, to taste

Peel the cooked beets. Dice into small, but not tiny pieces. Process in food processor until chopped into tiny pieces. Must not be puréed!

Add remaining ingredients and process until mixed. Mixture should be fairly thick. If not, add more bread crumbs.

Fill ravioli skins. Sheets of pasta can be purchased, or make your own, using any good pasta recipe.

Verrazano's

28835 Pacific Highway South, Federal Way. Phone 946-4122. Open Sunday through Thursday, 11:30 A.M. to 10:00 P.M.; Friday and Saturday, 11:30 A.M. to 11:00 P.M.

Diners at Verrazano's find excellent Italian food at family prices, with an added bonus: a gorgeous view of Puget Sound, looking west toward Maury and Vashon Islands with the Olympic Mountains as a backdrop. When the weather cooperates, there's also outside dining, from a menu with something for every taste.

• •

Roasted Veal Tenderloin with Dungeness Crab Risotto and Wild Mushrooms

RISOTTO:
2 tablespoons chopped shallots
1/4 cup butter
1 cup arborio rice
1/2 cup dry white wine
1 quart fish stock
1/4 teaspoon saffron threads
6 ounces Dungeness crab meat

Sauté shallots with butter until wilted. Add rice. Cook 1 minute. Add wine. Cook 2 minutes on high. Add fish stock and saffron threads. Bring to a boil. Reduce to simmer and cook until rice is a thick pudding consistency, about 35 minutes. Stir in crab meat. Keep warm while roasting veal.

VEAL:
2 tablespoons olive oil
2 8-ounce veal tenderloins
Salt and pepper, to taste

Basil
4-6 ounces chanterelle
    mushrooms
1/2 cup white wine
1/4 cup butter

Heat sauté pan to medium high. Add oil. Add veal. Sear for 2 minutes, seasoning with salt, pepper and basil. Add mushrooms to pan. Put pan in 425° oven to roast for approximately 8-10 minutes, or until meat thermometer reads 120°-125°. Remove veal from pan. Slice into thin medallions.

Add wine to mushroom pan to deglaze. Reduce liquid by one-half. Stir in butter to finish.

Spoon 6-8 ounces risotto on plate. Fan veal over risotto. Top veal with mushroom sauce. Garnish with fresh basil.

Serves 2.

• •

Wild Field Salad with Roasted Duck

**Field salad mixture (curly
  endive, bibb, romaine,
  radicchio, arugula, etc.)
  Premixed salad greens are
  available at the market.**
2 ounces Roquefort cheese
1/2 cup red currants
2 tablespoons oil
Flour
10-12 ounce breast of duck
Salt and pepper, to taste
Rosemary
4 ounces oyster mushrooms
Sprig of rosemary
1/2 cup raspberry vinegar

Arrange salad greens on 2 plates. Crumble 1 ounce cheese on each salad. Top with 1/4 cup red currants. Set aside.

Heat skillet to medium high. Add oil. Flour duck. Add to pan, skin side down. Cook 3 minutes, or until skin is dark brown and crispy. Turn duck over. Season with salt, pepper and rosemary. Add mushrooms to pan. Place in 425° oven for 6-8 minutes, or until medium rare.

Remove duck. Slice into thin strips.

To arrange, fan duck strips over salad greens. Garnish with the roasted oyster mushrooms and rosemary sprig. Deglaze roasting pan with vinegar and dress salad.

Serves 2.

Trattoria Mitchelli

84 Yesler Way, Seattle. Phone 623-3883. Open Sunday and Monday, 7:00 A.M. to 11:00 P.M.; Tuesday through Friday, 7:00 to 4:00 A.M.; Saturday and Sunday, 8:00 to 4:00 A.M.

Located in historic Pioneer Square, Trattoria Mitchelli - fittingly, given its location - lays claim to being Seattle's oldest trattoria. Expanded two years ago, "the Trat" is a favorite among local artists, actors, tourists and business people any time of day. Calzones, pizzas and other entrées from the wood-fired pizza oven are among the edibles, all done with typical Mitchelli flair.   The Mitchellis also own and operate the popular Bella Luna Trattoria, which is included in this book as well.

• •

Smoked Salmon Pizza with Fresh Spinach Sauce

10 ounces of your favorite pizza dough recipe or large purchased pizza crust, such as Boboli
1/4 cup Fresh Spinach Sauce (recipe follows)
1/4 pound grated mozzarella cheese
4 ounces nova cold smoked salmon, cut into quarter sized pieces
2 tablespoons capers, well drained, optional
2 ounces thinly sliced red onion

Roll pizza dough into 10-12 inch circle. Spread Fresh Spinach Sauce evenly over surface of dough, leaving 3/4 inch rim around the outer edge of the pizza. Sprinkle cheese evenly over sauce. Evenly distribute smoked salmon over cheese. Spread capers and red onions evenly over surface of pizza.

Place pizza on baking stone in the center of the oven. Bake in center of oven preheated to 450° until crust is golden brown and cheese is melted and bubbly.

Makes one 10-12 inch pizza.

FRESH SPINACH SAUCE:

2 tablespoons butter
1/2 teaspoon chopped garlic
1 tablespoon minced onions
1/2 cup fresh, finely chopped
    spinach
1/2 teaspoon salt
1/2 teaspoon fresh ground
    black pepper
2 tablespoons all-purpose flour
3/4 cup half and half

Melt butter in sauce pan. Add garlic and onions. Sauté over medium heat until onions turn translucent, but do not brown. Add spinach. Sauté until wilted. Add salt, pepper and flour. Stir until flour is evenly distributed. Add half and half. Bring to boil. Reduce heat. Simmer 5 minutes.

• •

Salvatore Ristorante Italiano

6100 Roosevelt Way, N.E., Seattle.   Phone 527-9301.   Open Monday through Thursday, 5:00 to 10:00 P.M.; Friday and Saturday, 5:00 to 11:00 P.M.; closed Sunday.

This small, family-run restaurant is a warm and friendly haven for Italian food lovers looking for a place to relax and feel at home.   Guests watch owner/chef Salvatore Anania at work in the open kitchen, preparing their meals, and they find that he enjoys sharing recipes and tips with them for those evenings at home. For over five years, Salvatore has earned a reputation for consistency, reliability, and warm, friendly service.

• •

Pollo ai Capperi

1/4 stick margarine
4 7-ounce chicken breasts, tenderized and pounded flat, floured
2 cloves of garlic, minced
3 ounces imported capers
2 tablespoons finely chopped parsley
1/4 cup dry Marsala
1/4 cup heavy cream
4 ounces part skim mozzarella cheese

In a large sauté pan, heat margarine. When pan is hot, add chicken breasts. Cook until lightly browned on both sides. Add garlic, capers and parsley. Sauté 15-30 seconds. Add Marsala and cream. Let the sauce reduce 2-3 minutes. Add cheese.

Bake in 400° oven 3-5 minutes, or until cheese melts. Pull from oven and remove chicken. Reduce the sauce to a very thick consistency. Pour over chicken breasts and serve. Buon Appetito! Enjoy.

Serves 4.

• •

Penne Puttanesca

1/2 cup olive pomace oil
8 flat filets of anchovy
3 cloves of garlic, minced
1/8 cup finely chopped parsley
1-1/2 tablespoons crushed red
    chilies
1/4 cup capers
24 Kalamata olives, pitted
Base Marinara (recipe follows)
24 ounces cooked penne or
    pasta of choice
1/4 cup Parmesan cheese

Heat oil in large sauce pan.
Add anchovies. Cook well, until
they disintegrate. Add garlic,
parsley and chilies. Let them
sizzle. Add capers and olives.
Sauté 15-20 seconds. Add Base
Marinara. Reduce 3-5 minutes, or
until oil separates from the
tomato. Add pasta and Parmesan.
Garnish with a light dusting of
Parmesan.
    Serves 4.

BASE MARINARA:
4 cloves of garlic
20 large fresh basil leaves
2 tablespoons salt
1 tablespoon pepper
1/4 cup cold water
16-ounce can crushed pear
    tomatoes

Combine all ingredients,
except tomatoes, in blender or
food processor. Mix at high speed
20-30 seconds. Combine mixture
with tomatoes, stirring well.

Sadighi's

921 Lakeway Drive, Bellingham. Phone 647-1109. Open Monday through Friday, 5:00 P.M. to closing; Saturday and Sunday, 4:30 P.M. to closing.

An intimate, quiet place, Sadighi's is a fine choice for special occasions, perhaps with a little romance involved. The menu is Mediterranean and American, and the food is well-prepared and beautifully presented. Owner Bill Sadighi and son Jeff clearly put themselves into their restaurant, and it shows. The cheesecake here is wonderful, so do try to reserve some room!

• •

Caesar Salad Dressing

1/3 cup red wine vinegar
2 medium eggs
1 ounce heavy cream
2 cloves of garlic
20 black peppercorns
1 teaspoon Dijon mustard
3 anchovies
1 cup olive oil, chilled

Combine vinegar, eggs, cream, garlic, peppercorns, mustard and anchovies in blender on highest setting. Slowly pour olive oil in a thin stream into blender while it is running until dressing thickens. Refrigerate up to 1 week.

Makes about 1-2/3 cups.

• •

Oysters Baked Italian

6 slices raw bacon, frozen
1 medium onion, diced medium
    small, less than 1/2 inch
    square
3 cloves of garlic, finely minced
1/2 teaspoon basil
1/2 teaspoon Greek oregano
1/2 teaspoon thyme
1/2 teaspoon white pepper
1/2 teaspoon black pepper
1/2 teaspoon cayenne pepper
1 tablespoon chopped parsley
12 medium white mushrooms,
    quartered
32 extra small, fresh oysters
2/3 cup shredded Romano
    cheese
White wine

Remove bacon from freezer. Cut into l/4 inch slices, end to end. Spray sauté pan with no-stick. Add bacon. Cook at medium low until bacon is brown and crisp, stirring to assure even cooking. Add onion and garlic. Mix and cook 3 minutes. Remove from heat. Add remaining spices. Mix well. Add mushrooms and oysters. Gently mix over medium heat 1 minute. Pour into baking dish. Top with cheese. Splash cheese with wine to prevent drying. Bake in 400° oven 5-8 minutes, or until cheese is lightly browned. Serve with crusty bread.

Serves 4.

Ave! Al Ristorante Italiano

4743 University Way N.E., Seattle.   Phone 527-9830.   Open for lunch Monday through Friday, 11:30 A.M. to 2:30 P.M.; open for dinner Sunday through Thursday, 5:00 to 10:00 P.M.; Friday and Saturday, 5:00 to 11:00 P.M.

Ave! has become something of an institution in the University District. Owner Gianfranco D'Aniello has endeavored to create a casual atmosphere in which his guests can relax and enjoy the authenticity of his Italian cuisine. Gianfranco sees to it that his food is of the highest quality and that his servers are competent and helpful, and says, "pleasing our customers is our priority."

• •

Penne con Salsa di Peperoni
(Penne in a Roasted Bell Pepper Sauce)

2 red bell peppers
1 clove of garlic, minced
2 tablespoons butter
1 tablespoon chopped, fresh
   Italian parsley
1/2 cup heavy cream
Salt and black pepper, to taste
8 ounces penne pasta
Parmesan cheese
Parsley

Place peppers in a baking dish and broil, turning until just black all over. Rinse under cold water, washing away the burned skin and seeds. Mince peppers.

Sauté garlic in butter until golden. Add peppers and parsley. Cook about 3 minutes. Add cream, salt and pepper. Cook, stirring constantly until a thickened, smooth consistency is obtained, usually about 10 minutes.

Cook penne in abundant, salted water until al dente. Add to the cream mixture. Serve hot with Parmesan cheese and parsley sprinkled on top.

Serves 2.

• •

Involtini di Vitello con Spinaci e Gorgonzola (Rolled Veal Scaloppine with Spinach and Gorgonzola)

2 cloves of garlic, finely minced
1/2 cup olive oil (not extra virgin), divided
6 ounces fresh spinach, cleaned
Salt, to taste
Pinch of hot crushed red pepper
4 veal slices, 3-4 ounces each, preferably tenderloin. If not, tenderize by pounding gently on both sides
Pepper, to taste
4 ounces Gorgonzola cheese, crumbled
1/2 cup dry white wine
Pinch of flour

In a large skillet, sauté garlic in 4 tablespoons olive oil until golden. Add spinach, salt and red pepper. Cook for 2-4 minutes, until spinach is soft and tender. Set aside.

Place veal slices on a flat working surface. Salt and pepper top side of each piece. Divide the Gorgonzola and spinach equally among the veal slices. Roll each slice and secure with a toothpick, lengthwise.

Add remaining oil to skillet on high heat. Cook veal, toothpick side down. Turn and cook another minute. Put heat on low. Cover and cook about 10 minutes, turning veal occasionally. Place veal on a serving dish. Take out toothpicks.

Place same skillet back on high heat about 30 seconds. Add wine and cook about 1 minute, stirring and scraping the bottom of the pan constantly. Add a pinch of flour. Keep stirring until slightly thickened. Pour over veal rolls.

Serves 2.

Lombardi's Cucina

2200 N.W. Market Street, Seattle. Phone 783-0055. Open for lunch Monday through Friday, 11:00 A.M. to 3:00 P.M.; open for brunch Saturday and Sunday, 9:00 A.M. to 3:00 P.M.; open for dinner Monday through Thursday, 5:00 to 10:00 P.M.; Friday and Saturday, 5:00 to 11:00 P.M.; Sunday, 4:30 to 9:30 P.M.

As you would expect, the pasta and ravioli are excellent at Lombardi's, since they operate their very own pasta company, Ribbons Pasta. Owner Diane Symms has dedicated Lombardi's to serving memorable, full-flavored, yet simple and affordable Italian food. That goal is achieved, both at this Ballard location and at another, located in Issaquah. Summer months open the outdoor seating option at sidewalk tables.

• •

Fettucine with Chicken and Portobello Mushrooms

2 cups rich, flavorful chicken
   stock
1 cup cream
2 ounces Marsala or dry
   sherry
1 pound portobello mushrooms,
   sliced
1 tablespoon minced shallots
4 tablespoons butter
1/4 cup flour
1/2 teaspoon fresh thyme leaves
1/2 teaspoon salt
1/2 teaspoon pepper
1 pound fresh fettucine, cooked

Heat together the chicken stock, cream and Marsala.

Sauté mushrooms with shallots in butter. When mushrooms are soft, add flour. Stir together over gentle heat 1 minute. Add thyme. Cook 1 minute. Add the stock mixture. Cook, stirring frequently, until sauce thickens. Add salt and pepper. Correct seasonings. Fold in cooked fettuccine.

Serves 2-4.

• •

Braised Rabbit

Rabbit
Flour
Oil
1 cup onions
1 tablespoon minced garlic
1/2 teaspoon fresh rosemary
1/2 teaspoon fresh thyme
1/2 cup white wine
1/2 cup chicken stock
3/4 cup whole tomatoes in juice,
 well mashed by hand
3 julienne cut pieces of red bell
 pepper
1/4 cup shitake mushrooms
Pinch of crushed pink and
 green peppercorns
Green onions

Cut rabbit into 4 legs and 4 pieces of saddle. Flour and brown in hot oil.

Add onions and garlic. Sauté until onions are translucent, being careful not to brown the garlic. Add rosemary, thyme, wine, stock, tomatoes, bell pepper, mushrooms, and peppercorns. Cover and braise 30-45 minutes. Add green onions to sauce for color.

Serve with polenta topped with Gorgonzola cheese.

Serves 4.

Ristorante di Ragazzi

2329 California Avenue S.W., Seattle.   Phone 935-1969.   Open for lunch Monday through Friday, 11:30 A.M. to 2:30 P.M.;   open for dinner Sunday through Thursday, 4:30 to 11:00 P.M.; Friday and Saturday, 4:30 P.M. to 1:00 A.M.

One recent reviewer stated that in Ristorante di Ragazzi, the conviviality of "Cheers" is combined with the rolling hills of the Tuscan countryside. It is a wonderfully cheerful place, and the decor, complete with golden murals of the Italian countryside, tapestry upholstery and green wicker chairs, is beautiful. The careful thought that obviously went into the ambiance is also evident in the rustic flavors of the food.

· ·

Agnello Braciole (Leg of Lamb Roasted and Stuffed with Fresh Herbs, Italian Meats and Dijon)

1/2 pound fresh Italian sausage
1/2 pound diced pancetta
4 sprigs of fresh rosemary, chopped
1 bunch of fresh marjoram, chopped
1 bunch of fresh oregano, chopped
1 bunch of fresh sage, chopped
Salt and pepper, to taste
1/2 cup Italian herbed bread crumbs
1 large egg
1/2 cup Dijon mustard
1 medium leg of lamb, boned

In a large pan, render off sausage. Drain and discard grease. Cook sausage until crumbly. Add pancetta and remove from heat.

Combine herbs, salt, pepper, bread crumbs, egg and mustard. Add to meat mixture.

Layer inside of lamb leg. Fold meat over stuffing. Tie string around leg. Cover pan with aluminum foil. Roast 1-1/4 hours in a preheated 325° oven. Remove from oven and let rest, covered, 15 minutes. Remove foil and slice thin.

Serves 6-8.

· ·

Rigatoni Demile

2 ounces sun-dried tomatoes,
  sliced
4 medium black Kalamata
  olives, pitted
1 ounce small capers
1 pat of butter
1 pint heavy cream
8 ounces rigatoni pasta

Sauté tomatoes, olives, and capers in butter. Add cream and reduce until mixture thickens. Set aside.

Boil off pasta 7-10 minutes. Drain.

Add pasta to cream mixture and reheat slightly.

Serves 2.

Testa Rossa

210 Broadway Avenue East, Seattle. Phone 328-0878. Open Monday through Thursday 11:00 A.M. to 11:00 P.M.; Friday and Saturday, 11:00 A.M. to midnight; Sunday, 1:00 to 11:00 P.M.

Visitors to Testa Rossa will be taken by the art-filled dining room and the pizzas - claimed to be the best in Seattle - which are offered in both deep dish (Chicago style) and thin crust styles. Pastas, salads, appetizers and "decadent" desserts round out the menu of this stylish eatery.

• •

Bruschetta & Sumptuous Spreads

BRUSCHETTA:
4 cloves of garlic, minced
1/2 cup extra virgin olive oil
1 loaf good Italian bread, sliced
　　1/2 inch thick
Olivada Spread (recipe follows)
Sun-dried Tomato Pesto (recipe
　　follows)
Herbed Montrachet Spread
　　(recipe follows)

　　Mix olive oil and garlic together. Brush both sides of bread with the garlic oil. Roast each side under broiler until golden. Present with spreads or pesto.
　　Serves 4-8.

OLIVADA SPREAD:
1 cup Kalamata olives
1/4 cup fresh parsley, chopped
1/4 cup toasted walnuts
2 tablespoons minced onion
1 teaspoon herbs de province
2 tablespoons extra virgin olive
　　oil

　　Chop olives in a food processor. Add parsley, walnuts, onions and herbs. Process 15 seconds on pulse. Slowly stream in oil with processor on.

SUN-DRIED TOMATO PESTO:
1 cup sun-dried tomatoes,
　　packed in oil
1/2 teaspoon red pepper flakes
1/2 teaspoon minced garlic
1 teaspoon balsamic vinegar
1 tablespoon fresh chopped
　　parsley
Salt and pepper, to taste
2 tablespoons toasted walnuts

　　Process all ingredients except walnuts until chunky. Add walnuts and process until smooth.

HERBED MONTRACHET SPREAD:
1/2 pound Montrachet cheese
1 small scallion, chopped
2 teaspoons fresh chopped
　　parsley
2 teaspoons fresh chopped basil
Cream, as needed

Process Montrachet 2-3 pulses. Add the scallion, parsley, and basil and process 30 seconds.

Thin with heavy cream, if necessary.

• •

Potato Pizza

Pizza dough, your favorite, enough for a 14 inch pizza
Olive oil
Pizza sauce, your favorite
Potato Slices (recipe follows)
Caramelized Onions (recipe follows)
Fresh grated Parmesan cheese
Fresh chopped Italian parsley

Roll out pizza dough to 1/8 inch thick (or your preference), 14 inches round (thin crust is the idea behind this pizza). Using a fork, gently make perforations all over dough crust to help prevent bubbles. Brush lightly with oil. Spread with a very light amount of pizza sauce, about 1/4 cup. Lay potato slices on top, starting in 1/4 inch from the edge and slightly overlapping each slice until the pizza is covered. Top with Caramelized Onions, and sprinkle with cheese.

Bake 7-10 minutes in a 475° oven, or until golden brown. Top with parsley.

Serves 2.

POTATO SLICES:
10 small red potatoes, sliced
2 teaspoons salt
2 teaspoons fresh ground black pepper
Half of the Caramelized Onions (recipe follows)
1 cup grated Parmesan cheese
1/2 cup olive oil
1/2 cup unsalted butter, at room temperature
2 teaspoons minced garlic

Gently mix all the ingredients together, being careful not to break the potato slices. Lay in a single layer on a lightly oiled sheet pan. Bake 10 minutes at 450°, or until light golden brown.

CARAMELIZED ONIONS:
1/4 cup olive oil
6 cups (about 3 pounds) thinly sliced yellow onions
Salt and pepper, to taste

Heat oil in a large, heavy skillet over medium to medium high heat. Add onions. Stir to coat with oil. Add salt and pepper. Stir occasionally, until onions are soft and a light caramel color, about 45 minutes.

• •

Il Fiasco

1309 Commercial, Bellingham. Phone 676-9136. Open for lunch Monday through Friday, 11:30 A.M. to 2:30 P.M.; open for dinner every day, 5:30 to 9:30 P.M.

New owner Andrew Moquin recently purchased this well-regarded Italian place and has busily set about making it even better. He sees Il Fiasco as an upscale, quality, full service restaurant and insists on the freshest Northwest ingredients and meticulous attention to detail to ensure that the product lives up to its promise.

• •

Mussels Tuaca

1 ounce unsalted butter
1 tablespoon minced shallots
1/8 cup sliced leeks
1/2 cup heavy cream
1/3 cup orange juice
1 shot of Tuaca
1 large or 2 small Roma
   tomatoes, diced
1 pound freshest mussels, rinsed
   and de-bearded
White pepper, to taste
Lemon juice
Salt, optional
Fresh chopped parsley or
   chives
Lemon wedges

In a sauce pan, heat butter until melted. Add shallots and leeks. Sauté 2 minutes on medium heat, or until leeks become wilted. Add cream, orange juice, Tuaca, and tomatoes. Turn heat up. Add mussels and steam open, removing as they open to a warmed bowl. Discard mussels that do not open after 2-3 minutes. Season sauce with pepper, lemon juice and salt.

An additional ounce of butter may be added if an extra rich sauce is desired.

Reduce sauce to desired consistency. Serve over mussels.

Sprinkle with parsley or chives. Serve with lemon wedges. Serves 2.

• •

Garlic and Chicken Soup

3-1/2 to 4 pound chicken
Salt and pepper, to taste
1 teaspoon dried thyme or 1
    sprig of fresh thyme
1 small yellow onion, quartered,
    plus 1 large yellow onion,
    chopped
1 small lemon, quartered
1/2 cup garlic cloves, peeled
1 tablespoon vegetable oil
3 bay leaves
1 carrot, sliced, plus 2 carrots
2 ribs of celery, sliced
2 leeks, chopped
1/3 pound unsalted butter
    plus 1/4 pound plus 2 ounces
1/2 gallon chicken stock
1/4 cup white flour
1 cup dry white wine
1 quart heavy cream
2 tablespoons minced fresh thyme
    or 1 tablespoon dried thyme
Lemon juice
Sour cream
Chives, chopped

Remove giblets, neck and other parts from cavity of chicken. Save for stock. Discard liver. Season cavity and outside of chicken with salt and pepper. Sprinkle cavity with thyme. Place quartered onion and lemon inside cavity. Tie legs together. Roast in 350° oven 2 hours, or until done.

Place garlic in small, oven-proof sauté pan with oil. Roast, covered, in oven with chicken. Stir garlic every 20 minutes until very soft. Remove. Allow to cool. Purée. Should yield 1/3 cup roasted garlic purée.

After roasted chicken has cooled, thoroughly pick off all meat, saving all bones, skin, fat and scraps including neck and giblets for stock. Cover scraps with 1 gallon cool water. Add bay leaves, sliced carrot and celery. Bring to boil. Skim off any foam that forms on top. Simmer 1-2 hours. Strain and skim fat. Dice all roasted meat.

Sauté leeks and chopped onion in 1/3 pound butter until limp. Purée. In separate pan, sauté 2 carrots, that have been pulsed in a food processor, in 1/4 pound butter until they are fairly small but not totally puréed.

Add puréed leeks and onions, sautéed carrot, and roasted garlic purée to chicken stock. Bring to boil, stirring constantly to avoid scorching.

Meanwhile, prepare a blond roux by melting 2 ounces butter. Stir in flour. Maintain over low heat 5-8 minutes. Allow to cool. Stir into simmering soup base, a bit at a time.

Add wine, cream, thyme, and chicken. Return to boil. Season with salt, pepper and lemon juice.

If cooled and reheated, soup may need to be re-seasoned.

Garnish with sour cream and chives.

Serves 6.

Pasta Bella

1530 Queen Anne Avenue North, Seattle. Phone 284-9827. Open Monday through Saturday, 11:00 A.M. to 10:00 P.M.; Sunday, 2:00 to 9:00 P.M.

Owner David Rasti says, "we believe good food starts with good ingredients," and at Pasta Bella they concentrate on selecting only the freshest and finest, from herbs and olive oils to legumes, pastas, meat and fish. The result is great food and atmosphere at reasonable prices. There is a second Pasta Bella located in Ballard, open for dinner only.

• •

Sea Scallops and Angelhair

1 pound large sea scallops
Seasoned flour
Olive oil
1 cup black olives, sliced
1 cup fresh tomatoes, diced
2 ounces capers
1 ounce minced garlic
Salt and pepper, to taste
1 teaspoon dried basil
4 ounces wine
1 pint marinara sauce
1 pound fresh angelhair pasta
2 tablespoons chopped fresh
    basil
Parmesan cheese
Basil

Toss scallops in seasoned flour. Sear over high heat in large sauté pan on both sides. Remove to plate.

In same pan, add olives, tomatoes, capers, garlic, salt, pepper, and dry basil. Heat until fragrant, 2-3 minutes. Add wine. Use spoon to remove anything sticking in the pan. As wine comes to boil, add marinara sauce. As sauce simmers, add sautéed scallops to warm and tighten to sauce consistency.

Cook pasta in boiling water. Cooks very quickly. Drain well.

Toss freshly chopped basil in sauce. Ladle over pasta. Garnish with Parmesan and basil.

Serves 4.

• •

Fresh Calamari Sauté
with Sun-dried Tomatoes

2 ounces olive oil
2 ounces butter
1 medium red onion, julienne
   cut
2 ounces sun-dried tomatoes,
   reconstituted, julienne cut
1 tablespoon minced garlic
1 teaspoon dried oregano
1 teaspoon dried marjoram
1 teaspoon salt
1/2 teaspoon pepper
1 tablespoon Dijon mustard
1/2 bunch of green onions,
   chopped
1/2 pound calamari, cleaned,
   chopped
2 ounces tomato sauce
2 ounces lemon juice
2 ounces white wine

In large sauté pan, heat oil and butter. Sauté onion and tomatoes over medium high heat 3-5 minutes. Add seasonings: garlic, oregano, marjoram, salt, pepper, and mustard. Heat until fragrant. Add green onions, calamari, tomato sauce, lemon juice and wine. Toss to heat quickly. Don't overcook. Serve immediately with crusty bread.

Serves 4 as an appetizer.

Cafe Piccolo

3040 Highway 20, Port Townsend. Phone 385-1403. Open daily, 5:30 to 9:00 P.M.

Owner Farnham Hogue's answer to the Italian restaurants of the big city is a small Port Townsend cafe with European atmosphere, friendly service, and a nice mix of traditional and contemporary Italian fare, with some Mediterranean specialties thrown in for good measure.   Needless to say, they also take advantage of the local availability of scrupulously fresh seafood.

• •

Polenta

1 large onion, diced
1/4 cup olive oil
3 cups polenta
11 cups chicken stock
1 tablespoon Italian herb blend
1 tablespoon salt
1 tablespoon white pepper
1 cup Parmesan cheese

Sauté onion in oil until soft. Add polenta. Stir in pan, coating cornmeal with oil. Add stock. Bring to boil, using constant stirring motion. Add herb blend, salt and pepper. As polenta thickens, add Parmesan cheese. Keep stirring to avoid sticking. When mixture reaches a good thickness, pour into 9 inch x 12 inch sheet pan. Cool in refrigerator until hard. Cut into any desired shape. Brown in sauté pan.

Cafe Piccolo notes that you may substitute any cheese you desire, or any other fresh or dry herb you wish. Also, they indicate, polenta can be served in its soft state, before chilling.

Makes 9 inch x 12 inch pan.

• •

Marinara Sauce

2 large onions, sliced
3 tablespoons chopped garlic
2 green bell peppers, sliced
24 mushrooms, sliced
1/2 cup olive oil
8 anchovy filets, diced
1 cup red wine
6 pints canned, diced tomatoes
10 leaves of fresh basil, minced,
    or 1 tablespoon dried
2 tablespoons fresh oregano,
    minced, or 1 tablespoon
    dried
Salt and pepper, to taste

Sauté onions, garlic, peppers and mushrooms in very hot oil. Add anchovies. Simmer. Add red wine. Cook down by half. Add tomatoes and herbs. Simmer 1 hour. Season with salt and pepper.

Farnham states that this recipe is "the original, one and only, according to an old Italian grandmother!"

Makes about 7 pints.

Rhododendron Cafe

553 Chuckanut Drive, Bow. Phone 766-6667. Open for lunch Wednesday through Sunday, 11:00 A.M. to 3:00 P.M.; open for dinner Wednesday through Sunday, 4:00 to 9:00 P.M; closed Monday and Tuesday. Also closed for lunch Wednesday and Thursday from September 15 to March 31.

The Rhododendron has quite a history. The building it occupies dates back to the early 1900's, when it housed a service station. Subsequent owners operated various combinations of service station, cafe and grocery store until current owners Don and Carol Shank purchased and fully renovated this local landmark in 1984 and transformed it into a charming country restaurant with an eclectic mix of cuisines, tilted toward the Italian and Mediterranean but with some Oriental and Northwest dishes adding to the variety. The Shanks take great pride in their own home-grown herbs and vegetables, as well as a very select group of food purveyors; needless to say, everything is prepared from scratch.

• •

Hummus

4 cups garbanzo beans, completely drained, juice reserved
1-1/3 cups tahina
5 cloves of garlic, pressed
1 teaspoon salt
1 cup lemon juice

Blend garbanzo beans, tahina, garlic and salt in food processor until smooth. With food processor running slowly, add lemon juice through feed tube.

If hummus is too thick, add some of the reserved liquid from the garbanzo beans, 1-2 tablespoons at a time until perfect. Present with pita bread.
Serves 6.

• •

Zarzuela
(Spanish Seafood Stew)

3/8 cup olive oil
2-1/2 cups onions
3 cloves of garlic, pressed
2 pints fish stock
1/4 cup parsley, chopped
1/2 #10 can of tomatoes, diced,
    or fresh tomatoes, diced
1/2 teaspoon salt
1/2 teaspoon pepper
1-1/2 tablespoons lemon juice
3/4 cup sherry
3/8 cup brandy
1 cup black pitted olives
1 pound snapper or other white
    fish
32 steamer clams
32 mussels
16 prawns
16 scallops
16 crab legs

Heat oil. Sauté onions and garlic until soft. Add fish stock, parsley, tomatoes, salt and pepper. Bring to low boil.

Add lemon juice, sherry, brandy and olives. Next add fish and clams. Cook on medium low heat 2-3 minutes. Add mussels, then prawns and scallops, and lastly crab.

The Rhododendron Cafe notes that the quantities of fish may be varied, depending on availability, and reminds us that the idea is to cook each seafood item only just long enough to be done.

Serves 8.

Bella Luna Trattoria

14053 Greenwood Avenue North, Seattle. Phone 367-5862. Open Monday through Thursday, 11:00 A.M. to 10:00 P.M.; Friday, 11:00 A.M. to 11:00 P.M.; Saturday, 8:00 A.M. to 11:00 P.M.; Sunday, 8:00 A.M. to 10:00 P.M.

Translated from the Italian, "Bella Luna" means "pretty moon," and that theme is reflected in the decor of this cozy neighborhood trattoria. A warm fireplace, sun room, and the friendly, relaxed atmosphere - not to mention an extensive wine list - complement the Italian cuisine. Owned by the Mitchelli family (which also owns Trattoria Mitchelli in Pioneer Square), Bella Luna is a favorite of north end restaurant goers.

· ·

Fettuccine con Pollo e Nocciole
(Fettucine with Chicken and Toasted Hazelnuts)

1/4 cup olive oil
8-10 ounces boneless, skinless
    chicken breast, diced 1/2
    inch x 1/2 inch
1/4 teaspoon dried basil
1/4 teaspoon dried thyme
1/4 teaspoon dried oregano
1 tablespoon chopped garlic
1 tablespoon chopped shallots
1/2 teaspoon salt
1/2 teaspoon fresh ground
    black pepper
1/4 cup toasted hazelnuts,
    broken in halves
1/2 cup dry white wine
1 pound fresh fettucine
1 gallon salted, boiling water
3/4 cup fresh Roma tomatoes,
    diced 1/2 inch x 1/2 inch
2 cups heavy cream
3/4 cup grated Romano or
    Parmesan cheese
1/4 cup chopped Italian parsley

Add oil to a large sauté pan. Sauté chicken until lightly browned. Transfer chicken to a warm plate. Set aside.

Add basil, thyme, oregano, garlic, shallots, salt, pepper and hazelnuts to the pan. Sauté until garlic is lightly browned. Add wine. Reduce until almost gone.

Add fettucine noodles to boiling water. Cook until al dente.

While pasta is cooking, add tomatoes and cream to sauté pan. Reduce by two-thirds. Add chicken back to sauce.

Drain pasta. Toss with sauce. Place on a warmed serving platter. Top with cheese and parsley.

Serves 4.

· ·

The Pink Door Ristorante

1919 Post Alley (Pike Place Market), Seattle. Phone 443-3241. Open Tuesday though Saturday, 11:30 A.M. until "the wee hours."

Tucked away in the Pike Place Market, The Pink Door is a cozy little Italian place that's romantic and fun. Known for its Northwest seafood stew, cioppino (a bib might be wise) and its medium price range, The Pink Door has attracted a loyal following of locals, while tourists happen on it as they wander around the popular Pike Place Market.

• •

Baked Tomatoes and Basil on Spaghetti

Olive oil
**16 Roma tomatoes, sliced
  lengthwise in half**
**1/4 cup cloves of garlic, finely
  chopped**
1/4 cup finely chopped parsley
Salt and pepper, to taste
1 pound spaghetti
**2 tablespoons unsalted butter,
  softened**
16 basil leaves, torn
Parmesan cheese

Oil baking sheet. Place tomato halves on sheet, cut side up.

Sprinkle with garlic, parsley, salt and pepper. Drizzle with olive oil. Bake 60 minutes in preheated 425° oven, or until browned on edges and soft.

Cook spaghetti until al dente. Place half of the cooked tomatoes and butter into a pasta bowl. Mash into a sauce. Toss the hot pasta with the sauce, and top with the remaining tomatoes.

Sprinkle with basil leaves and serve with Parmesan cheese.

Serves 4.

• •

Insalata di Mozzarella e Rucola con Olive Nere (Arugula, Mozzarella & Black Olive Salad)

2 bunches of arugula
1/2 pound mozzarella, cubed
Salt and pepper, to taste
16 black olives, slivered
**1/2 large red onion, very thinly
  sliced**
Extra virgin olive oil

Arrange arugula in 4 bowls. Divide mozzarella cubes among bowls. Salt and pepper to taste. Top with olives and onion. Drizzle with olive oil.

Serves 4.

• •

Yanni's Lakeside Cafe

7419 Greenwood Avenue North, Seattle. Phone 783-6945. Open Monday through Saturday, 4:00 to 10:00 P.M; closed Sunday.

Your nose will tell you that you've found an authentic restaurant when you arrive at Yanni's; the delicious aromas of traditional Greek food permeate the place. They like to say that their recipes come from home, not a cook book; good, honest food at reasonable prices, and a fun atmosphere are the results at this friendly, family-operated restaurant.

• •

Kotopoulo Me Patates
(Roast Chicken with Potatoes)

1 whole chicken, approximately
   3 pounds
1/3 cup fresh lemon juice
Salt and pepper, to taste
Garlic powder
Oregano
8 small potatoes or 4 medium
   potatoes, cut in half
   lengthwise
1 tomato, quartered, optional
1/2-1 cup water

Several hours before cooking, place chicken in a roasting pan. Sprinkle lemon juice, salt, pepper, garlic powder and oregano in cavity and on outside of chicken. Cover. Refrigerate 1-2 hours.

Arrange potatoes and tomato around chicken. Roast at 400° 1 hour, or until juices run clear when pierced. Turn and baste occasionally. Add water to pan to increase juices, if necessary. Use pan drippings to baste chicken.

Serves 4.

• •

Brizoles Yiahni
(Braised Lamb Steaks)

4 lamb steaks, trimmed
Salt and pepper, to taste
1/8 teaspoon oregano
2 tablespoons olive oil
1 tablespoon minced shallots
2 cloves of garlic, minced
1/4 cup fresh lemon juice
1/4 cup tomato sauce
1/4 cup water
1/2 cup white wine

Sprinkle steaks with salt, pepper and oregano. Heat oil in a skillet. Brown meat on both sides. Remove from skillet.

Add shallots and garlic to skillet. Sauté until golden.

Return meat to skillet. Combine lemon juice, tomato sauce, water and wine. Pour over meat. Correct seasonings. Cover and simmer 45 minutes, basting occasionally.

Serves 4.

Kafe Neo

21108 Highway 99, Edmonds. Phone 672-3476. Open Monday through Thursday and Saturday, 11:00 A.M. to 8:30 P.M.; Friday, 11:00 A.M. to 9:00 P.M; closed Sunday.

Edmonds has its own corner of Greece, located at the Kafe Neo. Owner Sofeea Koures is adamant about using only the freshest ingredients, with everything made to order. Their offerings are traditional Greek, with the recipes having been handed down for generations.

* *

Spanakopita

3 bunches of green onions,
   finely chopped
1/2 cup olive oil
6 eggs, beaten
1/3 cup chopped parsley
1/3 teaspoon dillweed
1 teaspoon pepper
3 pounds spinach, fresh or
   frozen, finely chopped
4 cups feta cheese, grated
1 cup butter, melted
1 pound fillo dough. Keep
   frozen until 8 hours before
   using.

Sauté green onions in olive oil until tender.

Combine eggs, parsley, dillweed, and pepper. Add spinach, green onions and feta cheese.

Prepare one sheet of fillo at a time. With a pastry brush, lightly butter a sheet of fillo, then fold it into thirds (see diagram).

Spread 2 tablespoons (2-3 ounces) of spinach mixture on corner of fillo. Fold corner over to form a triangle, as if folding a flag (see drawings below). Continue to fold fillo in triangles, to make one triangle.

Arrange triangles on a baking sheet. Brush tops with melted butter. Bake 25-30 minutes at 350°, or until golden brown.

Serves 8-12.

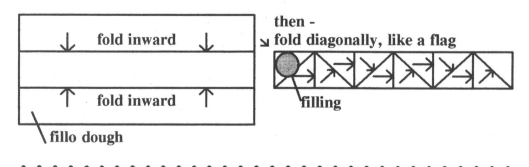

* *

Baklava

SYRUP:
2-1/4 cups sugar
2 cups water
2-3 strips of lemon peel, 2
    inches long
6 whole cloves
1 cinnamon stick
1 tablespoon fresh lemon juice
1/2 cup honey

BAKLAVA:
6 cups walnuts, chopped
1/2 cup sugar
2-1/4 teaspoons cinnamon
1/8 teaspoon nutmeg
1 teaspoon cloves
1-1/2 cups butter, melted
1 pound fillo dough
Whole cloves

Make syrup first. In a large sauce pan, combine all syrup ingredients. Bring to a boil, lower heat and simmer for 15 minutes. Cool.

Next, mix walnuts, sugar, cinnamon, nutmeg and cloves. Set aside.

Most fillo dough comes sized 11 inches x 17 inches. If you have this size pan, use it; if not, use a 9 inch x 13 inch cake pan.

Using a pastry brush, butter the pan lightly. Place one layer of fillo in the pan. Lightly brush with butter. Layer 10 fillo sheets this way. Sprinkle the 10th layer with about 1/2-3/4 cup of walnut mixture. Cover with a sheet of fillo. Brush with butter. Layer one more sheet of fillo. Butter it. Cover with 1/2-3/4 cup of the walnut mixture. Continue this process until all the walnut mixture is gone.

Then, layer 12-14 sheets of fillo on top, buttering each sheet. If there is a lot of fillo on the edges of the pan, cut it off. Take a dull knife and gently push fillo down the edges of the pan (the baklava will be much prettier this way).

With a sharp knife, cut baklava into squares, then cut the squares in half diagonally, cutting all the way through it.

Put a whole clove in the middle of each piece of baklava. Brush with remaining butter.

Bake 1 hour at 350°, or until golden brown. Pour cooled syrup over hot baklava. Sofeea intimates that the secret to using syrup and fillo dough is to pour cool syrup over a hot fillo dish, or hot syrup over a cool fillo dish. Otherwise, the dish will become soggy!

Makes one 11 inch x 17 inch pan.

Spyros Gyros

21851 Marine View Drive South, Des Moines.   Phone 870-1699.   Open Monday through Saturday, 10:00 A.M. to 9:00 P.M.

This tiny, very unpretentious little taverna is hidden away in Seattle's south end burbs, but they've attracted an enthusiastic following for their limited, but well-prepared, menu.   Prices are very reasonable.   When the weather cooperates, there is outside dining; inside seating is limited.   Demetra Rouvas says that's due to change this fall, when an expansion is planned.

• •

Bourtheto

3/4 cup olive oil
3 medium onions, sliced
6 cloves of garlic
2 tablespoons tomato paste
Red pepper, to taste (try a
    tablespoon of paprika and a
    teaspoon of cayenne)
Water
1 kilo of fish (halibut or cod
    filets preferred)

Heat oil in oven proof pan. Add onion and garlic. Cook until soft. Stir in tomato paste and red pepper. Fry gently about 2 minutes. Add about 1 cup of water. Simmer 5 minutes.

Add fish and more water, if necessary, to cover fish and onion mixture.

Bake in 350° oven for about 40 minutes, or until sauce is a good consistency and oil has separated. Fish should be tender. Let stand covered about 5 minutes before serving.

Delicious with steamed greens and fresh garlic. Dress greens with olive oil and lemon juice. Accompany with your favorite bread for soaking up the sauce.

Serves 4.

• •

Sofrito

1 kilo veal or beef filet
Flour
2/3 cup olive oil
Salt and pepper, to taste
5 cloves of garlic
1 tablespoon chopped parsley
Pinch of fresh chopped mint
2 tablespoons strong wine
    vinegar
4 tablespoons brandy, optional
1-1/4 cups water

Cut meat into individual servings and pound thin. Dredge in flour. Heat oil in frying pan. Fry meat, turning once, until lightly brown on both sides. Leaving oil and meat in pan, add remaining ingredients, stirring a little. Simmer until sauce thickens.

Serve at once with potatoes or pasta as side dish.

Serves 4-6.

Byzantion Restaurant

601 Broadway East, Seattle. Phone 325-7580. Open Monday through Thursday, 11:00 A.M. to 11:00 P.M.; Friday, 11:00 A.M. to midnight; Saturday, 9:00 A.M. to midnight; Sunday, 9:00 A.M. to 11:00 P.M.

Proprietor Bekris Anastasia (who also owns the popular Aegean Restaurant) says, "If you're up for a little foreign adventure, try the Byzantion!" A wide variety of Greek dishes, from roast lamb to casseroles, chicken and fish is offered, with a warm atmosphere that will make any guest feel right at home.

• •

Psari Plaki (Baked Fish)

1/4 cup cooking oil combined
    with 1/4 cup olive oil
2 large onions, thinly sliced
1 cup diced carrots
1 cup chopped celery
1 clove of garlic, chopped
1 cup white cooking wine
16-ounce can tomato sauce
2 pounds salmon, cod or halibut
Salt and pepper, to taste
Lemon slices
3 tablespoons fresh chopped
    parsley

Heat oil in skillet. Add vegetables and garlic. Slowly sauté. Add wine and tomato sauce. Simmer 30-35 minutes.

Pour the mixture into a large baking pan or dish. Place the fish over the top of the sauce. Season with salt and pepper. Bake 1 hour at 350°. Garnish with lemon slices and parsley.

Bekris advises that "fish lovers will find this a truly delicious way to prepare baked fish. Using either cod, salmon or halibut, it is a seafood delight!"

Serves 6-8.

• •

Moussaka (Baked Eggplant and Ground Beef Dish)

1 large eggplant, trimmed and
    sliced in 1/2 inch slices
3 tablespoons flour
1/4 cup cooking oil
1-1/2 pounds ground beef
1 medium onion, diced
1 teaspoon dried oregano
2 8-ounce cans tomato sauce
Salt and pepper, to taste
1 cup grated cheddar or jack
    cheese
1 tablespoon grated Parmesan
    cheese
2 large eggs, well-whipped

Dredge slices of eggplant in flour. Fry in oil until light brown. Remove and drain on paper towels.

In another skillet, put the ground beef, onion and oregano. Fry until meat is done. Add tomato sauce. Simmer until thick. Season with salt and pepper. Remove from heat.

In a large, deep baking dish, place a layer of eggplant. Spoon one-half of meat mixture over it. Sprinkle one-half of the cheddar cheese over that. Repeat with another layer of eggplant, meat and cheese. Sprinkle with Parmesan. Bake 35 minutes in 350° oven.

Remove from oven and drain excess grease. Pour beaten eggs over top. Return to oven to bake 15 minutes.

Dish out and serve with a Greek salad or French bread.

"This is a traditional dish," claims Bekris, "that you will find almost anywhere you travel in Greece. Easy to prepare and a real palate pleaser. If you are not a fancier of eggplant, zucchini can be substituted," he suggests, "to make an equally delicious dish."

Serves 4.

Athenian Inn

1517 Pike Place Market, Seattle. Phone 624-7166. Open Monday through Saturday, 6:30 A.M. to 6:30 P.M.; closed Sunday.

Located in the heart of the Pike Place Market (in the old main arcade on the water side, between Pike and Pine Streets), the Athenian Inn seems as much a part of Seattle as does the market itself. Although Greek food is not - as the name may imply - the mainstay of the menu, it is a part of the tradition and thus deserves part of the billing. Visitors to the Athenian enjoy a lovely view of Elliott Bay and the Olympics. The service is friendly, the food is simple and very well-prepared, and a visit here is always fun.

• •

Greek Pizza

1 package, 4 each Boboli Pizza
   Dough
1 cup sliced mozzarella cheese
2 cups pizza sauce
1 cup diced tomatoes
10 black olives, sliced
1/2 cup sliced artichoke hearts
1/4 cup diced green onions
1/3 cup feta cheese
8 anchovy filets, optional

Cover each pizza dough with mozzarella cheese. Pour on the pizza sauce. Top with tomatoes, olives, artichoke hearts, green onions and feta cheese.

Bake 10 minutes in preheated 350° oven. Before serving, add anchovies.

Makes 4 pizzas.

• •

Hearty Greek Salad

1 cup red vinegar
1 cup salad oil
1/3 cup lemon juice
1 cup mayonnaise
Salt and pepper, to taste
Ground oregano
1 head of lettuce
1 pound salad mix (lettuce, red
    cabbage, carrots)
4 eggs, hard-boiled, sliced
2 tomatoes, cut into 16 wedges
16 black olives
4 pepperoncini
1 cup sliced artichoke hearts
12 pieces of anchovy,
    approximately 4 ounces
1/2 cup diced green onions
1 cup feta cheese

Combine and whip the vinegar, oil, lemon juice, mayonnaise, salt, pepper and oregano. Set aside.

Line 4 salad bowls with lettuce leaves. Fill the center of each bowl with 1/4 pound salad mix. On top of the salad mix, artistically arrange the remaining ingredients: 1 sliced, hard-boiled egg, 4 wedges of tomato, 4 black olives, 1 pepperoncini, 1/4 cup artichoke hearts, 3 pieces of anchovy, sprinkle of green onions and feta cheese. Present with dressing.

Serves 4.

Continental Greek Restaurant

4549 University Way N.E., Seattle. Phone 632-4700. Open Monday through Saturday, 7:00 A.M. to 11:00 P.M.; Sunday, 8:00 A.M. to 11:00 P.M.

The Continental is among the oldest of Seattle's Greek restaurants, serving traditional Greek foods in a relaxed, cafe-like setting. Owner/chef George Lagos - born in the Greek Isles - serves up old favorites like Spanakopita and Souvlaki, as well as his own creations. At the same time, the Continental emphasizes healthy, nutritional food.

• •

Horiatiki (Village) Salad

2 tomatoes, preferably vine ripened, sliced into wedges
1 small cucumber, chopped
1 small onion, chopped
1 green bell pepper, chopped, optional
Olive oil
2 eggs, hard-boiled, sliced into wedges
Feta cheese, chopped
Kalamata olives
Oregano
Salt and pepper, to taste

Place the tomatoes, cucumber, onions and peppers in a deep dish. Pour in some olive oil. Gently mix the vegetables. Add the eggs, cheese, and olives. Top with sprinkles of oregano, salt and pepper. More olive oil can be added to taste.

Serve with hearty Italian bread.

Serves 2.

• •

Taso's Greek Rice Salad

**1 head of romaine lettuce,
chopped**
1/2 cup raisins
**2 cups cooked brown or white
rice**
Olive oil
1 vine ripened tomato, sliced
1 egg, hard-boiled, sliced
Feta cheese, diced
Olives
Oregano

Place lettuce, raisins and rice in salad bowl. Pour in some olive oil and stir gently. Place tomato slices on top. Then add the egg, cheese and olives. Top with oregano. Add more olive oil if needed.

Serves 2-4.

Aegean Restaurant

1400 First Avenue, Seattle. Phone 343-5500. Open Sunday through Thursday, 11:00 A.M. to 10:00 P.M.; Friday and Saturday, 11:00 A.M. to 11:00 P.M.

There is a little bit of Greece in downtown Seattle, and you will encounter it at the Aegean. In addition, you'll find very authentic Greek food, wine, and music, served up with care and friendly courtesy, at reasonable prices. Bekris Anastasia, who also owns the Byzantion Restaurant on Broadway, promises, "You are going to be hooked forever!"

• •

Kota Me Bamyes
(Chicken and Okra)

1-1/2 pounds fresh okra (or 2 10-ounce packages frozen okra)
1/2 cup vinegar
2 tablespoons salt
6 tablespoons butter
1 cup chopped onion
3 to 3-1/2 pound chicken, cut up
15-ounce can solid packed tomatoes
2 tablespoons tomato paste
Salt and pepper, to taste

Sprinkle okra with vinegar and salt. Soak 30 minutes. Rinse thoroughly and drain.

In a heavy sauce pan, sauté okra lightly in butter. Remove and set aside. Add onion to pan. Brown slightly. Add chicken; brown. Add tomatoes, tomato paste, salt and pepper. Simmer about 45 minutes. Add okra; cook 30-40 minutes, or until tender.

Serves 4-5.

• •

Bouti Arniou Psitó
(Roast Leg of Lamb)

5-6 pound leg of lamb
6 small cloves of garlic
1/4 teaspoon oregano
1/4 teaspoon thyme
Salt and pepper, to taste
2 tablespoons olive oil
1 cup water
Juice of 2 lemons
Oregano
Roasted Potatoes (recipe
 follows)

With a pointed knife, make 6 slits (total) on top and bottom of meat. Insert 1 clove of garlic in each slit.

Combine oregano, thyme, salt and pepper, and sprinkle some in each slit. Rub lamb with oil. Sprinkle with additional salt and pepper.

Place in a roasting pan. Add water to pan. Roast 45 minutes at 425°, turning occasionally as each side browns lightly. Reduce oven temperature to 325°. Turn lamb to rest on its flat side. Continue baking 90 more minutes. Sprinkle with lemon juice and oregano and return to oven. Roast about 30 minutes longer, or until meat thermometer inserted near center registers 175°. Baste occasionally. Let stand about 20 minutes before carving (allowing juices to retreat back into tissues and ensuring juicy slices of meat).

For a variation, substitute 1/2 cup of tomato sauce diluted in 1/4 cup of water for lemon juice.

Roasted potatoes are usually served with roast lamb, as follows.

Bekris reminds us that "in Greece, the most festive of all meats is lamb. Whether your choice of cooking lamb is 'psitó' (oven roasted) or 'souvlas' (broiled on a spit), this meal will draw compliments. Traditionally, the Greeks enjoy their lamb roasted well done."

Serves 6.

ROASTED POTATOES:
2 pounds small potatoes, pared
Salted, boiling water
1/3 cup fresh lemon juice
1/2 cup clarified butter or 1/4
 cup olive oil
Salt and pepper, to taste
Generous pinch of oregano

Parboil potatoes in water 4 minutes. Drain thoroughly. Mix with remaining ingredients.

Arrange in a baking dish. Bake at 450° 15 minutes. Turn potatoes. Continue baking 15 minutes longer.

Costas Opa Greek Restaurant

3400 Fremont Avenue North, Seattle. Phone 633-4141. Open Sunday through Thursday, 11:00 A.M. to 10:00 P.M.; Friday and Saturday, 11:00 A.M. to 11:00 P.M.

An authentic - and affordable - Greek restaurant, Costas Opa is a warm and friendly place located in Seattle's Fremont District. Greek wines are a specialty. At lunch time, they serve Greek as well as American sandwiches, but at dinner, they concentrate on the traditional Greek dishes on which they built their reputation.

• •

Horiatiki Salata
(Greek Village Salad)

1 onion, thinly sliced lengthwise
3 tomatoes, cut into wedges
1 green bell pepper, cut into
    rings
1 cucumber, pared and sliced
1 cup black Kalamata olives
1/2 pound feta cheese,
    crumbled
1/4 cup olive oil
2 tablespoons red wine vinegar
1/4 teaspoon oregano
Salt and pepper, to taste

Toss first 6 ingredients in salad bowl.

Combine oil, vinegar, oregano, salt and pepper to form a dressing. Toss with vegetable mixture.

Serves 3-4.

• •

Africa,
the Middle East
and India

Kokeb Ethiopian Restaurant

926 - 12th Avenue, Seattle. Phone 322-0485. Open for lunch Monday through Friday, 11:00 A.M. to 2:00 P.M.; open for dinner Monday through Saturday, 5:00 to 11:00 P.M.; closed Sunday.

Diners looking for something different and exotic will find it at Kokeb. Owners Belete and Yeshi Shiferaw, husband and wife, fled their native Ethiopia fifteen years ago as political refugees. They settled in Seattle, worked hard, and finally opened their own restaurant, thereby introducing fortunate Seattle residents and visitors to a cooking tradition not seen here before them. The fact that Kokeb has thrived is testimony to the fact that Americans enjoy this unique cuisine as well.

• •

Tibs
(Stir-Fried Beef Cubes)

1 red onion, chopped
4 tablespoons niter kibbeh
1-1/2 pounds lean beef, cubed
1/2 teaspoon black pepper
1 teaspoon cardamom
1/2 teaspoon salt
1 jalapeño pepper, chopped,
    optional

Stir onions in pan about 2-3 minutes at medium heat. Add niter kibbeh. When it begins to splutter, add beef, black pepper, cardamom and salt. Add jalapeño, if desired, for additional flavor. Continue stirring until beef is tender.
Serves 2-3.

• •

Doro Wat
(Chicken Stew)

1 whole chicken, cut into 8
    pieces
2 tablespoons strained fresh
    lemon juice
2 teaspoons salt
2 cups finely chopped onions
1/4 cup niter kibbeh
1 tablespoon scraped, chopped
    fresh ginger root
1/4 teaspoon pulverized
    fenugreek seeds
1/4 teaspoon ground cardamom
1/8 teaspoon ground nutmeg
    (preferably fresh grated)
1/4 cup berbere
2 tablespoons paprika
1/4 cup red wine
1 cup water
4 eggs, hard-boiled
1/2 teaspoon ground black
    pepper

Pat chicken dry. Rub with lemon juice and salt. Set aside.

In a heavy 3-4 quart enameled casserole, cook onions over moderate heat 5-6 minutes, or until soft and dry, stirring constantly. Stir in niter kebbeh. When it begins to splutter, add ginger root, fenugreek seeds, cardamom and nutmeg, stirring well after each addition. Add berbere and paprika. Stir over low heat 3-5 minutes. Pour in wine and water, still stirring. Bring to boil over high heat. Continue cooking until liquid has reduced to the consistency of heavy cream. Drop chicken into simmering sauce, turning pieces about until coated on all sides. Reduce heat to the lowest point. Simmer 15 minutes.

With the tines of a fork, pierce 1/4 inch deep holes over the entire surface of each egg. Add eggs to pan. Turn gently about in sauce. Cover and cook 15 minutes, or until chicken is tender.

Serves 4.

Mamounía Moroccan Restaurant

1556 East Olive Way, Seattle. Phone 329-3886. Open every day, 5:00 to 10:00 P.M.

Owner/chef Mehdi Ziani is one of those instinctive chefs who cook by feel, taste and smell rather than by precise measurements. "Never use a cupful, always a handful," he says (Mehdi made an exception with the recipe below). Even though most of us would have a hard time turning out a well-prepared meal following that advice, it's hard to argue with the results he obtains: beautifully prepared meals with the rich flavors of Morocco.

• •

Couscous with Lamb, Vegetables and Raisins

3-1/2 ounces black raisins
1 pound medium onions, minced
1/8 teaspoon cinnamon
Water
3 pounds couscous
1 bunch of parsley, finely
   chopped
2 pounds lean boneless lamb
   shoulder, trimmed and cut
   into 1-1/2 inch chunks (can
   also substitute beef)
1 teaspoon salt
1 teaspoon fresh ground black
   pepper
3/4 cup oil
7 ounces butter
1 teaspoon saffron
1/2 teaspoon powdered
   coriander
1/2 teaspoon powdered ginger
4-5 zucchini, cut into 1 inch x 2
   inch lengths
1/2 pound squash, peeled and
   cut into pieces 2 inches x 1/4
   inch
6-ounce box dried garbanzo
   beans, soaked 10-12

hours, drained, rinsed,
simmered in water, covered
1 hour, drained again, and
shelled, or 2-3 cups canned
garbanzo beans
3 large firm tomatoes, cut into 2
   inch pieces
1 pound carrots, peeled, heart
   cut out and discarded, cut
   into 2 inch lengths
4 green bell peppers, sliced into
   pieces 1 inch x 2 inches
1/2 pound small white turnips,
   peeled and cut into 1 inch
   pieces
Hot sauce, optional

Place raisins, onions, cinnamon and 1/3 cup cold water in sauce pan. Cook over medium high heat, stirring frequently until water is almost evaporated. Place in bowl and set aside.

To prepare couscous, place in a large shallow pan. Add 4 cups of water. Stir with hands or wood spatula. Drain through a sieve.

Place back in the pan, spreading even. Let pellets set 15 minutes to swell. Sprinkle couscous with 1 ounce of water. Rub moistened grains between palms of hands until well separated.

In the lower half of a couscoussier (or deep kettle or casserole), place raisins and onion mixture, parsley, lamb, salt, pepper, oil, butter, saffron, coriander, ginger and 3-4 cups of cold water (enough to completely cover the ingredients by 1 inch). Cook until the mixture comes to a boil and steam begins to rise. Reduce heat to medium. Set the top part of the couscoussier in place over the lower level (for the top part of the couscoussier, you can substitute a colander lined with cheesecloth and placed over the top of the kettle or casserole). The top of the pan should not touch the water in the bottom.

While the ingredients continue to steam, place the pellets in the top level, rubbing between the palms of the hands and dropping them gently into the strainer in upper level. Steam uncovered 20 minutes. Remove the strainer with the pellets. Continue cooking the vegetables and meat in the lower level. When tender, transfer to a bowl and set aside in a warm area. Again, place the pellets in a shallow pan. Sprinkle lightly with salt. Rinse in 4-5 cups of water. Drain excess water through a sieve.

Place the zucchini, squash, garbanzo beans, tomatoes, carrots, green peppers and turnips in lower level. Add water to cover completely. Bring to boil over high heat. Set the upper level of the couscoussier back in place over the steaming vegetables. Reduce heat to medium. Again, add the couscous to the top level of the couscoussier, rubbing the grains between the palms of the hands and gently dropping them back into the strainer. Continue to steam 20 minutes more, or until tender.

When couscous is cooked, place in a large serving platter and dot the top with butter.

Place previously cooked vegetables and lamb back into the broth of the couscoussier. Reheat over high temperature 2 minutes.

Place meat over the couscous. Arrange vegetables on top. Pour 2 ladles of broth over the surface of the ingredients. This dish may be served with hot sauce if desired.

Serves 10.

• •

Ali Baba Restaurant

707 East Pine Street, Seattle. Phone 325-2299. Open Monday through Friday, 11:30 A.M. to 10:00 P.M.; Saturday, noon to 10:00 P.M.; Sunday, 5:00 to 9:00 P.M.

With music and belly dancing and a lot of atmosphere - not to mention the food - owner Anwar Aboul-Hosn has created in the Ali Baba a place where the overall experience of Middle Eastern cuisine can be enjoyed and savored.

• •

Baba Kanouj

1 large eggplant
1/2 cup tahina
Juice of 3 lemons
1 clove of garlic, minced
Salt, to taste
2 tablespoons oil
Parsley
Tomato slices

Bake eggplant in 500° oven until tender. Split open. Scoop out the pulp and juices and discard. Mash eggplant. Set aside.

Combine the tahina, lemon juice, garlic and salt to make a sauce. Add eggplant and mix.

Place on platter. Pour oil over the top. Garnish with parsley and tomato slices.

Serves 2-6.

• •

Stuffed Cabbage

1 medium head of cabbage,
   about 2 pounds
1 cup uncooked rice
1 pound lamb shoulder or beef,
   ground
1/8 teaspoon cinnamon
1/4 teaspoon allspice
Salt and pepper, to taste
3 large cloves of garlic, diced
1 large clove of garlic, mashed
1 tablespoon dried mint
1/4 cup lemon juice

Core and parboil cabbage until the leaves are limp and easy to roll. Place in a colander. Separate leaves. Slice each leaf in half on the rib.

In a bowl, mix rice, meat, cinnamon, allspice, salt and pepper. Place a tablespoon of the mixture on each leaf. Spread lengthwise along the rib and roll as for a jelly roll. Gently squeeze each roll when placing in pan. Arrange in compact rows over layer of cabbage ribs. Sprinkle a little diced garlic between each layer. Cover rolls with water 1/2 inch higher than the top. Cover pan. Cook on medium heat 15-18 minutes.

Mash 1 clove of garlic with mint and a little salt. Add lemon juice and mix well. Pour over cabbage rolls. Simmer 20 minutes, or until rice is done.

Serves 4-6.

Mediterranean Kitchen

4 West Roy Street, Seattle. Phone 285-6713. Open Sunday through Thursday, 5:00 to 10:00 P.M.; Friday and Saturday, 5:00 to 11:00 P.M.

Kamal Aboul-Hosn, co-owner of the Mediterranean Kitchen, says that his restaurant "has been proudly injecting Seattle with garlic for fifteen years. The smell of garlic and delicious spices can lead you to us from miles away." The menu consists of dishes from throughout the Mediterranean region, especially the Middle East, all at reasonable prices.

● ●

Lentil Soup

9 cups water
1 pound lentils, rinsed and
    drained
1/2 cup salad oil
1/2 cup extra virgin olive oil
2 onions, diced
3 teaspoons allspice
1 teaspoon black pepper
2 teaspoons ground cinnamon
1 bunch of cilantro, chopped
Cloves of garlic, blended with
    lemon juice

Bring water to boil; add lentils. Simmer 15 minutes or more, to desired consistency.
In another pan, heat oils. Sauté onions until golden. Add allspice, pepper, cinnamon, and cilantro. Cook 5 minutes. Add to lentil mixture. Boil 5 minutes.
Add garlic and lemon juice blend to soup, a little at a time. Serve immediately.
Serves 4.

● ●

Meenar Restaurant

12359 Lake City Way N.E., Seattle. Phone 367-5666. Open Monday through Wednesday, 11:00 A.M. to 10:00 P.M.; Thursday and Friday, 11:00 to 2:00 A.M.; Saturday, 4:00 P.M. to 2:00 A.M.; Sunday, 4:00 to 10:00 P.M.

The Meenar Restaurant is difficult to classify, since it serves a wide variety of cuisines - Pakistani, Indian, Persian and Middle Eastern. Owner Riaz Qureshi, a native Pakistani, states with pride that his dishes - over 70 at last count - are very authentic and would be typical of what you would find in each of these locales, unlike some restaurants, which "Americanize" their cooking to try to appeal to a larger, but less knowledgeable, clientele.

• •

Lamb Curry

4 ounces vegetable oil
2 large onions, chopped
8 cloves of garlic, crushed
3 large tomatoes, sliced
1-1/2 teaspoons ground ginger
 root
1-1/2 teaspoons salt
1 teaspoon ground coriander
3/4 teaspoon ground cumin
1/2 teaspoon ground cinnamon
1/4 teaspoon turmeric
1/4 teaspoon red hot pepper
1/4 teaspoon curry powder
2 pounds boneless lamb, cut
 into bite-size pieces
2-1/2 cups water

Heat oil in large pot. Add onions and garlic. Cook until onions are browned. Add tomatoes, ginger, salt, coriander, cumin, cinnamon, turmeric, red hot pepper and curry powder. Sauté 5 minutes. Add lamb. Sauté 20 minutes. Add water. Bring to a boil. Reduce heat. Simmer until lamb is tender, adding more water if necessary to produce sauce.

Riaz suggests that basmati rice is a perfect accompaniment to this flavorful curry.

Serves 8.

• •

Phoenecia at Alki

2716 Alki Avenue S.W., Seattle. Phone 935-6550. Open Tuesday through Friday, 11:00 A.M. to 10:30 P.M.; Saturday and Sunday, 8:00 A.M. to 10:00 P.M.; closed Monday.

Long an institution at its original location near the Seattle Center, a decision to demolish the building that housed it (in favor of a supermarket!) resulted in a move to a new area, at Alki in West Seattle. The food - which introduced many Seattle diners to the pleasures of Mediterranean and Lebanese cuisine - is, as always, excellent.

• •

Tabbouleh
(Cracked Wheat Salad)

1/2 cup bulgur
1 cup chopped green onions
3 tomatoes, chopped
2 cups chopped parsley
1/2 cup chopped fresh mint or
**   2 tablespoons dried mint**
Salt and pepper, to taste
8 teaspoons extra virgin olive oil
6 teaspoons lemon juice

Soak bulgur in cold water to cover. Drain well. Place in large bowl. Mix in onions, tomatoes, parsley and mint. Season with salt and pepper. Stir in oil and lemon juice. Allow to stand 1/2 hour before serving.

The Phoenecia points out that this is one of the national dishes of the Middle East.

Serves 2-4.

• •

Tandoor Restaurant

5024 University Way N.E., Seattle. Phone 523-7477. Open Sunday through Thursday, 11:00 A.M. to 10:00 P.M.; Friday and Saturday, 11:00 A.M. to 10:30 P.M.

Tandoor has become a well-established favorite among fanciers of Indian cuisine. Customers are evenly divided between students from the nearby university, local residents and business people. All seem taken with the food, both the affordable luncheon buffets and the fine cuisine served at dinner time. Owners Lakhvinder and Mohinder Mroke take considerable pride in the following they have earned, both here and in a sister restaurant they own and operate in Spokane.

• •

Butter Chicken

1/2 cup butter
8-ounce can stewed tomatoes
16-ounce can peeled
    tomatoes
1 tablespoon sugar
1 tablespoon salt
1 pint half and half
2 teaspoons cumin powder
1-1/2 teaspoons coriander
    powder
1 teaspoon ground fenugreek
Salted water
2 pounds boneless, skinless
    chicken pieces
Parsley, chopped

Melt butter in sauce pan. Add tomatoes. Bring to a boil. Add sugar, salt and half and half. Continue to boil until sauce thickens. Add cumin, coriander and fenugreek.

In another pan, bring salted water to boil. Add chicken pieces. When chicken is tender, drain off liquid. Pour butter sauce over chicken pieces. Sprinkle with parsley.

Serves 4.

• •

Shamiana

10724 N.E. 68th Street, Kirkland.   Phone 827-4902.   Open for lunch daily, 11:00 A.M. to 2:30 P.M.; open for dinner daily, 5:00 to 10:00 P.M.

At Shamiana, authentic flavors of India, Pakistan and East Africa are expertly presented by an American brother and sister team who grew up there.   Owners Eric and Tracy Larson were determined to recreate the foods they loved in their youth, and the happy result is a dining adventure. The atmosphere is authentic as well;   Shamiana is decorated with Indian folk art and the colorful cotton tents from the region that give this restaurant its name.

• •

Masala Ginger Lamb or Beef

2 pounds lamb or beef stew
   meat
3 tablespoons puréed ginger root
1 quart Masala Sauce (recipe
   follows)
Chopped coriander

Place stew meat in Dutch oven. Add ginger root and Masala Sauce. Mix together. Bake in 350° oven 45 minutes, checking occasionally and adding a little water to keep meat moist. Garnish with chopped coriander.
   Serves 4.

MASALA SAUCE:
28-ounce can diced tomatoes
   with juice
1/2 pint plain yogurt
1/2 tablespoon garam masala
1/2 tablespoon curry powder
1/2 tablespoon ground coriander
1/2 tablespoon red chili powder
   or cayenne pepper
1 teaspoon turmeric
1-1/2 tablespoons vegetable oil
1 large yellow onion, chopped
1 tablespoon finely chopped
   garlic
Salt, to taste

In food processor, blend tomatoes and yogurt together. Set aside.
   Combine spices and set aside.
   Heat oil in sauce pan. Add onion. Cook until dark brown, but not burned. Add garlic and spice mixture. Cook 2 minutes. Add processed tomatoes and yogurt and stir. Purée all ingredients in food processor. Season with salt.

• •

Mulligatawny Soup

1/4 cup ghee or vegetable oil
3 cups chopped yellow onions
5 cloves of garlic, peeled and
    minced
1 teaspoon turmeric
1-1/2 tablespoons garam masala
1-1/2 teaspoons ground
    coriander
1/2 teaspoon red chili powder or
    cayenne pepper
2 bay leaves
2 cups red lentils, washed and
    drained
3-4 cups chicken stock
1 cup canned unsweetened
    coconut milk
Juice of 1 lemon
1 cup diced, cooked chicken
Salt, to taste
1 cup basmati or long grain
    rice, cooked
Lemon wedges

Heat the ghee in a large pan.
Add onions. Cook until brown.
Add garlic. Cook 2-3 minutes.
Add spices and bay leaves. Cook 1
minute. Stir in lentils. Add stock.
Bring to boil. Simmer 20
minutes, or until lentils are
tender. Remove from heat,
discarding bay leaves.

Purée mixture until smooth.
Pour back into the pan. Add
coconut milk, lemon juice,
chicken and salt. Simmer to heat
through.

Ladle soup over cooked rice.
Garnish with lemon wedges.

Serves 8.

Raga Cuisine of India

555 - 108th Avenue N.E., Bellevue. Phone 450-0336. Open for lunch Sunday through Friday, 11:30 A.M. to 2:00 P.M.; open for dinner Sunday through Thursday, 5:00 to 10:00 P.M.; Friday and Saturday to 10:30 P.M.

Raga Cuisine of India has received consistently fine reviews since it opened its doors. That's no surprise to owner Bill Khanna, who set out to create a serene, sophisticated and inviting restaurant that would showcase Indian dishes to a market that had not had much exposure to that cuisine. Attentive service and irresistible desserts complement the dinner menu, and on Sundays, a popular buffet brunch is offered.

• •

Chicke Tikka

2 cups yogurt
1 ounce heavy cream
1 teaspoon ground pepper
1 teaspoon garam masala
3 cloves of garlic, mashed
1 small piece of ginger root, mashed
1 teaspoon vinegar
1 teaspoon lemon juice
1/2 teaspoon each red and yellow food coloring
1 pound boneless, skinless chicken breasts, cut into small cubes, about 1-1/2 inches x 1-1/2 inches

Combine first 9 ingredients. Fold in chicken cubes. Marinate 10-12 hours in the refrigerator. Thread the chicken onto skewers. Set on an oven proof tray covered with aluminum foil.

Prepare the clay oven (tandoor), or preheat a conventional oven to 350-400°.

In a tandoor, cook 7 to 10 minutes, turning occasionally. In a conventional oven, cook about 20 minutes, turning frequently.

Present with rice or bread. Serves 2-3.

• •

Eggplant Bhartha
(Eggplant Purée)

1 eggplant
1 tablespoon oil
2 onions, cut into small cubes
1/4 teaspoon turmeric
1 teaspoon paprika
2 tomatoes, cut into small cubes
1 teaspoon garam masala
2 tablespoons chopped
   coriander leaves

Bake eggplant in a 350° oven 15-20 minutes, turning frequently. Remove. Peel off skin under running water. Purée and set aside.

Heat oil. Add onions and fry for a few minutes. Add turmeric and paprika. Fry a few more minutes. Add tomatoes and eggplant purée. Cook over low heat, stirring occasionally, until a golden brown color.

Sprinkle with garam masala and coriander leaves.

Serves 2-4.

Jewel of India

3520 Pacific Highway E., Fife. Phone 922-2697. Open daily, 10:00 A.M. to 10:00 P.M.

Just north of Tacoma, the Jewel of India serves up sumptuous curries and tandoori dishes in the proud Indian culinary tradition to its guests. For the less adventurous, owner Mohan Walia also offers a selection of American dishes. A blazing fireplace and candlelit tables add a romantic ambience, and the food is excellent and authentic.

• •

Lamb Biryani

1/2 pound yogurt
6 cloves
4 black cardamom seeds
2 teaspoons cumin seeds
4 cloves of garlic
Red chili
Salt, to taste
2 pounds boneless lamb, cut
   into cubes, washed and
   dried
6 tablespoons oil
9 ounces chopped onions
2 pounds basmati rice, washed
   and soaked 45 minutes
2-1/2 quarts water

Make a paste of yogurt, cloves, cardamom, cumin, garlic, chili and salt. Rub into lamb and set aside for 2 hours.

Heat oil. Add chopped onions. Cook until golden brown. Add lamb. Cook until tender. Add rice and water. Cook on a slow heat until water is evaporated. Stir with handle of spoon. Serve hot. Serves 4.

• •

Tandoori Murgha (Tandoori Chicken)

1 small chicken, about 2 pounds
2 teaspoons salt, divided
Tomato coloring
2 tablespoons lemon juice
12 cloves of garlic
2 teaspoons allspice
3 tablespoons fresh lime juice
1 teaspoon red pepper
8 ounces yogurt
1 teaspoon dried powdered
   mango
Butter
Green onions, sliced
Chilies
Lemon wedges

Remove the skin, wash and dry the chicken. Make cuts. Rub 1 teaspoon salt, pinch of tomato coloring and lemon juice into the cuts and all over the chicken. Set aside 30 minutes.

Make a paste of the garlic, allspice, 1 teaspoon salt, lime juice, red pepper, yogurt, pinch of tomato coloring and mango. Rub into chicken cuts and all over the chicken. Set in refrigerator 12 hours.

Remove excess paste and place in heated oven at 350°-400° for 15 minutes. Remove. Rub with butter. Cook 10 minutes more. Remove from oven.

Serve hot, garnished with onions, chilies, and lemon wedges.

Mohan Walia states that "Tandoori is the last word in cookery. It is the showpiece of the Indian culinary art and is a true demonstration of the height of perfection to which an art can be raised." He insists, "It is marvellous and is perhaps one of the world's most delicious preparations. A visit to India can never be complete without sampling this great dish."

Serves 2.

Bite of India

15600 N.E. 8th, Suite #9, Bellevue (Crossroads Shopping Center). Phone 643-4263. Open Monday through Thursday, 10:00 A.M. to 9:00 P.M.; Friday and Saturday, 10:00 A.M. to 10:30 P.M.; Sunday, noon to 6:00 P.M.

Owner Usha Reddy proudly claims that Bite of India is the only restaurant in the greater Seattle area to serve cuisine from south India. Dishes are cooked home style, and the curries are made from recipes that have been in the family for ages. The dosas are a favorite dish here (vegetarian, spicy, healthy and simply delicious).

• •

Vegetable Curry

1-1/2 tablespoons vegetable oil
1 small onion, chopped
1-1/2 inch piece ginger root, minced
3 cloves of garlic, minced
1/8 teaspoon turmeric
1/2 teaspoon ground cayenne pepper
1/2 teaspoon ground coriander
1/8 teaspoon garam masala
Salt, to taste
1/2 cup plain yogurt
2 medium size potatoes, diced
1/2 cup frozen green peas
2 medium size tomatoes, cubed
1/2 cup cauliflower flowerettes

Heat oil in a 3 quart sauce pan. Add onion and sauté until golden brown. Add, one at a time, the ginger root, garlic, turmeric, pepper, coriander, garam masala, salt and yogurt. Cook 2 minutes. Add the potatoes, peas, and tomatoes. Cook 15-20 minutes. Add cauliflower and mix well. Reduce heat to low. Cover and cook 5 minutes, stirring occasionally.

Serve warm with steamed rice or with Indian breads.

Serves 4.

• •

Chicken Curry

1 pound boneless chicken breasts
2 tablespoons vegetable oil
1 medium size onion, chopped
3 cloves of garlic and 2 inch
    piece of ginger root, minced
    together to form paste
2 cloves
2 whole cardamom
1 inch cinnamon stick ground
    with 2 tablespoons slivered
    almonds
1/4 teaspoon cayenne pepper
1/8 teaspoon turmeric
1 teaspoon ground coriander
Salt, to taste
1/2 cup yogurt
1/2 cup water
Steamed rice

Wash and dry the chicken with paper towels. Cut into pieces. Set aside.

Heat oil in a 2 quart sauce pan over medium heat. Add onion and sauté 2 minutes. Add ginger root paste and sauté 1 minute. Reduce temperature to medium low. One by one, add the spices and yogurt. Sauté 2 minutes.

Add chicken. Stir well so that the chicken is coated with spice mixture. Leave on low heat for 5 minutes, stirring occasionally. Increase the heat to medium high. Cook another 5 minutes, stirring often. Add water and cook 10 minutes.

If more gravy is needed, add another 1/2 cup water. Cook another 5-10 minutes. Accompany with rice.

Serves 2.

India Palace

13025 Aurora Avenue North, Seattle.   Phone 361-9710.   Open Sunday through Thursday, 11:00 A.M. to 9:00 P.M.; Friday and Saturday, 11:00 A.M. to 10:00 P.M.

The fact that quality Indian restaurants have not only reached the suburbs but are prospering there is perhaps a measure of just how far that country's cuisine has come in gaining wide acceptance in the Puget Sound area. India Palace is a case in point; the aromas are intense, the food authentic and full of exotic flavors (curry is just the beginning), and owner Amrik Kamoh has created a menu that is diverse enough to provide something for every taste.

• •

Prawn and Tomato Curry

1 pound prawns (about 3 cups), uncooked, shelled and deveined
Salt, to taste
1/4 cup butter or ghee
3 large tomatoes, peeled and sliced
3 onions, finely chopped
1/4 teaspoon garlic powder
1/4 teaspoon ground ginger root
1 teaspoon chili powder
2 teaspoons ground coriander
1/2 teaspoon ground turmeric
3 tablespoons shredded coconut
2/3 cup water
2 teaspoons garam masala

Sprinkle prawns with salt. Lightly fry in butter. Add tomatoes, onions, garlic, ginger, chili, coriander, and turmeric. Continue to cook 5 minutes. Add coconut and water. Simmer until prawns are almost cooked.

Sprinkle on the garam masala. Cook until prawns are tender.

Serve with plain boiled rice and a selection of side dishes.

Serves 3-4.

• •

Kheer (Rice Pudding)

3 quarts milk
1/2 cup long grain rice
3/4 cup sugar
1/2 cup chopped almonds
1/4 teaspoon ground cardamom
    seed
Toasted chopped almonds

Bring milk to boil in large sauce pan (a wide, shallow pan will work better than a deep one). Add rice. Cook over medium low heat, stirring frequently and watching carefully to prevent milk from boiling over, until consistency of heavy cream and mixture begins sticking to bottom of pan, about 2-1/4 hours. Stir in sugar, 1/2 cup of almonds, and cardamom. Continue cooking 3-4 minutes, stirring constantly.

Serve warm or chilled, sprinkled with almonds.

Serves 8.

Asia

House of Hong

409 - 8th Avenue South, Seattle. Phone 622-7997. Open Monday through Thursday, 11:00 A.M. to 10:00 P.M.; Friday, 11:00 A.M. to midnight; Saturday, 10:30 A.M. to midnight; Sunday, 10:30 A.M. to 10:00 P.M.

The House of Hong is one of the most reliable and upscale Chinese restaurants in Seattle, and that is no small feat. A fixture in the International District for over 35 years, the House of Hong is a favorite for dim sum lunches, and has an extensive menu for lunch and dinner as well. Owner/chef Paul Lee has made the House of Hong a quietly elegant place, with decor as handsome as the food is delicious.

• •

Spice Ma Pou Bean Curd

2 boxes of bean curd, cut into 1
  inch cubes
2 teaspoons salad oil
2 ounces ground pork
3 cloves of garlic, chopped
1 teaspoon hot bean paste
2 teaspoons soy sauce
1 teaspoon salt
1/4 teaspoon MSG, optional
6 ounces chicken stock
1 bunch of green onions, chopped
2 teaspoons cornstarch
1 teaspoon sesame oil

Boil bean curd in water about 1 minute, or until the inside is hot. Set aside.

Heat oil and fry ground pork until well cooked. Add garlic, hot bean paste, soy sauce, salt, MSG, stock and reserved bean curd. Cook 5 minutes.

Sprinkle mixture with green onions. Thicken with cornstarch. Stir in sesame oil.

Serves 2.

• •

Mongolian Beef

2 teaspoons soy sauce
1 teaspoon red wine
1/2 pound choice beef flank
    steak, sliced thin
4 teaspoons salad oil
3 cloves of garlic, chopped
1/2 pound green onions, cut into
    1 inch pieces
1 teaspoon white vinegar
3 teaspoons brown sugar
1 teaspoon ground black pepper
1 teaspoon sesame oil

Combine the soy sauce and wine. Add the flank steak. Marinate 30 minutes.

Heat the salad oil in a frying pan until very hot. Add the garlic and then the beef, stir-frying for 5 minutes. Add green onions, vinegar, brown sugar and pepper, continuing to stir-fry until the beef is thoroughly cooked. Add sesame oil.

Chef Paul Lee advises that the secret to this dish is to use very high heat and cook quickly ... that's what makes the beef juicy and tender.

Serves 2.

Jemmy's Wok

16212 - #D Bothell-Evertt Highway, Mill Creek. Phone 742-8858. Open Tuesday through Thursday, 11:00 A.M. to 9:00 P.M.; Friday and Saturday, 11:00 A.M. to 11:00 P.M.; Sunday, 4:00 to 9:00 P.M.

Jemmy's Wok (and yes, there is a Jemmy) is a smallish Chinese restaurant in the Seattle suburb of Woodinville that has earned a big reputation and a devoted following for its Szechwan, Hunan and Mandarin cuisine. Everything is cooked fresh to order, and customer preferences as to how spicy they would like their meals are duly noted. Diners concerned about MSG need not worry here; it's never used.

• •

Coral Shrimp

6 tablespoons oil, divided
1/4-1/2 cup baby corn
1/4-1/2 cup sliced carrots
1/4-1/2 cup broccoli flowerettes
1/4-1/2 cup sliced mushrooms
1/2 pound shrimp, 26-30 size
1 teaspoon cooking wine
1-1/2 teaspoons preserved black
    beans
1/3 teaspoon chopped garlic
5 teaspoons chicken broth
5 teaspoons soy sauce
2 teaspoons sugar
1/4 teaspoon chili oil
1/4 teaspoon sesame oil
1/4 teaspoon white pepper
1-1/2 teaspoons cornstarch,
    dissolved in 1 tablespoon
    water
1/2 teaspoon chopped green
    onions

Heat 2 tablespoons oil in wok or skillet. Stir-fry corn, carrots, broccoli and mushrooms 1 minute. Remove from pan.

Reheat wok with 2 tablespoons oil. Add shrimp. Stir-fry 1-2 minutes. Add wine. Remove from pan.

Reheat wok with 2 tablespoons oil. Add black beans and garlic. Stir-fry 30 seconds. Add broth, soy sauce, sugar, oils and pepper, along with reserved vegetables and shrimp. When mixture is hot, add cornstarch and mix well. Sprinkle with onions when ready to serve.

Serves 2-3.

• •

Sesame Beef

3-1/2 teaspoons soy sauce
1/4 teaspoon white pepper
4 teaspoons sugar
1-1/2 teaspoons vinegar
1/2 teaspoon chopped garlic
1/3 teaspoon chili oil
1/4 teaspoon sesame oil
12 ounces flank steak, sliced
 approximately 2 inches x 4
 inches x 1/2 inch
1 green onion, sliced
2 teaspoons sesame seeds,
 toasted

Combine soy sauce, pepper, sugar, vinegar, garlic, chili and sesame oils in a bowl. Add steak pieces. Marinate approximately 2 hours, turning the meat over occasionally. Broil meat over hot coals. Sprinkle with green onions and sesame seeds just before serving.

Serves 2.

Hing Loon Seafood Restaurant

628 South Weller Street, Seattle. Phone 682-2828. Open Sunday through Thursday, 10:00 A.M. to midnight; Friday and Saturday, 10:00 to 2:00 A.M.

This recent addition to Seattle's International District serves some of the finest Chinese cuisine to be found anywhere this side of the Great Wall, including a wonton soup (recipe below) that is not to be missed. Hing Loon is owned by two brothers, Paul Fung and Chu Ngai Hang, and their watchful eyes make sure that the food is consistently excellent and that customers are served quickly and competently.

• •

Wonton Soup

BROTH:
4 ounces dried shrimp
Pinch of coarsely ground pepper
2 quarts water
1/2 filet of dried sole (Tai Tee Yuee), grilled, then finely chopped to powder state
1/4 pound chicken bones
1/4 pound pork bones
3 teaspoons salt
1 ounce rock sugar
1/3 teaspoon MSG, optional

Combine the dried shrimp, pepper, water and sole in large pot. Bring to boil, reduce heat, and simmer 1 hour. Add chicken and pork bones. Bring back to boil and cook another 2 hours. Strain and remove bones. Stir in salt, rock sugar and MSG.

WONTONS:
3/4 pound shrimp, 71-90 size, shelled, chopped
Pepper, to taste
1/2 pound pork, coarsely ground

3 teaspoons salt
1 teaspoon dried sole (Tai Tee Yuee) powder from broth recipe
1-1/2 teaspoons sugar
1/3 teaspoon MSG, optional
1 egg yolk
1/2 ounce sesame oil
1/4 teaspoon white pepper
1 tablespoon cottonseed or salad oil
1 tablespoon brown sesame seeds
Wonton skins (preferably Hong Kong style, very thin)

Shake shrimp in pepper. Add ground pork, salt, sole, sugar, MSG, egg yolk, sesame oil, pepper, salad oil and sesame seeds. Combine well. Refrigerate 30 minutes to make it easier to handle. Fill wonton wrappers.

Drop wontons into simmering broth. Cook 5 minutes. Serve wontons in bowl with broth surrounding them.

Serves 4-6.

• •

Kau Kau Barbecue & Seafood Restaurant

656 South King Street, Seattle. Phone 682-4006. Open Sunday through Thursday, 10:00 A.M. to 10:00 P.M.; Friday and Saturday, 10:00 A.M. to midnight.

Kau Kau has been a landmark of Seattle's International District for many years. Thoroughly remodeled not long ago, Kau Kau now has a fresh new face to go with its long tradition of Chinese cuisine. Especially well-known for barbecued pork, roasted pig and duck, owner Wai Eng says they also barbecue whole turkeys for customers on request; these barbecue items are sold over the counter as well as for dining in the restaurant.

• •

Pork Fried Rice

1-2 tablespoons oil, more if needed
1 egg
4 cups cooked rice
2-3 ounces chopped barbecued pork, or any other cooked meat
2-3 ounces bean sprouts
Soy sauce, to taste
Handful of chopped green onions

Heat oil in frying pan or wok over high flame. Add egg and scramble. Add rice and mix well. Add meat, sprouts and soy sauce. Stir-fry until well combined and very hot. Sprinkle with green onions.

Serves 3-4.

• •

Linyen Restaurant

424 Seventh Avenue South, Seattle.   Phone 622-8181.   Open Monday through Saturday, 2:30 P.M. to 1:30 A.M.; Sunday, 2:30 to 11:00 P.M.

Located in the heart of Seattle's International District, Linyen is an old favorite among diners who love Chinese food. Owner Elaine Young sees to it that Linyen's traditional Cantonese dishes are prepared and served with meticulous care in a warm and friendly atmosphere.

• •

Crystal Shrimp

1-1/2 pounds shrimp
3 tablespoons coarse kosher salt
3 tablespoons favorite oil:
   Mazola, peanut, etc.
3 cloves of garlic, chopped
1 piece of ginger root, thinly
   sliced
4-5 green onions or scallions,
   chopped
1 tablespoon dry sherry
1 tablespoon soy sauce

Devein shrimp. Place in salt, coat well and let stand 1 minute. Rinse and drain. Repeat this step twice more. Dry with paper towels.

Shrimp may be stir-fried with any number of vegetables, or stir-fried alone several hours in advance and used as an appetizer.

To stir-fry, heat oil in the wok, add shrimp and quickly stir so they are well coated with the oil. Add the garlic, ginger root and onions. Stir-fry together for just moments. Add sherry and soy sauce. Total cooking time should be no more than 2 minutes.

Serves 4.

• •

Satin Chicken

1 whole roasting chicken,
    approximately 4 pounds
1 onion, quartered
1 small piece of ginger root,
    sliced
1 tablespoon salt
Water
2 cloves of garlic
36 ice cubes
Sauce (recipe follows)

Place chicken in cauldron with onion, ginger root, salt, and enough water to cover. Simmer, skimming surface, about 12 minutes. Cover and gently simmer 15 minutes.

Remove from burner. Let stand approximately 30 minutes (size of chicken determines time of steeping; a smaller chicken would need less time). Simmer 10 minutes more if you want well done.

Place chicken in large bowl. Fill with ice cubes and water. Chill thoroughly. Dry well with paper towels and refrigerate. When ready to serve, slice as you would a roasting chicken. Serve with sauce in separate dishes.

Serves 4.

SAUCE:
1/4 cup Mazola or peanut oil
1 teaspoon sesame oil
1 piece of ginger root, finely
    chopped
10 sprigs of cilantro or parsley
1 clove of garlic, chopped fine
3 tablespoons salt

Heat the oil in a small pan until it smokes blue, then pour oil over ginger root, cilantro, garlic and salt. Stir and serve at room temperature.

New Hong Kong

212 - 12th Ave. So., Seattle. Phone 324-4091. Open daily, 10:00 A.M. to 10:00 P.M.

Located just east of the International District, where 12th meets Jackson, this smallish Chinese restaurant is among the most authentic you'll find anywhere. Owner Ray Suu has built a solid clientele with great food, an extensive and varied menu, and moderate prices.

• •

Deep Fried Crispy Chicken

1 whole chicken
Boiling water
2 teaspoons salt
1 teaspoon five-spice
   powder
1/2 cup white vinegar
1/4 cup Chinkiang vinegar
2 tablespoons malt syrup
1-1/2 cups water
Oil for deep frying

Clean chicken, removing and discarding internal organs from cavity. Pour boiling water over chicken. Combine salt and five-spice powder, and sprinkle inside cavity. Combine the vinegars, syrup and water. Cook over low heat until boiling. Pour over chicken. Hang chicken up and allow to dry.

Heat oil in deep container to 350-375°. Carefully lower chicken into oil. Fry until skin is brown and crispy, turning with spatula as needed. Remove from oil and drain on paper towels. Cut into small pieces.

Serves 2-4.

• •

Black Pepper Beef

1 pound flank steak, cut into
   3 inch x 1 inch x 1/2 inch
   pieces
1 teaspoon cornstarch
1 teaspoon oyster sauce
1/2 teaspoon mushroom soy
   sauce
1 teaspoon cooking wine
Oil for deep frying
Black Pepper Sauce (recipe
   follows)

Combine the steak pieces with the cornstarch, oyster sauce, mushroom soy sauce and wine, mixing well. Heat oil to 350-375° in a deep container. Fry meat one piece at a time until well done. Remove and drain on paper towels. Mix with Black Pepper Sauce.

Serves 2-4.

BLACK PEPPER SAUCE:
1 teaspoon cheehau sauce
1/2 teaspoon satay sauce
1/3 teaspoon black bean sauce
1/3 teaspoon garlic sauce
1/3 teaspoon black pepper
1/2 teaspoon sugar
1 teaspoon cornstarch, dissolved
   in 1 tablespoon water
1 cup water

Combine ingredients in sauce pan. Bring to boil and continue cooking until sauce thickens.

The Proud Bird

4234 University Way N.E., Seattle.   Phone 632-7248.   Open Sunday through Thursday, 11:00 A.M. to 10:00 P.M.; Friday and Saturday, 11:00 A.M. to midnight.

The Proud Bird has come a long way from its origins as a char-broiled chicken restaurant. The Chan brothers - Jim, Nathan and Bor - decided to change their University District eatery into a full-service Chinese restaurant four years ago, and the result is some of the best, and most authentic, Chinese food to be found outside the International District. One welcome difference is the use of true Chinese vegetables, rather than their North American versions. A wide variety of noodle dishes complements traditional main course entrées such as Mongolian beef, chicken with black bean sauce, and some new dishes, such as General TSO's chicken.

• •

Broccoli with Prawns

1/4 cup vegetable oil
1/8 teaspoon salt
1 clove of garlic, finely chopped
12-16 shrimp, unshelled
10 ounces broccoli, cut into
   bite-sized pieces
1/2 cup chicken broth or water
1 teaspoon sesame oil
1 tablespoon cooking sherry
2 teaspoons cornstarch,
   dissolved in 1/4 cup cold
   water

Turn heat to highest setting. Pour oil into wok or frying pan. Heat oil until it almost smokes. Add salt to oil. Add garlic to wok. Stir-fry 5 seconds. Add shrimp and broccoli to wok. Stir-fry until half done. Add broth to wok. Heat until broth boils. Add sesame oil and cooking sherry. Slowly add cornstarch, until a light gravy is formed.
Serves 4.

• •

Chicken with Black Bean Sauce

1/4 cup vegetable oil

1/8 teaspoon salt

1/2 teaspoon preserved black
    beans, finely chopped

1 clove of garlic, finely chopped

3-4 slices of ginger root, finely
    chopped

2-1/2 ounces green bell pepper,
    cut into small pieces,
    approximately 1 inch square

2-1/2 ounces onion, cut into
    small pieces, approximately
    1 inch square

12 ounces boneless chicken, cut
    into nugget form,
    approximately 30 pieces

1 cup chicken broth or water

1 teaspoon sesame oil

1 tablespoon cooking sherry

2 teaspoons cornstarch,
    dissolved in 1/4 cup cold
    water

Turn heat to the highest setting. Pour oil into a wok or frying pan. Heat oil until almost smoking. Add salt to oil. Add black beans, garlic, and ginger root. Stir-fry 5 seconds. Add pepper, onion and chicken. Stir-fry until chicken is slightly brown on outside. Add broth to wok. Heat until broth boils. Add sesame oil and cooking sherry. Slowly add cornstarch, until a light gravy is formed.

Serves 2-3.

Singapore Restaurant

17549 - 15th Avenue N.E., Seattle. Phone 365-3474. Open Monday through Friday, 11:00 A.M. to 10:00 P.M.; Saturday, 1:00 to 10:00 P.M.; closed Sunday.

Frank Lau opened the Singapore Restaurant in 1980, and it has earned a loyal and enthusiastic following. It's a family style restaurant, serving hot and spicy Szechwan cuisine and curry dishes that are as pleasing to the eye as they are to the palate.

• •

Jing Du Spareribs

1/2 tablespoon soy sauce
1/2 teaspoon salt
1 teaspoon sugar
1/2 tablespoon rice wine
1/2 tablespoon chopped garlic
1-1/3 pounds small spareribs
3 tablespoons cornstarch
1/2 teaspoon baking soda
6 cups oil
1 tablespoon Worcestershire
   sauce
1 tablespoon tomato ketchup
1/2 tablespoon sugar
1/4 teaspoon sesame oil
2 tablespoons water
1 tablespoon oil
Tomato slices

Combine first 5 ingredients. Set aside.

Cut spareribs into 20 sections. Combine with soy sauce mixture. Marinate 20 minutes. Mix with cornstarch and baking soda.

Heat oil and deep fry spareribs 4 minutes over medium heat. Remove. Heat oil until very hot. Return spareribs to oil and fry for 1 minute. Remove and drain.

Combine Worcestershire sauce, ketchup, sugar, sesame oil and water in a small pan. Heat until boiling. Add spareribs and 1 tablespoon oil. Toss lightly to coat spareribs with sauce. Remove spareribs and drain.

Garnish dish with tomato slices.

Serves 2-3.

• •

Szechwan Green Beans

1 teaspoon rice wine
1/2 tablespoon soy sauce
1/2 teaspoon sugar
1/4 teaspoon MSG
1/2 tablespoon water
1 pound string beans
3 cups oil
1 ounce chopped pork
2 tablespoons chopped dried
    shrimp
4 tablespoons chopped
    Szechwan pickled mustard
    greens
1/2 tablespoon chopped green
    onions
1/2 teaspoon sesame oil

Combine first 5 ingredients and set aside.

Remove ends from beans. Pull away any "veiny" strings.

Rinse and drain. Cut into 3 inch sections.

Heat oil for deep frying. Deep fry string beans over medium heat for 5 minutes. Remove and drain.

Discard all but 3 tablespoons of oil from pan and reheat. Add pork to pan and fry until it changes color. Add shrimp and Szechwan pickled mustard greens. Stir-fry 30 seconds. Add string beans along with the rice wine mixture. Stir-fry until the sauce is dry.

Add green onions and sesame oil. Toss lightly to combine ingredients.

Serves 6.

Atlas Chinese Restaurant

424 Maynard Avenue South, Seattle.   Phone 623-0913.   Open Monday through Thursday, 11:00 A.M. to 11:00 P.M.; Friday and Saturday, 11:00 A.M. to midnight; Sunday, noon to 10:00 P.M.

The Atlas has long been a standard in Seattle's International District, serving up good and plentiful food at reasonable prices. Hing and Eling Wong are hands-on owners, and the quality of the food and service shows it; orders are served up promptly and well-prepared.

. . . .

Hot and Sour Soup

1 pint water
2 ounces diced pork
1/5 tofu cake, diced
20 green beans
5 lily flowers, diced
5 black fungi, diced
1/4 teaspoon salt
1/2 teaspoon sugar
1/2 teaspoon MSG
3 teaspoons soy sauce
1-1/2 teaspoons hot sauce
6 teaspoons vinegar

1-1/2 teaspoons cornstarch,
    dissolved in 3 ounces water
1 egg, beaten

Bring water to a boil. Add pork, tofu, green beans, lily flowers, and fungi. Add salt, sugar, MSG, soy sauce, hot sauce and vinegar. Bring back to boil. Add cornstarch mixture. Stir. Turn off heat. Lightly stir in egg.
Serves 2.

. . . .

Clams with Hot Garlic Sauce

1 tablespoon oil
3 green onions, cut into 3-4 pieces
2 ounces preserved black beans
1 clove of garlic, diced
1-1/2 pounds clams
1 pint water
1/2 teaspoon hot sauce
1/4 teaspoon salt
1 teaspoon sugar
1 teaspoon MSG
1/2 teaspoon soy sauce

1 teaspoon cornstarch, dissolved
    in 1 tablespoon water

Place oil in wok. Add green onions when hot. Add black beans and garlic. Stir thoroughly. Add clams and water. When clams open, add hot sauce, salt, sugar, MSG, and soy sauce. Cook 2 minutes. Add cornstarch mixture and allow liquid to thicken.
Serves 4.

. . . .

Takara

1501 Western Avenue, Seattle. Phone 682-8609. Open Monday through Saturday, 11:30 A.M. to 9:00 P.M.; Sunday, noon to 7:00 P.M.

Tucked away below the Pike Street hillclimb (the elevator and skybridge that access the Pike Place Market from Western Avenue), Takara is a Japanese oasis for harried downtown business people and foot-weary market visitors. A really first-rate sushi bar complements table seating for traditional Japanese cuisine, consistently among the best in Seattle.

• •

Sake Kasu

Black cod filet
Salt, to taste
Sake (the cheaper the better)
Sake kasu (sake less)
White miso paste

Lightly salt filet and refrigerate overnight. Wash off filet with sake.

Combine sake kasu and miso (ratio is 1:1), enough for cod to be completely surrounded and soaked. Marinate at least 2 days.

Before grilling, clean off cod with dry towel. Remove paste completely, but gently, so you do not end up with small pieces.

Grill the cleaned cod on very hot, lightly oiled grill. When you oil the grill, it should dissipate oil and smoke. Caution: Do not overcook the fish!

Serves 1.

• •

Butter Itame

Geoduck
Salt and pepper, to taste
Flour
Butter or margarine
Green onions, very thinly sliced
Ponzu sauce

Remove the shell and skin from the geoduck. Slice as thin as possible, about 1/16 inch thick. Lightly salt and pepper. Roll in flour, shaking off excess.

Melt butter or margarine in a hot pan. Sauté geoduck until lightly browned over medium to high heat. Add green onions. Wait 2-3 seconds, then add ponzu sauce.

Caution: Ponzu sauce will become bitter if you overcook with the sauce in the pan!

Serves 4.

• •

Koraku Restaurant

419 Sixth Avenue South, Seattle. Phone 624-1389. Open Monday through Friday, 11:30 A.M. to 5:00 P.M.; closed Saturday and Sunday.

Long a favorite for lunch in the International District, Koraku hosts business people, tourists, and local residents with a wide range of midday Japanese foods, prepared with consistency and obvious attention to detail.

• •

Saba Misoni

3 cups water
2 tablespoons hon dashi
1 cup soy sauce
2-3 slices of ginger root
1 cup sugar
2-3 pieces of mackerel
Miso Sauce (recipe follows)

Combine water, dashi, soy sauce, ginger root, and sugar in sauce pan. Bring to a boil. Add fish and cook until done. Put on a serving plate. Cover with Miso Sauce.
Serves 2.

MISO SAUCE:
1 cup miso
3 cups water
2 tablespoons hon dashi
2 cups sugar, more or less to
 taste

Mix all ingredients together. Bring to a boil.

• •

Tofu Steak

Flour
Black pepper, to taste
**1 package of tofu, cut into 5
   pieces**
Oil
Steak Sauce (recipe follows)
Green onions
Red ginger

Combine flour and pepper. Roll tofu in flour mixture. Fry in small amount of oil until lightly browned on each side. Remove to plate. Add Steak Sauce. Garnish with green onions and red ginger.
Serves 2.

STEAK SAUCE:
3 cups water
2 tablespoons hon dashi
1/2 cup soy sauce
Salt, to taste
1 cup sugar
1 tablespoon grated ginger root
1/3-1/2 cup cornstarch

Combine the first 6 ingredients. Bring to a boil. Add cornstarch to thicken while boiling.

Bush Garden

614 Maynard Avenue South, Seattle. Phone 682-6830. Open for lunch Monday through Friday, 11:30 A.M. to 2:00 P.M.; open for dinner Monday through Saturday, 5:00 to 10:00 P.M.; Sunday, 5:00 to 9:00 P.M.

Many Seattle residents and visitors were first introduced to the delights of Japanese cuisine at the Bush Garden, a landmark of the International District for forty years. Traditional Japanese foods are served by kimono-clad waitresses in the traditional way, in private tatami rooms, with seating on the floor. Conventional seating is offered, if you prefer, and there is also the sushi bar where you can watch the preparation.

Mr. Seko's Sukiyaki

1 cup soy sauce
1 cup water
1/2 cup sake
3 tablespoons sugar
1 small can yam noodles
1 small can bamboo shoots
3 large dry onions, sliced
4 bunches of green onions, cut in 1-1/2 inch lengths
2-1/2 pounds sukiyaki beef strips (beef sliced 1/8 inch thick from the eye of prime rib)

Combine the soy sauce, water, sake, and sugar in small bowl. Set aside.

Place the yam noodles, bamboo shoots, dry onions and green onions in a large frying pan. Spread the beef evenly over the vegetables to a thickness of about 1/8 inch. Pour enough of the reserved sauce over the vegetables and meat so that the ingredients will be half submerged in liquid.

Put the frying pan on the stove and heat the contents. Bring to a simmer, uncovered, and continue cooking until the meat is about three-fourths done. Mix the entire contents with a chopstick and turn the burner off. Allow to stand 3-5 minutes before serving, during which time the meat will finish cooking.

Serves 8.

Daimonji

5963 Corson Avenue South, #194, Seattle. Phone 762-7820. Open for lunch Monday through Friday, 11:00 A.M. to 2:00 P.M.; open for dinner Monday through Saturday, 5:00 to 10:00 P.M.

Tucked away in Seattle's Georgetown industrial area is Daimonji, a small gem of a Japanese restaurant. Popular with workers from nearby Boeing Field (and often their Japanese guests), Daimonji is becoming known more widely outside the immediate area as well. A good sushi bar, a varied and authentic menu, and a selection of Japanese beers round out the bill of fare.

• •

Tonkatsu (Breaded Pork Cutlet)

3-1/2 ounce pork cutlet, tenderized
Salt and pepper, to taste
1-3 tablespoons flour
1 egg, beaten with 1 tablespoon water
1/3 cup panko
Vegetable oil for deep frying
Cabbage, shredded
Red leaf lettuce, shredded
Tonkatsu sauce

Sprinkle cutlet with salt and pepper. Dust with flour, dip into egg wash, then immediately into panko. Heat oil to about 350°. Deep fry cutlet about 7 minutes, or until golden brown.

Present on platter accompanied with cabbage, lettuce and tonkatsu sauce. Serves 1.

• •

Okonomiyaki (Japanese Style Pancake)

1 cup flour
1 cup water
2 eggs
1/2 ounce baby shrimp
1 ounce chopped squid
1/2 ounce finely sliced beef
2 ounces shredded cabbage
Pickled red ginger, julienne cut
Mayonnaise, tonkatsu or okonomiyaki sauce

Combine flour, water and egg to make batter. Stir in shrimp, squid, beef and cabbage. Pour the thick mixture onto well-greased, 350° griddle. Cook until golden, about 10 minutes, turning once.

Top with ginger, a small amount of mayonnaise, tonkatsu or okonomiyaki sauce. Serves 1.

• •

Hisago Japanese Restaurant

543-I Northgate Way N.E., Seattle. Phone 363-1556. Open for lunch Tuesday through Friday, 11:30 A.M. to 2:00 P.M.; open for dinner Tuesday through Saturday, 5:00 to 9:30 P.M.; Sunday, 5:00 to 9:00 P.M.; closed Monday.

For 10 years, Hisago has offered north end residents and business people looking for authentic Japanese food and atmosphere with an alternative to the drive into Seattle's International District. This small (62 seat) restaurant offers a sushi bar, private tatami rooms, and a complete range of well-prepared Japanese foods, including a very popular bento box, which features a lunch-size assortment of Japanese dishes from the garden, mountain and sea.

• •

Sukiyaki

10 tablespoons chicken broth
3 tablespoons soy sauce
3 tablespoons sugar
3 tablespoons sake
Dash of bonito
4-1/2 tablespoons water
1 block of tofu, cut into 1 inch
    cubes
1/2 small head of Chinese
    cabbage, cut into 1/2 inch
    slices
1 small onion, cut in half and
    then into 1/2 inch slices
1/2 cup sliced carrots
8-ounce can bamboo shoots
8 dried mushrooms, soaked 1
    hour in warm water
1 pound beef, sliced paper-thin
7-8 green onions, cut into 1/2
    inch slices

Combine broth, soy sauce, sugar, sake, bonito, and water to make sauce. Place in bottom of pan. Arrange tofu and vegetables in sauce. After vegetables are almost cooked, add beef and green onions. Cook until beef is done.

The Hisago Restaurant reminds us that the ingredients for Sukiyaki vary from time to time. Experiment and find the combination that pleases you.
Serves 2.

• •

Chicken Teriyaki

Ground ginger root
1 clove of garlic, ground
1 tablespoon sugar
1/2 cup soy sauce
2 boneless, skinless chicken
   breasts

Combine ginger root, garlic, sugar and soy sauce to make a teriyaki sauce. Pour over chicken breasts, moving poultry around until well coated. Allow to marinate 24 hours. Remove chicken from marinade and bake.

Place marinade in sauce pan. Boil several minutes. Pour a little of this sauce over the cooked chicken breasts. Serve remainder of sauce on the side.

Serves 2.

Toyoda Sushi

12543 Lake City Way N.E., Seattle. Phone 367-7972. Open Wednesday through Saturday, 5:00 to 10:00 P.M.; Sunday and Monday, 5:00 to 9:00 P.M. (9:30 in summer); closed Tuesday.

As you would expect from the name, this small north end Japanese restaurant has a fine sushi bar, but there is much more here than that. The restaurant side seats 49 people and serves them with the gamut of Japanese cuisine, including some of the best homemade gyoza (potstickers) anywhere. Owners Natsuyoshi and Helen Toyoda have built a remarkable place. Natchan (his nickname) comes from the Japanese Alps and learned the art of sushi from a master, starting at age 18. Both have an uncompromising approach to quality and a commitment to treat every customer as if he were a guest in their home. The traditional Japanese country inn decor has some interesting twists, including a collection of over 200 personalized wooden sake cups, each of them for a regular customer.

• •

Black Cod Kasuzuke
(Black Cod Marinated in Sake Paste)

Salt, to taste
Black cod (or salmon or other
    fish) filet, cut into pieces
    about 1/2 inch thick
2 pounds sake kasu
1/4 pound miso paste
1/4 cup sugar
1/2 cup sake

Lightly salt both sides of fish. Let sit about 1 hour in refrigerator. Rinse and pat dry thoroughly with cheesecloth.

Combine sake kasu, miso paste, sugar and sake.

Carefully cover fish pieces with sake paste. Place in a shallow rectangular plastic container and cover. Marinate at least 1-2 days. Will last a week or more.

When ready to prepare, remove fish from paste. Carefully wipe each piece. Bake or broil in the oven about 10 minutes, or until done. Accompany with steamed rice.

Serves 4.

• •

Teriyaki Chicken

1/4 cup mirin
1/4 cup sugar
1/2 cup soy sauce
1/2 ounce garlic, crushed
1/2 ounce ginger root, crushed
Chicken, any cut is okay

Combine mirin, sugar, soy sauce, garlic and ginger root in bowl.

Place chicken in shallow pan. Pour mirin mixture over chicken. Let sit in refrigerator 1 day.

Bake chicken in 400° oven about 20 minutes, or until done. Present with steamed rice.

Serves 2.

Nikko

Westin Hotel, 1900 Fifth Avenue, Seattle. Phone 322-4641. Open for lunch Monday through Friday, 11:30 A.M. to 2:30 P.M.; open for dinner Monday through Saturday, 5:00 to 10:00 P.M.; Sunday, 4:30 to 9:00 P.M.

In its long, proud history in Seattle (which, under a different name, dates back to World's Fair days), the Westin Hotel has earned a reputation for doing things right. The Nikko restaurant had also earned a fine reputation, at its old location on King Street. Thus, it only followed that when a new Nikko was constructed in the Westin, the result would be spectacular. And it is. The decor is sumptuous and elegant, the menu almost overwhelming in its variety, the execution painstakingly correct and the service flawless.

• •

Sukiyaki

Beef fat or salad oil
1 bunch of green onions
1 block of tofu
Shitake mushrooms
Enoki mushrooms
Nappa cabbage
Sliced bamboo shoots
Crysanthemum leaves or spinach
Sukiyaki Sauce (recipe follows)
Udon noodles
Shiratake noodles
1/2 pound or more thinly sliced
    beef

SUKIYAKI SAUCE:
1/2 cup chicken broth
1/2 cup water
3/8 cup soy sauce
1/2 cup sugar
1/4 cup sake

Combine all ingredients.

Use either a sukiyaki pan on a propane burner at the table or a frying pan. Grease with beef fat or oil, if preferred. Arrange vegetables attractively in pan, starting with the vegetables that take the longest to cook. Add Sukiyaki Sauce, then noodles. Cover with beef. Cook until done.
    Serves 2-4.

• •

Arita Restaurant

8202 Greenwood Avenue North, Seattle. Phone 784-2625. Open for lunch Monday through Friday, 11:30 A.M. to 2:00 P.M.; open for dinner, Monday through Thursday, 5:00 to 9:00 P.M.; Friday and Saturday, 5:00 to 9:30 P.M; closed Sunday.

Jerry Yang, a native of Taiwan, was brought up with Chinese traditions, but studied Japanese cookery under the watchful eye of Daiki Matsueda, the owner of Arita, and now Jerry manages the restaurant. He has become a student of the long history of Japanese cuisine, dating back to the 8th and 9th centuries, when the Chinese came to Japan and introduced, among other things, chopsticks and soy sauce. In the 13th century, there was another Chinese export to Japan: Zen Buddhism, which brought with it a strict vegetarian regimen. A long period of isolation followed, until the 19th century, when diplomats from the West established contact with Japan, and brought with them new foods and cooking techniques. This sense of history and tradition is evident in the cuisine at Arita Restaurant.

• •

Salmon Teriyaki

2 tablespoons grated ginger root
1/4 cup soy sauce
1 tablespoon sake
1/2 teaspoon sugar
1 clove of garlic, crushed
6-1/2 ounce salmon filet

Combine ginger root, soy sauce, sake, sugar and garlic to form a teriyaki sauce. Marinate salmon in this sauce. Cook in your favorite fashion: baking, grilling or frying.
Serves 1.

• •

Tempura

2 eggs
1-1/2 cups ice water
2 cups all-purpose flour
An assortment of seafood and
    vegetables
1-3/4 cups dashi
1/3 cup soy sauce
1/3 cup mirin

To form a batter, combine eggs, water and flour. Coat seafood and vegetables, then deep-fry.
To form a dipping sauce, combine dashi, soy sauce and mirin.
Serves 4.

• •

Provinces Asian Restaurant

201 Fifth Avenue South (Old Mill Town), Edmonds. Phone 744-0288. Open Monday through Thursday, 11:30 A.M. to 9:30 P.M.; Friday and Saturday, 11:30 A.M. to 10:30 P.M.; Sunday, 4:00 to 10:00 P.M.

This relaxed and comfortable north end restaurant isn't easy to classify. Rather than concentrating on one nation or region's cuisine, Provinces' territory includes most of Asia; Cantonese, Szechwan, Hunan, Hong Kong, Vietnamese and Thai dishes are all included on the diverse menu and well-prepared in the kitchen. For diners, the result is lots of variety at one unique restaurant.

• •

Thai Basil Scallops

3/4 pound medium sea scallops, rinsed (do not substitute bay scallops)
1 tablespoon cottonseed oil
1 green onion (white part only), diced
3 cloves of garlic, minced
1 tablespoon hoisin sauce
1/2 teaspoon tom yum paste
3 sprigs of Thai basil (red stems with green leaves), stems removed, leaves chopped coarsely to release flavors
1/2 sweet onion, sliced thin
1/2 cup carrots, julienne cut or grated
1/2 cup pea pods
1 tablespoon sake
1 teaspoon fish sauce
1 teaspoon oyster sauce
Chicken broth, as needed
1/2 teaspoon sesame oil

Bring a large pot of water to a boil. Parboil scallops 2 minutes, drain, and set aside.

With wok on high heat, add oil. Turn heat down to medium high. Add green onion and garlic. Stir-fry just to color, not brown.

Stir in the hoisin sauce and tom yum paste to liquefy. Add basil along with the rest of the vegetables. Increase heat, and add scallops. Drizzle sake around the edge of the ingredients.

Stir in the fish and oyster sauces. Cover wok and cook 1-2 minutes, until food steams. If liquid has evaporated a bit, add 1 tablespoon chicken broth. Stir in sesame oil and serve immediately.

If a spicier flavor is desired, add ground Thai chilies or fresh small Thai chilies to taste.

The chef at Provinces points out that prawns may be substituted, but do not parboil.

This delectable dish can also be served as a salad. Line platter with chilled chunks of iceberg or romaine lettuce. Cut one large tomato in half and slice the halves. Peel a cucumber to produce a striped look, cut in half lengthwise, then slice the halves diagonally to match the thickness of the tomato slices. Place hot Thai Basil Scallops in the center and surround with tomato and cucumber slices. Garnish with a few cilantro sprigs on top of the scallops, then a lemon wedge on the side for drizzling. This makes for a very colorful and refreshing presentation.

Serves 2.

• •

Pacific Rim Restaurant

100 South 9th Street, Tacoma. Phone 627-1009. Open Monday through Thursday, 11:00 A.M. to 10:00 P.M; Friday, 11:00 A.M. to 11:00 P.M.; Saturday, 5:00 to 11:00 P.M.; closed Sunday.

A neo-classical building with a past and a present is home to a unique and elegant restaurant specializing in the cuisines of the Pacific Rim. Difficult to classify, executive chef Diana Prine's offerings are an eclectic amalgam of many cuisines, utilizing the best and freshest Northwest ingredients in a highly varied menu with flair and flavor. The street floor of Pacific Rim is casual and often hosts live music; the upstairs is a bit more formal and has a nice view out over Commencement Bay.

• •

Dungeness Crab and Saffron Chowder

Olive oil
2 onions, diced small
3 stalks of celery, diced small
Pinch of saffron
2 potatoes, diced small
3 cups chicken stock
1/2 cup corn
Salt and pepper, to taste
Thyme
1 cup milk or heavy cream
5 ounces Dungeness crab meat

Heat the oil in a sauce pan. Sauté the onions and celery until they begin to soften. Add saffron. Sauté another minute. Add potatoes, stock, corn and seasonings. Simmer until vegetables are tender.

Put through a strainer. Reserve liquid. Reserve two-thirds of the solids and purée one-third. Return the liquid, the solids and the purée to the sauce pan. Add milk and crab meat. Bring to a simmer. Adjust consistency and seasonings.

Serves 2-4.

• •

Pan Roast Ahi Tuna with Black Bean Ginger Sauce and Papaya Chili Salsa

Ahi tuna, 5 ounce portion per
person
Salt and pepper, to taste
Olive oil
Black Bean Ginger Sauce
(recipe follows)
Papaya Chili Salsa (recipe
follows)

Season tuna with salt and pepper. In a very hot sauté pan with olive oil, sear the tuna on both sides. Finish in oven until medium rare.

To serve, cover the entire plate with the Black Bean Ginger Sauce. Place tuna on the sauce and garnish with Papaya Chili Salsa.

BLACK BEAN GINGER SAUCE:
Olive oil
1/4 yellow onion, diced small
1 tablespoon cumin
1 tablespoon peeled, chopped
ginger root
1 cup cooked black beans
1/2 cup chicken stock
Salt and pepper, to taste

Heat a small amount of oil in a heavy bottomed pot. Add onions and sauté until they begin to turn translucent. Add cumin and ginger root. Sauté 2 minutes. Add beans, stock, salt and pepper. Simmer 10 minutes.

Remove two-thirds of the sauce and reserve. Purée the remaining one-third. Stir the purée back into the reserved sauce.

PAPAYA CHILI SALSA:
1/2 red bell pepper
4 tomatillos
1 tomato
1/2 red onion
1 papaya
1 jalapeño pepper
3 tablespoons chopped cilantro
Zest and juice of 2 limes
2 teaspoons Asian chili paste
Salt, to taste

Dice the red pepper, tomatillos, tomato, red onion and papaya into 1/4 inch pieces. Cut jalapeño in half, remove seeds, and dice. Place these ingredients in a mixing bowl.

Add cilantro, lime zest and juice, chili paste and salt. Mix gently. Let flavors blend 2 hours before serving.

Wild Ginger
Asian Restaurant and Satay Bar

1400 Western Avenue, Seattle. Phone 623-4450. Open for lunch Monday through Saturday, 11:30 A.M. to 3:00 P.M.; open for dinner Sunday through Thursday, 5:00 to 11:00 P.M.; Friday and Saturday, 5:00 P.M. to midnight. Satay bar open Monday through Saturday, 11:30 A.M. to 1:30 A.M.; Sunday, 5:00 P.M. to 1:00 A.M.

At Wild Ginger, Pacific Northwest ingredients and the cooking techniques and spices of southeast Asia combine to offer the adventurous some exciting and exotic fare. The dishes derive from Cambodia, Thailand, Malaysia, Singapore and Vietnam. Satays, by the way, are smaller, snack-size portions, which give the diner an opportunity to try several different things. Either way, satay or entrée, the food here is delicious and interesting.

• •

Steamed Salmon Cantonese Style

8 ounces fresh salmon
Several thin slices of fresh
ginger root
2 tablespoons Shaoxing rice wine
2 tablespoons fish sauce
2-3 tablespoons peanut oil
1 clove of garlic
Scallion, 2 inches of white part
only, fine julienne cut
2 sprigs of cilantro

For easy steaming, fashion 2 old chopsticks into an "X" by cutting a groove midpoint on one of them. Place inside wok. Fill wok with water to a level just below the chopsticks, about 3 cups. Place lid on wok. Turn burner on high.

Place salmon in a Pyrex pie plate. Cover with ginger. Pour rice wine and fish sauce over salmon and ginger.

When water has come to boil, place pie plate on top of chopsticks and replace lid. Steam, covered, approximately 7 minutes, or until a toothpick goes through the salmon easily.

While steaming, heat oil in wok or small skillet on high. When hot enough to make a small piece of garlic sizzle, add the whole clove of garlic. Cook until browned. Discard clove but do not turn off heat until you use the oil; it must be very hot to sear the fish.

As soon as the salmon is cooked to perfection, transfer to a serving plate. Place scallion strips on top of ginger and sear with the hot garlic oil. Garnish with whole sprigs of cilantro.

Serves 1-2.

• •

Vietnamese Hot and Sour Soup

8 cups cold water
4-5 pounds fresh fish bones
    (halibut, snapper, rockfish,
    or other white fish)
1 medium onion, quartered
2 cloves of garlic, crushed
2 carrots, sliced
1 teaspoon black peppercorns,
    crushed
1/2 pound white fish, sliced into
    1/2 inch x 1 inch pieces
1/2 pound fresh sea scallops,
    cut in half if large
1/2 pound fresh mussels,
    scrubbed and de-bearded
1/2 pound squid, cleaned, cut
    into 1 inch x 1 inch pieces

4-5 shallots, thinly sliced
1/2 cup peanut oil for frying
4 cups fish stock
2 cups pineapple juice
1/3 cup white vinegar
1 teaspoon red chili pepper
    flakes, crushed
2 ounces sugar
1 tablespoon fish sauce
2 teaspoons dried tamarind,
    dissolved in 1/2 cup hot
    fish stock
2 tomatoes, cut into 18 small
    wedges
1 cup bean sprouts
Fresh taro root, 2-3 thin
    slices per serving
Fried shallot flakes
1/3 cup chopped rice paddy herb

Place water and fish bones in large stock pot. Turn stove on to high. When stock starts to simmer, skim off white foam. Turn heat down before the soup comes to a boil, so as to get a clear stock (cloudiness does not, however, affect the taste). Add onion, garlic, carrots and peppercorns. Simmer uncovered 2-1/2 to 3 hours, or until reduced by half.

When reduced, turn heat up to medium high. Take each type of seafood and place into long handled wire mesh basket. Poach seafood separately in the hot stock 2-3 minutes, or until cooked to rare. Place a few pieces of each type of seafood into individual serving bowls. Strain stock through cheesecloth and reserve.

Fry shallots in oil until golden. Drain on paper towels. Set aside.

Add to heated fish stock, the pineapple juice, vinegar, chili flakes, sugar, fish sauce, and tamarind stock. Taste to correct. Soup should taste first sour, then hot, and finish sweet.

Just before serving, set out the serving bowls with the seafood. Add the following ingredients to each bowl: 3 tomato wedges, a small handful of bean sprouts, and 2-3 pieces of taro root. Ladle in the piping hot soup. Garnish with fried shallot flakes and chopped rice paddy herb.

Serves 6.

* *

Pacific Cafe

100 N. Commercial, Bellingham. Phone 647-0800. Open for lunch Monday through Friday, 11:30 A.M. to 2:00 P.M.; open for dinner Monday through Saturday, 5:30 to 9:00 P.M. (occasionally earlier - please call ahead).

East meets West at the Pacific Cafe in Bellingham, where owner Robert Fong blends Northwest regional ingredients with the culinary traditions of the Orient and Europe in innovative ways. This charming restaurant is sophisticated but not pretentious, and guests can expect fine and original dining (and an extensive wine list).

* *

Ginger Prawn Black Bean

Oil
2 teaspoons chopped ginger root
2 teaspoons preserved black
    beans, mashed
2 tablespoons chopped scallions
4 mushrooms, sliced
1/2 red bell pepper, thinly sliced
2 tablespoons white wine
10 large prawns, peeled and
    deveined
1 teaspoon soy sauce
Pinch of fresh cilantro, chopped
Pinch of salt
1 cup chicken or vegetable stock
Green onions, diagonally sliced

Heat oil. Add ginger root, black beans, scallions, mushrooms, bell pepper and wine. Cook 15-30 seconds.

Stir in prawns and cook 1 minute. Add soy sauce, cilantro, salt and stock. Cook an additional 30-60 seconds. Garnish with green onions.

Serves 2.

* *

Punjabi Chicken Curry

6 pieces of chicken (thighs, legs or breasts - with or without skin)
Flour
Oil
2 cups Curry Sauce (recipe follows)

Dredge chicken in flour and cook in oil until browned. Add Curry Sauce. Simmer 20 minutes, or until cooked thoroughly.
Serves 2.

CURRY SAUCE:
1 cup vegetable oil
3 cups chopped onions
3 tablespoons chopped garlic
2 tablespoons chopped ginger root
1 tablespoon cumin
2 teaspoons turmeric
1 tablespoon coriander
1-1/2 tablespoons ground hot red pepper
1 teaspoon ground fennel
1-2 cups chicken stock, separated
1-1/2 cups canned tomatoes, drained, chopped
1 cup yogurt
Salt, to taste
2 teaspoons garam masala
1/4 cup chopped fresh cilantro
Lemon juice

Heat oil. Add onions, garlic and ginger root. Sauté until onions are soft and golden brown, about 7-8 minutes.

Reduce heat to low. Add cumin, turmeric, coriander, red pepper, fennel, and 2-3 tablespoons of chicken stock. Cook for 1 minute, stirring constantly.

Add tomatoes, yogurt and salt. Increase heat to medium and pour in 1 cup of chicken stock. Bring to a boil.

Sprinkle with garam masala and cilantro. Reduce heat to low and cover tightly. Simmer 20 minutes, adding more stock if necessary. Add lemon juice and additional salt if required.

Makes about 1-1/2 quarts of sauce. Leftover sauce can be frozen.

Bangkok Cafe on 15th

345 - 15th Avenue East, Seattle. Phone 324-9443. Open for lunch Monday through Friday, 11:00 A.M. to 3:00 P.M.; open for dinner Sunday through Thursday, 5:00 to 10:00 P.M.; Friday and Saturday, 5:00 to 11:00 P.M.

The first Thai restaurant in the Capitol Hill area, the Bangkok Cafe has been delighting its customers since 1984 with authentic Thai food, served in or out. A casual, unpretentious place, the Bangkok has earned some excellent reviews as well as a lot of repeat business. Owner Orapim Puidpard is justifiably proud of her extensive menu of over 100 items.

• •

Peanut Sauce

1-1/2 cups coconut milk
1 teaspoon red curry paste
4 tablespoons peanut butter
1-1/2 teaspoons fish sauce
1-1/2 tablespoons sugar

Heat coconut milk until boiling. Add red curry paste, peanut butter, fish sauce and sugar. Stir until well blended. Place in flat dish for serving.
Makes about 1-1/2 cups sauce.

• •

Khao Neo Dum (Black Rice Pudding)

1-1/2 cups black rice
6 cups water, divided
3/4 cup sugar
1/2 teaspoon salt
1/2 cup cooked fruit
   (longan or sweet corn)
12 tablespoons coconut milk

Soak rice in 3 cups of water overnight. Drain. Combine with remaining water and bring to a boil. Lower temperature and cook until rice is done, about 15 minutes, stirring frequently. Add sugar, salt and fruit, and mix well. Apportion into bowls. Add coconut milk as topping.
Serves 6.

• •

Bai Tong Thai Restaurant

15859 Pacific Highway South, SeaTac. Phone 431-0893. Open for lunch Monday through Friday, 11:00 A.M. to 3:00 P.M.; open for dinner Monday through Saturday, 5:00 to 10:00 P.M.; Sunday, 5:00 to 9:00 P.M.

Bai Tong is something of an institution among the growing legions of Thai food fanciers in the Puget Sound area. Originally started as a restaurant to serve the crews of Thai Airlines, who found it difficult to find good Thai food close to the airport, Bai Tong wasn't "discovered" by the public until owner Chanpen Lapangkura expanded and opened his restaurant to all comers. The food is superb and among the most authentic you'll find.

* *

Tom Yam Koong

3 cups chicken stock
1 lemon grass stem, cut into
    short sections
6 large shrimp, cleaned, shelled
    and washed thoroughly
3 tablespoons lemon juice
5-6 hot chilies, broken with pestle
1 tablespoon fish sauce
2-3 kaffir lime leaves, torn
2 coriander plants, chopped
    coarsely

Heat stock to boiling. Add lemon grass and shrimp. Season with lemon juice, chilies and fish sauce. Add kaffir lime leaves and coriander. Remove from heat and serve hot.

For variety, substitute 1 teaspoon ground pepper for chilies, or replace the shrimp with chicken.

Serves 2.

* *

Thai Style Iced Coffee or Tea

2 tablespoons ground coffee or
    powdered tea leaves
1-1/2 cups boiling water
4 tablespoons sugar
1/4 cup unsweetened condensed
    milk

Place coffee or tea leaves in a cloth bag. Place bag in mug. Pour boiling water into the bag. Allow to steep a few moments. Lift bag to a second mug. Pour contents of first mug into the bag. Repeat until desired strength is reached. Remove bag. Add sugar and milk, stirring until sugar dissolves. Pour into ice-filled glasses.

Serves 2-4.

* *

Bahn Thai

409 Roy Street, Seattle. Phone 283-0444. Open for lunch Monday through Friday, 11:30 A.M. to 3:00 P.M.; open for dinner Monday through Thursday, 4:30 to 10:00 P.M.; Friday, 4:30 to 11:00 P.M.; Saturday, 4:00 to 11:00 P.M.; Sunday, 4:00 to 10:00 P.M.

One of the oldest Thai restaurants in the Seattle area, Bahn Thai was serving up Thai food to its customers before many of its more recent competitors had realized there was a market for it. Ten years (and many favorable reviews) later, the pleasures of Thai food are widely known and appreciated, while Bahn Thai continues the same approach it had from the beginning: high quality Thai food, served authentically and with style.

• •

Kai Yang (Thai Style Barbecued Chicken)

2 tablespoons chopped ginger
   root
2 tablespoons chopped lemon
   grass
2 tablespoons coriander
2 cups light soy sauce
1 teaspoon sugar
2 teaspoons pepper
1-1/2 teaspoons curry powder
2 pounds chicken pieces

Combine the ginger root, lemon grass, coriander, soy sauce, sugar, pepper, and curry powder in a blender. Pour into stainless bowl. Add chicken pieces and stir to coat well. Allow to marinate in the refrigerator at least 6 hours.

When ready to cook, remove chicken from marinade. Broil slowly over a low fire until well done.

Serves 4-6.

• •

Phud Thai with Prawn

3 tablespoons cooking oil
1 tablespoon chopped garlic
1 egg
3 ounces prawns
4 tablespoons diced firm yellow
   bean curd
7 ounces rice noodles
3 tablespoons sugar
2 tablespoons fish sauce
4 tablespoons vinegar
1 teaspoon plus 2 tablespoons
   chopped roasted peanuts
1/4 teaspoon ground chilies
6 ounces bean sprouts
1/3 cup green onions, cut into 1
   inch lengths
1 lime, sliced

In a large frying pan, heat oil over medium high heat. Sauté the garlic. Add egg, stirring continually. Add prawns, bean curd and noodles. Season with sugar, fish sauce, vinegar, and 1 teaspoon peanuts. Toss and cook until noodles turn soft. Add chilies, bean sprouts and green onions. Stir a few more minutes. Garnish with remaining chopped peanuts and lime slices.

Serves 2-3.

Ayutthaya Thai Restaurant

727 East Pike Street, Seattle. Phone 324-8833. Open Monday through Thursday, 5:00 to 9:30 P.M.; Friday and Saturday, 5:00 to 10:00 P.M.

On the increasingly lengthy list of Thai restaurants in the Puget Sound region, owner Tim Fuangaromya's Ayutthaya ranks among the top on just about everyone's. The reasons are not unusual: insistence on fresh ingredients, adherence to traditional methods, and lots of attention to detail.

• •

Yum Neau (Beef Salad)

1 pound tender beef steak
1/4 cup sliced red onions
1 tomato, cut into wedges
1/4 cup sliced cucumber
1/4 cup thinly sliced red and
    green Thai chili peppers,
    optional
1/4 cup mint leaves
1/4 cup fish sauce
1/4 cup lime juice
2 tablespoons minced garlic
2 tablespoons chopped cilantro
1/4 cup chopped green onions,
    cut into 1 inch pieces

Barbecue beef over charcoal, or broil/grill until medium to well done. Slice thinly. Set aside.

Combine onions, tomato, cucumber, chili peppers and mint leaves. Add to beef.

Combine fish sauce, lime juice, garlic, cilantro and green onions. Toss with beef mixture just before serving.

Ayutthaya Thai points out that this recipe is one of the favorites in Bangkok restaurants and home kitchens alike.

Serves 4.

• •

Gai Pad Khing (Ginger Chicken)

2 tablespoons oil
8 ounces boneless chicken
   breast, thinly sliced
2 cloves of garlic, minced
2 tablespoons fish sauce
1 tablespoon oyster sauce
1 tablespoon sugar
Pinch of black pepper
1/8 cup slivered ginger root
1/8 cup sliced green bell pepper
1/8 cup sliced red bell pepper
1/8 cup sliced mushrooms
1/8 cup sliced onion
Cilantro, optional

Heat a large skillet. Add oil, chicken and garlic. Cook 2 minutes. Add remaining ingredients except cilantro. Stir-fry 3 minutes. Transfer to serving dish. Garnish with cilantro.

This is a quick and easy recipe for a healthy meal, notes Ayuttahaya Thai, and one of the most popular dishes in Thai restaurants. It is equally suitable for home kitchen preparation.

Serves 1-2.

Thai Kitchen

14115 N.E. 20th St., Bellevue. Phone 641-9166. Open daily, 11:00 A.M. to 10:00 P.M.

The Thai Kitchen is a relative old timer among Thai restaurants, having been established in 1981. Thus, it was among the first eateries to introduce this spicy, and often hot, cuisine to Northwest diners, and has developed a loyal following among "eastsiders" ever since. It's a family style restaurant, with moderate pricing and a casual, comfortable atmosphere.

• •

Green Chicken Curry

10 fresh jalapeño peppers
2 tablespoons chopped lemon
   grass
1 teaspoon chopped coriander
   root
1 tablespoon chopped red onion
1 tablespoon chopped garlic
1 teaspoon chopped galangal
1 teaspoon salt
3 teaspoons vegetable oil
2 14-ounce cans of coconut milk
2 cups chunked chicken
1/2 cup fresh basil leaves
   (preferably Thai basil)
1 cup zucchini chunks
1 cup sliced bamboo shoots
Steamed rice

In a blender, combine the jalapeño peppers, lemon grass, coriander root, red onion, garlic, galangal and salt. Blend into a paste.

Heat the oil in a medium size sauce pan. Stir the paste in the oil until it is lightly brown, or until the aroma becomes strong. Add 1/2 can of coconut milk and bring to a boil. Add the chicken and remaining coconut milk. Bring back to a boil. Add basil, zucchini, and bamboo shoots. Continue cooking until all is thoroughly heated. Taste, adding more salt if necessary.

Accompany with rice.
Serves 2-4.

• •

Chili Pepper Fried Rice

3 tablespoons vegetable oil
2 teaspoons chopped garlic
2 cups sliced chicken
1 teaspoon salt
8 cups steamed white rice
2 tablespoons Japanese soy
  sauce
2 cups broccoli flowerettes
Chili powder or chopped
  jalapeño peppers

Heat the oil in a wok until nearly smoking. Stir in the garlic. Sauté until light brown. Add chicken and salt. Stir until the chicken is nearly done. Stir in rice, adding soy sauce as you go. Add the broccoli and stir-fry until everything is well blended.

Add the chili powder or jalapeños. Stir-fry a bit more. Taste, and add more chili if needed.

Serves 4-6.

Sea Thai Restaurant

2313 North 45th Street, Seattle. Phone 547-1961. Open Monday through Saturday, 11:30 A.M. to 10:00 P.M.; Sunday, 5:00 to 9:00 P.M.

Arrapin Chancharu, the owner of this small but charming restaurant, is a Thai national come to this country who prides himself on the authenticity of his home style cuisine. Each dish is made to order, using only the freshest ingredients, and recipes that have been in his family for many years.

• •

Yum Neau

Lettuce
Tomatoes
Cucumbers
6 ounces lean beef steak
2 tablespoons lime juice, fresh
   squeezed
2 tablespoons fish sauce
1/2 teaspoon sugar
1 teaspoon chili powder
2 small shallots or 2
   tablespoons sliced red onions
1 small scallion, chopped or cut
1 sprig of coriander,
   coarsely chopped

Arrange the lettuce, tomatoes, and cucumbers on a serving plate.

Preheat grill or broiler. When really hot, grill or broil steak to taste (traditionally, medium rare). Slice thinly. Set aside.

In a bowl, mix together the lime juice, fish sauce, sugar, and chili powder. Add shallots, scallions and beef. Stir quickly. Turn onto serving dish. Sprinkle with coriander.

Serves 1.

• •

Steamed Scallops with Garlic

3 tablespoons light soy sauce
1 inch piece of ginger root,
    finely chopped
1 teaspoon sugar
1 small red chili, finely chopped
6 scallops on the shell, cleaned
3 tablespoons oil
3 cloves of garlic, finely
    chopped
1 small red or green chili,
    sliced into fine rings
2 tablespoons scallions, sliced
    into small rings

Combine soy sauce, ginger root, sugar and chili to form a sauce. Set aside.

Set the scallops in their shells in a steamer over 1-2 inches of water.

In a small frying pan, heat the oil, add garlic and sauté until brown. Pour a spoonful of oil and garlic over each scallop, and add a little sliced chili. Cover and steam over medium heat until the scallops are cooked (10 to 15 minutes). When cooked, remove from the steamer and place on a serving plate with the scallions. Serve remaining sauce on the side.

Serves 1.

Thai Terrace

21919 - 66th Avenue West, Suite D, Mountlake Terrace. Phone 774-4556. Open Monday through Thursday, 11:00 A.M. to 9:00 P.M.; Friday, 11:00 A.M. to 10:00 P.M.; Saturday, 4:00 to 10:00 P.M.; closed Sunday.

This small Thai restaurant, located in the suburbs north of Seattle, is a real find. The cooking is Thai home style, and manager Chai Nanta says with pride that he brought the recipes with him when he came to this country. And he doesn't aspire to a larger place: "I am happy to run a small operation so that I can maintain the high quality of my food." With an attitude like that, it's little wonder that he has developed a loyal base of regular customers.

• •

Paad Thai

1 ounce package of Thai rice
   noodles
Warm water
Cold water
1/2 cup vegetable oil
2 eggs
10 medium size prawns
2 tablespoons tomato ketchup
1-1/2 tablespoons sugar
2 tablespoons fish sauce
1 teaspoon ground chilies,
   optional
2 tablespoons ground, roasted
   peanuts, divided
2 cups bean sprouts, washed
   and drained, divided
Green onions, sliced

Soak rice noodles in warm water 15 minutes. Drain and wash with cold water. Drain again. Set aside.

Heat oil in frying pan or wok over medium heat. Add the eggs, breaking the yolks, and stirring. Add the prawns. Stir 2-3 times. Add noodles. Stir. Add ketchup, sugar, fish sauce, and chilies. Stir, and cook until noodles turn light brown. Add 1 tablespoon peanuts and 1 cup bean sprouts. Stir 1-2 times.

Place on serving dish with remaining bean sprouts on the side. Sprinkle the top with remaining peanuts and green onions.

Serves 2.

• •

Thai Terrace Garlic Pork

3 cloves of garlic, chopped
Oil for deep frying
2 tablespoons oil
8 ounces boneless pork, sliced
    according to taste
1/2 teaspoon salt
1/2 teaspoon pepper
1/2 tablespoon sweet soy sauce
1/2 teaspoon thin soy sauce
2 tablespoons chicken broth
Cabbage, chopped
Carrots, sliced

Deep fry garlic in hot oil until golden. Drain and set aside.

In wok, heat 2 tablespoons oil over medium heat. Add pork, garlic, salt, pepper, both soy sauces and chicken broth. Stir-fry until meat is golden brown. Turn out onto serving plate lined with cabbage and carrot and serve immediately.

Serves 1-2.

Siam on Broadway

616 Broadway East, Seattle. Phone 324-0892. Open Monday through Thursday, 11:30 A.M. to 10:00 P.M.; Friday, 11:30 A.M. to 11:00 P.M.; Saturday and Sunday, 5:00 to 11:00 P.M.

Thai food is hugely popular in Seattle, and one good reason is Siam on Broadway, a small oasis where owner John Siriwatanarong offers authentic and flavorful cuisine in the true Thai tradition: some cool, some hot, always delicious and a delight to the eye as well as the tastebuds.

• •

Panang Kai (Stir-Fried Chicken Curry)

3 ounces coconut milk
2 tablespoons fish sauce
2 tablespoons sugar
6 kaffir lime leaves
1 tablespoon oil
2 tablespoons red curry paste
8 ounces chicken, sliced
1/8 cup sliced green bell pepper
1/8 cup sliced red bell pepper
1/4 cup sliced onions
2 tablespoons ground, roasted
    peanuts
1 tablespoon coconut milk
1 kaffir lime leaf, sliced very
    thin

Combine coconut milk, fish sauce, sugar and lime leaves. Set aside.

Heat large skillet. Add oil and curry paste. Cook 1 minute on low heat. Return temperature to high. Sauté chicken, adding the reserved sauce. Cook until sauce is thick. Add bell peppers, onions, and peanuts. Cook 2 minutes.

Pour mixture into serving bowl. Top with 1 tablespoon coconut milk and lime leaf strips.

Serves 2.

• •

Phad Thai Noodles

8 ounces rice noodles
3 tablespoons oil
3 cloves of garlic, minced
6 medium shrimp
1/4 cup fish sauce
1/4 cup sugar
2 tablespoons tamarind sauce
2 tablespoons tomato paste
1/2 cup fried tofu
2 tablespoons dried turnip,
   minced
1 egg, beaten
1/4 cup ground, roasted peanuts
1/4 cup sliced green onions, 1
   inch lengths
1 cup bean sprouts
Lime

Soak rice noodles in cold water 30 minutes, or until soft. Drain and set aside.

Heat a large skillet until hot. Add oil. Add garlic and shrimp and stir-fry. Add noodles and stir-fry until translucent. Lower heat if mixture is cooking too quickly and noodles are sticking.

Add the fish sauce, sugar, tamarind and tomato paste. Stir-fry until thoroughly combined. Stir in tofu, turnip and egg. Turn heat to high.

Cook until egg sets, stirring gently. Thoroughly combine the mixture.

Continue cooking over medium high heat about 2 minutes, until most of the liquid is reduced.

Sprinkle peanuts and green onions on top of dish. Place bean sprouts along side noodles. Garnish with lime.

Siam on Broadway proudly notes that this is their #1 dish!

Serves 4.

Rama on Post

83 Spring Street, Seattle. Phone 340-9047. Open Monday through Thursday, 11:00 A.M. to 10:00 P.M.; Friday, 11:00 A.M. to 11:00 P.M.; Saturday, 3:00 to 11:00 P.M.; closed Sunday.

"Elegant, but casual, Thai dining" is the way co-owner Frank Mizer describes his restaurant, Rama on Post. He points out that head chef (and, coincidentally, his wife), La-iad Mizer has been preparing Thai cuisine commercially for 12 years and personally trained many of the Thai chefs now working elsewhere in the Seattle area. The food, as you would expect, is great, and the menu offers a wide selection. The dilemma: what to choose?

• •

Thai Beef Salad

1 cup sliced celery
1/2 red onion, sliced diagonally
5 mint leaves
1 tomato, sliced
1/2 cucumber, sliced
1 teaspoon salt
1 tablespoon fish sauce
1 teaspoon sugar
2 tablespoons lime juice
1 teaspoon nam pik pao
3 tablespoons vegetable oil
2 cups sliced beef round steak
1 teaspoon chopped garlic
1/4 head iceberg lettuce,
    broken into salad size pieces
1/2 teaspoon ground red chili
    pepper
3 sprigs of cilantro

In a bowl combine the celery, onion, mint, tomato, cucumber, salt, fish sauce, sugar, lime juice and nam pik pao. Set aside.

Heat oil. Add beef and garlic, cooking until the beef is medium rare. Remove from pan and add to the bowl, mixing thoroughly.

To serve, place lettuce on individual salad plates. Spoon the meat mixture on top of the lettuce. Sprinkle with ground red chili pepper and garnish with cilantro.

Serves 4.

• •

Chicken Curry

4 dried kaffir lime leaves
1 can coconut milk, divided
2 tablespoons red curry paste
1 tablespoon sweet paprika
2 teaspoons ground coriander
1 teaspoon cumin
1 clove of garlic, chopped
2 cups boneless, skinless
   chicken, cut into small
   chunks
2 tablespoons fish sauce
1 tablespoon sugar
1 cup chicken stock
1 cup sliced bamboo shoots
2-3 sprigs of sweet basil
3 dried whole red chili
   peppers
Red bell peppers, sliced

Soak the dried kaffir lime leaves in water until soft. Cut into thin strips. Set aside.

Bring one-half of the coconut milk to a boil in a medium size sauce pan. Lower the heat to medium. Add the curry paste, paprika, coriander, cumin and garlic. Simmer for approximately 2 minutes. Add the chicken chunks, fish sauce, sugar, the remaining one-half can of coconut milk and the chicken stock. Mix slightly, cover, and cook at medium temperature until boiling. Add the bamboo shoots. Simmer 10 minutes, or until the chicken is completely cooked. Add basil, red peppers, and reserved lime leaf strips. Cook 1 minute.

Serve over steamed rice with red bell pepper slices for decoration.

Serves 2-3.

Viet My Restaurant

129 Prefontaine Place South (Corner of 4th Avenue South and Washington Street), Seattle. Phone 382-9923. Open Monday through Friday, 11:00 A.M. to 8:30 P.M.

Those looking for fancy decor won't find it here, but there is excellent Vietnamese food and generous portions at very reasonable prices. The place is usually packed at lunch. Those who become addicted to the curries can purchase the special curry powder at the restaurant; it's a unique formula made in Vietnam and imported exclusively by them.

• •

Viet My Fish Sauce

3 cups boiling water
1-1/2 cups fish sauce
8 tablespoons sugar
2 tablespoons vinegar
1 tablespoon minced garlic
1 tablespoon ground chili paste

Combine all ingredients together in a bowl. Stir well.

Viet My suggests that this sauce is great with many dishes, including pasta!

Makes about 4-1/2 cups.

• •

Saté

Oil
1/2 teaspoon minced garlic
1 portion of meat or seafood of
   your choice
Fresh onions
Bell peppers
1 tablespoon sugar
1 tablespoon fish sauce
2 teaspoons chopped lemon
   grass
1/2 teaspoon saté chili paste

Add a little oil to wok or frying pan. Add garlic, then meat or seafood. Stir-fry until meat is nearly done. Add some onions and bell peppers along with sugar, fish sauce, lemon grass, and chili paste. After these ingredients are all added, stir-fry until done, or about 30 seconds.

Serves 1.

• •

Quoc Huong Restaurant

1200 S. Jackson Street, Seattle. Phone 323-8689. Open Wednesday through Monday, 9:00 A.M. to 9:00 P.M.; Tuesday, 9:00 A.M. to 3:00 P.M.

Surely among the most authentic traditional Vietnamese restaurants you'll find, Quoc Huong is an unpretentious place with a big menu and great food. Some of their most popular dishes are roll-ups, with veggies and meats being assembled on thin, moist rice paper wrappers, then dipped in sauces and eaten. They're tricky at first - definitely something you do with hands, not utensils - but you'll gradually catch on, and they are delicious.

• •

Chicken Salad

2 tablespoons fish sauce
2 tablespoons sugar
2 tablespoons water
2 tablespoons vinegar
1 teaspoon hot pepper
2 cloves of garlic, minced
5 pieces (halves) boneless,
   skinless chicken breast
1 small cabbage, shredded
1 small onion, sliced
1 bunch of mint, finely chopped

Prepare the salad dressing by combining fish sauce, sugar, water, vinegar, hot pepper and garlic in small bowl. Set aside.

Boil chicken. Tear into small pieces. Combine with cabbage, onion and mint. Pour reserved dressing over all when ready to serve.

Serves 4.

• •

Lemon Grass Chicken

1 piece of lemon grass, chopped
Hot pepper, to taste (1/2
   teaspoon is medium)
1 tablespoon sugar
1/2 teaspoon salt
1/2 teaspoon MSG, optional
1 clove of garlic, minced
3 pieces (halves) boneless,
   skinless chicken breast,
   cut into small pieces
1/2 teaspoon salad oil
1/2 cup water

Combine lemon grass, hot pepper, sugar, salt, MSG and garlic. Add chicken breast and marinate 30 minutes.

Pour oil into pan. Stir-fry marinated chicken. Add water. Allow to simmer until chicken pieces are thoroughly cooked. Present with rice or rice noodles.

Serves 3-4.

• •

Andre's Restaurant

14125 N.E. 20th Street, Bellevue. Phone 747-6551. Open for lunch Monday through Friday, 11:30 A.M. to 3:00 P.M.; open for dinner Tuesday through Thursday, 5:30 to 9:00 P.M.; Friday and Saturday, 5:30 to 10:00 P.M.

Strip mall restaurants can sometimes be a bit ordinary, but that's not the case with Andre's. Vietnamese cuisine is often French-influenced, due to the long French presence in that country. Here, though, French gets equal - and in many cases, separate - billing. Andre's is neither pretentious or pricey, but the food is consistently good and is often unique.

• •

Canh Chua (Tamarind Soup)

4 cups shrimp stock
1/2 cup diced celery
1 package Knorr tamarind
    powder
1 ounce sugar
1/2 ounce fish sauce
1 cup pineapple, fresh or
    canned
1/2 cup large diced tomato
1/2 cup bean sprouts
4 mushrooms, sliced
12 prawns, shelled and deveined
1/2 teaspoon chopped mint

Bring the shrimp stock to a boil in a soup pot. Add celery, tamarind powder, sugar, and fish sauce. Heat 2 minutes. Add remaining ingredients and cook until shrimp are done.
    Serves 4-6.

• •

Hue Prawns

1 tablespoon oil
1/2 yellow onion, thinly sliced
1/4 teaspoon chopped garlic
12 large prawns
1/4 teaspoon chopped ginger
  root
1/4 teaspoon curry paste
1/2 tablespoon chopped lemon
  grass
1 cup chopped mushrooms
1 teaspoon chopped fresh basil
1 teaspoon soy sauce
1/2 tablespoon peanut butter
1/2 cup coconut milk

Heat oil in hot wok. Add onion and garlic and sauté. Add prawns and cook until about half done. Add ginger root, curry paste, lemon grass, mushrooms and basil. Stir well to blend. Add remaining ingredients, stirring very quickly and cooking until prawns are finished. Accompany with rice.

Serves 2.

Saigon West

1208 Sylvan Way, Bremerton. Phone 396-2946 or 377-2611. Open Monday through Friday, 4:00 to 9:00 P.M.; weekends and holidays, 11:00 A.M. to 9:00 P.M.

For fanciers of Vietnamese food, this tiny (400 square feet) restaurant is a real find, tucked away in Bremerton. With obvious pride, owner Huey White promises service with a smile, home style cooking with crispy fresh veggies, and "no disappointments ever!" He also points out that no MSG is used here. All meals are individually cooked to order, never in advance.

• •

Almond Chicken

Cloves of garlic, finely chopped
Onion, finely chopped
1 tablespoon olive oil
1-2 pounds boneless, skinless
   chicken, cut into bite-size
   pieces
1/2 teaspoon seasoned salt
1 teaspoon soy sauce
1 teaspoon Maggi
Vegetables of your choice:
   carrots, celery, onions, red
   bell peppers, green bell
   peppers - all cut into
   bite-size pieces
1 cup water
1 teaspoon cornstarch, dissolved
   in 1/2 cup water
1/2 cup almonds, roasted in
   300° oven until brown

Sauté garlic and onion in oil until golden brown. Add chicken pieces. Cook until about half way done. Sprinkle with salt, soy sauce and Maggi. Add vegetables and cook, stirring until chicken is done. Add water and cornstarch mixture. Bring to a boil, allowing sauce to thicken. Stir in almonds. Accompany with steamed rice.
   Serves 4-6.

• •

Out-of-This-World Salad

STEP 1:
1 head of red leaf lettuce,
    thinly sliced
1/4 pound bean sprouts
1 cucumber, peeled and finely
    shredded

Toss together.

STEP 2:
5 quarts water
14-16 ounce package of rice
    stick noodles

Bring water to boil. Add rice stick noodles and cook 2 minutes. Drain in colander. Run cold water over noodles until they are cool. Allow to drain in colander for about 20 minutes.

STEP 3:
1 onion, sliced
1/2 clove of garlic, finely
    chopped
4 tablespoons olive oil
2 pounds boneless, skinless
    chicken meat, sliced for
    stir-fry. Pork, beef, shrimp
    or tofu may be substituted.
1 teaspoon seasoned salt, or
    regular salt, if preferred
1 teaspoon soy sauce
1 green or red bell pepper,
    thinly sliced, or 1/4 pound
    snow peas, optional

Over medium heat, sauté onion and garlic in oil until lightly browned. Add chicken, salt and soy sauce. Cook, stirring constantly, about 8 minutes. Add vegetables. Continue cooking and stirring 2 minutes.

STEP 4:
10 branches of cilantro and/or
    peppermint leaves
4 tablespoons chopped, roasted
    peanuts

Finely chop the cilantro and/or peppermint leaves.

STEP 5:
1/4 cup soy sauce/fish sauce/
    Maggi (choose any or all)
1/8 cup lemon juice/lime juice/
    vinegar
1/8 cup sugar or substitute
1/8 teaspoon cayenne pepper

Combine all ingredients.

STEP 6:
In large individual soup bowls, layer a portion of Step 1, then Step 2, then Step 3. Garnish with sprinkles of Step 4. Sprinkle with Step 5 before eating.

Mix it all up, suggests the Saigon West, so the sauce can be in every bite as you are enjoying this wonderful salad. It's their No. 1 favorite dish!

Serves 4-6.

Asia Express Restaurant

219 Broadway East, Seattle. Phone 329-1991. Open Monday through Friday, 11:00 A.M. to 9:30 P.M.; Saturday, noon to 9:30 P.M.; closed sunday.

Asia Express offers both traditional Chinese and Vietnamese dishes to its patrons, and prides itself on service. Their food is also bargain priced, with most dishes under $5.00. Owner Frank Le reminds customers concerned about MSG that it can be omitted from any dish at their request.

• •

Lemon Grass Chicken

1 teaspoon salt
1 tablespoon sugar
1 teaspoon MSG
1 teaspoon hoisin sauce
2 tablespoons soy sauce
2 tablespoons vegetable oil
1/4 onion, sliced
Garlic, minced
Lemon grass
12 ounces chicken, diced
1 teaspoon cornstarch
Hot sauce, optional

Combine salt, sugar, MSG, hoisin sauce and soy sauce. Set aside.

Heat wok. Add oil. Cooking over high heat, add onion, garlic and lemon grass, then chicken. When chicken has changed color to almost dark brown, pour reserved sauce into wok. Cook about 8 minutes, continuing to stir to prevent burning. Add cornstarch to make a thick gravy. Add hot sauce to produce a spicier dish, if desired.

Serves 1-2.

• •

Teriyaki Chicken

1/2 cup sugar
1/4 cup soy sauce
Ginger root, minced
Chicken thighs
Sesame seeds

Pour sugar and soy sauce into a big bowl. Add ginger root and mix thoroughly. Put chicken in bowl. Refrigerate about 4 hours. Remove chicken and place on oven proof tray. Reserve sauce. Broil chicken, turning over for better cooking.

Pour reserved sauce into deep pan and boil.

Remove chicken from oven. Cut into small pieces. Pour the boiled teriyaki sauce over chicken. Sprinkle with sesame seeds.

Serves 4.

Pho 88 Restaurant

1038 #A South Jackson Street, Seattle. Phone 325-0180. Open Monday through Thursday, 8:00 A.M. to 7:00 P.M.; Friday through Sunday, 8:00 A.M. to 8:00 P.M.

Daniel Vu's small Vietnamese restaurant is among the most authentic you will find. The name Pho (actually pronounced like the musical note "fa") is a Vietnamese word literally translated as "with noodle." Popularly, it means a hearty beef noodle soup that could well be the national dish. Like many Vietnamese dishes, part of the fun is adding various ingredients in your own way. An assortment of roll-ups and other items are offered as well.

. . . .

Beef Stew

1 tablespoon oil
4 cloves of garlic, minced
2 pounds beef stew meat, cut
   into large cubes
12 ounces tomato sauce
3/4 teaspoon salt
2 teaspoons sugar
1/4 tablespoon pepper
5 pieces of star anise
5 cups water

Heat oil in medium size sauce pan. Fry garlic gently until golden. Add beef cubes and fry, stirring continuously, 3 minutes. Add remaining ingredients, bring to a boil, and reduce heat. Allow to simmer uncovered 2 hours.

Present in bowls accompanied by rice noodles, egg noodles, or rice vermicelli noodles and French bread. Serves 4-6.

. . . .

Garlic, Chili & Fish Sauce

2 red chili peppers
2 cloves of garlic
1 teaspoon sugar
Juice and pulp of 1 lime
1/4 cup vinegar
1/4 cup water
1/2 cup fish sauce

Remove seeds from chili peppers. Cut into small pieces.

Pound peppers and garlic together until a paste-like consistency is achieved. Add remaining ingredients and pour into small bowls. This basic Vietnamese sauce is ever-present at meals, and goes well with many Vietnamese dishes, even being used as a salad dressing from time to time! Makes about 1 cup.

. . . .

Da Thao Cafe

15116 - 8th Avenue SouthWest, Seattle.   Phone 248-1155.   Open Monday through Friday, 11:00 A.M. to 7:00 P.M.; Saturday, 11:00 A.M. to 6:00 P.M.

This small Vietnamese cafe in the Burien area may be unpretentious, but the food is authentic, fresh, and tasty, and the prices are surprisingly low. Popular with locals for lunch and early dinner, diners new to Vietnamese cuisine find their first try is rarely their last.

. . . .

Snow Peas with Shrimp

1 tablespoon oil
1/2 onion, sliced
1/2 pound shrimp, 21-25 size
1 pound snow peas
1 teaspoon sugar
1/4 teaspoon salt
1 teaspoon fish sauce
2 green onions, cut into 2 inch
    lengths
Hot sauce, optional

Heat pan and add oil. Add onion and stir-fry. Add shrimp. Stir-fry 3 minutes. Add snow peas, sugar, salt, and fish sauce. Stir-fry 1 minute. Add green onions. Stir-fry 1 minute. Add hot sauce, if a spicy dish is desired.

Serves 1-2.

. . . .

The Americas

Burk's Cafe
Creole & Cajun

5411 Ballard Avenue N.W., Seattle. Phone 782-0091. Open Tuesday through Saturday, 11:00 A.M. to 10:00 P.M.; closed Sunday and Monday.

If one were to think of a likely place to find first-rate Cajun and Creole cuisine in the Puget Sound area, it's unlikely that Ballard - with its strong Scandinavian heritage - would be on anyone's list. No matter. Burk's has been quietly serving up great Southern food at moderate prices for over ten years, and now draws its clientele from all over the Seattle area. They assure us that no one ever leaves hungry!

• •

Mussels in Tomato Court Bouillon

14 ounces diced tomatoes
8 ounces tomato purée
48 ounces clam juice
1 cup sliced onions
1 cup sliced green onions
8 cloves of garlic, minced
2 tablespoons allspice
3 bay leaves
1 tablespoon cayenne pepper
2 tablespoons coriander
1 tablespoon thyme
1 teaspoon cloves
1 teaspoon mace
1 cup white wine
1 cup Brown Roux (recipe
    follows)
2-3 pounds mussels

In a sauce pan, combine tomatoes, purée and clam juice. Bring to a boil.

Sauté onions, green onions and garlic until translucent. Add to sauce pan.

Heat spices in onion pan to release essential oils. Scrape into sauce pan.

Deglaze onion pan with white wine and add to sauce pan. Simmer 1 hour.

Slowly stir in the Brown Roux. Simmer 10 minutes.

De-beard and scrub the mussels. Steam in the sauce until just opened, about 5 minutes.

Serves 4.

BROWN ROUX:
1/2 cup flour
1/2 cup peanut oil

Combine flour with peanut oil in a pan. Bring to a low boil over moderate heat. Stir frequently until roux thickens and turns the color of peanut butter. Take care to avoid scorching in the final minutes. Cool.

• •

BBQ Prawns

**6 tablespoons Flavored Butter
 (recipe follows)**
6 jumbo prawns
**1 teaspoon homemade chili
 sauce**

Place butter in a skillet over
high heat. When it begins to
sizzle, fry the prawns about 2
minutes per side. Add one
teaspoon of homemade chili sauce
and swirl briefly. Present in a
bowl with ample sauce.
  Serves 1.

FLAVORED BUTTER:
1 pound butter
2 lemons, sliced
4 ounces ginger root, chopped
1 tablespoon minced garlic
1/2 teaspoon cayenne pepper
1 teaspoon paprika
**1 teaspoon Worcestershire
 sauce**
1 teaspoon black pepper
Fresh rosemary

Place butter in a heavy
bottomed sauce pan on very low
heat. Add the lemon slices, ginger
root, garlic, cayenne, paprika,
Worcestershire sauce, pepper and
rosemary.
  Simmer 20 minutes. Strain
through fine sieve, pressing with
a wood spoon. Discard the pulp.
  The flavored butter may be
used immediately, or refrigerated
for up to 1 week.

Cajun Corner Cafe

Alexis Hotel, 90 Madison Street, Seattle. Phone 624-4844. Open Monday through Thursday, 11:30 to 12:30 A.M.; Friday and Saturday, 11:30 to 1:30 A.M.; Sunday, 5:00 to 11:30 P.M.

Seattle has a new Cajun place, and manager Raymond Carey has set out to make it as authentic as you'll find anywhere. The menu is supplemented by daily specials to provide new culinary treats to regular visitors. Chef de cuisine Hayden Smissen uses techniques from Cuban, French and Southern cuisines to create both traditional and unique dishes that represent the wide diversity of Cajun food.

• •

Four Meat Bourbon Chili

1 pound pork shoulder
1 pound beef chuck roast
1 pound chicken meat
1 pound hot Creole-style sausage
4 large white onions
4 bay leaves
1 cup ancho chili powder
4 tablespoons salt
4 tablespoons black pepper
4 tablespoons cayenne pepper
2 tablespoons powdered mace
1 cup olive oil
4 large cloves of garlic, coarsely
    chopped
1 teaspoon liquid smoke
    seasoning
1 cup beer
2 cups bourbon
1 cup maple syrup

Cut pork shoulder, chuck roast, chicken, sausages and onions into 1 inch dice and set aside.

Combine the bay leaves, chili powder, salt, black pepper, cayenne pepper and mace in a bowl. Set aside.

Heat oil in large pot until smoking. Add meats, onions and garlic. Stir constantly until the meats are thoroughly browned and almost sticking to the sides of the pot. Add dry seasonings, stirring until meats are well coated. Add the liquid smoke seasoning, beer, bourbon and maple syrup. Bring to a boil. Reduce heat and simmer about 1-1/2 hours, or until chili is thick and the meats begin to break up and have a "shredded" look.

Manager Carey recommends accompanying this spicy chili with cold beer and your favorite corn bread.

Serves 6-8.

• •

Catfish Symphony

4 5-ounce catfish filets
Blackening Spice (recipe
    follows)
12 mussels
12 large tiger prawns
Creole Rum Sauce (recipe
    follows)
Rice (recipe follows)
Lemon wedges
Scallions, chopped

Sprinkle catfish filets liberally with Blackening Spice and broil 5 minutes. Steam mussels and prawns in Creole Rum Sauce 2 minutes.

Scoop Rice onto individual plates. Ladle a portion of the Creole Rum Sauce on top. Arrange 3 steamed mussels and 3 prawns around edge of rice and place catfish filet directly on top of the rice. Garnish with lemon wedges and chopped scallions.

Serves 4.

BLACKENING SPICE:
4 tablespoons salt
4 tablespoons pepper
2 tablespoons cayenne pepper
2 tablespoons thyme
4 tablespoons onion powder

Mix together very thoroughly in a small bowl.

CREOLE RUM SAUCE:
2 white onions, diced
5 cloves of garlic, minced
3 bell peppers, diced
1 tablespoon cayenne pepper
1 tablespoon black pepper
2 tablespoons salt
3 tablespoons brown sugar
2 bay leaves
16-ounce can diced tomatoes
1 cup rum

Sauté onions, garlic and bell peppers until soft. Add cayenne and black peppers, salt, sugar and bay leaves. Stir and continue cooking until the sides of the pan begin to brown. Add tomatoes and rum. Simmer 20 minutes.

RICE:
6 cups chicken stock (canned is
    okay)
3 cups white rice
1 white onion, finely diced
1 tablespoon salt
1/4 cup minced parsley

Bring stock to a boil. Add rice. Stir. Add remaining ingredients. Cover and simmer 15-20 minutes.

Cafe Melange

12305 - 120th Avenue N.E., Kirkland. Phone 821-1212. Open Monday through Friday, 11:00 A.M. to 3:00 P.M. for lunch, 5:00 to 9:00 P.M. for dinner; Saturday, noon to 9:00 P.M.

The dictionary defines 'melange' as 'mixture', and it is a fitting name for this bright, cheery - and unique - little restaurant, where the seemingly diverse cuisines of China and the Cajun south come together as naturally as you please. Owner Debbie Collier is Chinese herself and hails from New Orleans, so she's had plenty of exposure to both. Servings are generous, the prices reasonable, and the food here is consistently good.

• •

Orange Chicken

1/2 tablespoon oyster sauce
1-1/2 tablespoons hoisin sauce
1/2 tablespoon vinegar
1 tablespoon fresh minced garlic
1 tablespoon white wine
2 boneless, skinless chicken
   breasts, about 1 pound total
1/2 cup flour
1 tablespoon cornstarch
Water
1 egg
Oil for frying
Orange, sliced
Steamed broccoli, optional

Prepare sauce by combining the oyster sauce, hoisin sauce, vinegar, garlic and white wine in a sauce pan. Cook over medium heat until hot. Keep warm while preparing chicken.

Cut chicken into bite-sized pieces. Combine the flour, cornstarch, water and egg in a bowl to form a batter. Dip chicken pieces into batter and fry in hot oil.

To serve, top chicken pieces with orange sauce. Garnish with 2 orange slices and broccoli. Debbie adds that if you like, you can stir pieces of orange peel into the sauce.

Serves 2.

• •

Red Beans and Rice with Andouille Sausages

1 pound dry red kidney beans
Water
3-1/2 to 4 pounds ham hocks
2-1/2 cups chopped celery
2 cups chopped onions
2 cups chopped green bell
    pepper
5 bay leaves
2 teaspoons white pepper
2 teaspoons dried thyme leaves
1-1/2 teaspoons garlic powder
1-1/2 teaspoons dried oregano
    leaves
1 teaspoon ground red pepper
1/2 teaspoon black pepper
1 tablespoon Tabasco sauce
1 pound Andouille sausages
4-1/2 cups hot white rice

Cover beans with water, extending the water well above beans. Let stand overnight.

Place ham hocks, 10 cups of water, celery, onions, green peppers, bay leaves, white pepper, thyme, garlic, oregano, red pepper, black pepper, and Tabasco in large Dutch oven. Cover and bring mixture to a boil. Reduce heat. Simmer at least 1 hour, or until ham hocks are tender, stirring often. Remove ham hocks. Set aside.

Drain beans. Add to Dutch oven along with 4 cups of water. Bring to boil. Reduce heat and simmer 30 minutes, stirring often. Add 2 cups of water. Simmer another 30 minutes, continuing to stir often. Stir in sausages. Simmer 35 minutes, stirring often. Push 4 large spoonfuls of the beans against the side of the pan and mash.

Remove meat from hocks. Discard skin and fat. Cut meat into bite-size pieces. Add to bean mixture.

Place 2 scoops of white rice in center of each plate. Spoon beans and sausage around rice. Garnish with parsley.

Serves 6-8.

Triangle Tavern

3507 Fremont Place North, Seattle. Phone 632-0880. Open Monday through Friday, 11:30 to 2:00 A.M.; Saturday and Sunday, noon to 2:00 A.M.

Not long ago, this neighborhood tavern started serving an eclectic mix of very reasonably priced ethnic dishes - Cajun, Creole, Caribbean and Italian - and earned itself rave reviews in the local press. It's still a tavern, after all, and a lively one at that (co-owners James Weimann and Alice Hughes describe it as a "hoppin' night spot"), but the food's great, the portions are ample, and they have a good selection of local micro-brews on tap.

• •

Caribbean Eggplant Chutney

5 tablespoons olive oil
1 teaspoon grated ginger root
1 tablespoon chopped garlic
1 teaspoon turmeric
1 teaspoon coriander seed, crushed
2 teaspoons cumin
1 teaspoon crushed red chili pepper
2 eggplants, diced
1 onion, chopped fine
2 beets, sliced
3 tablespoons brown sugar
Juice of 2 limes
Salt, to taste

Heat oil in large sauté pan. Add ginger root, garlic, turmeric, coriander, cumin and red chili pepper. Reduce heat, being careful not to burn garlic. Add eggplant, onion and beets. Sauté until eggplant is tender. Remove beet slices and discard. Add brown sugar, lime juice and salt. Cool in refrigerator. Serve at room temperature.

Present this chutney with grilled fish such as tuna or ling cod. The Triangle Tavern notes that they serve it over fish hot on a cold, wild green salad. They point out that the beets add an unusual flavor and brilliant color to the condiment.

Serves 2-4.

• •

Cajun Style Black Bean Burgers

1 cup black beans, cooked until
    tender
1/4 cup all-purpose flour
2 tablespoons olive oil
2 teaspoons cumin
1/8 teaspoon cayenne pepper
1 tablespoon chopped garlic
1 teaspoon salt
1/4 cup sour cream or plain
    yogurt
Kaiser rolls
1 tablespoon chopped cilantro
Garnishes

Coarsely grind beans, flour, oil, cumin, pepper, garlic and salt in a food processor, adding water if necessary to form a mixture that can be worked into patties.

Form into burgers. Dust with flour. Grill over flame, brushing with olive oil, until browned.

Serve with sour cream or yogurt on rolls with cilantro and your favorite burger garnishes (tomato, lettuce, etc.).

Serves 2.

La Mediterranean Delicatessen

528 Broadway, Seattle. Phone 329-8818, Open Monday and Tuesday, 11:30 A.M. to 5:00 P.M.; Wednesday through Friday, 11:30 A.M. to 6:00 P.M.

The name is something of a misnomer; La Mediterranean actually specializes in Caribbean, Creole and African foods. Owner/chef Jocelyn Owens explains that when the restaurant opened in 1972, Mediterranean foods were their specialty; although they remain today as an option for customers of the catering business, the restaurant menu was changed years ago to Caribbean and Creole. New dishes gleaned from Jocelyn's travels are frequently added to the bill of fare. La Mediterranean also hosts an annual - and popular - Caribbean and Country Bar-B-Q Festival at Myrtle Edwards Park in Seattle.

• •

Jamaican Jerk Grilled Steaks

4 scallions
1 medium onion, chopped
4 cloves of garlic, minced
2 teaspoons fresh thyme,
   chopped
1 teaspoon salt
1 tablespoon brown sugar
1 teaspoon allspice
1/2 teaspoon nutmeg
1/2 teaspoon cinnamon
1 hot Scotch bonnet or chili
   pepper, chopped
3 tablespoons soy sauce
1 tablespoon vinegar
4 New York or rib steaks

Combine the first 12 ingredients. Place steaks in liquid. Refrigerate 2 hours. Drain, reserving marinade.

Prepare charcoal grill. When coals glow dusty red, place steaks on grill. After 6 minutes cooking on each side, turn, baste with marinade, and continue cooking until done.

La Mediterranean recommends using this same marinade on chicken, shrimp, boneless pork and ribs.

Serves 4.

• •

Caribbean Papaya Salad

1/2 fresh pineapple
2 medium oranges
2 medium papayas
1 medium avocado
3 tablespoons lemon juice
1/8 teaspoon ground allspice
1/8 teaspoon ground cloves
1/8 teaspoon paprika
1/8 teaspoon ground ginger
Iceberg lettuce
Cherries
Bananas, sliced and dipped in
    lemon juice
Coconut, grated

Rinse pineapple. Twist off top. Slice into spears, then into chunks. Peel and section oranges, reserving juice. Dice and cube. Halve papayas lengthwise. Cut into cubes. Halve avocado lengthwise. Cut into cubes. Set aside.

Combine reserved orange juice, papaya, avocado and lemon juice. Toss to coat.

In a mixing bowl, combine pineapple, oranges, papaya, avocado and spices. Toss gently.

Serve on lettuce bed. Decorate with cherries, bananas and coconut.

Serves 4.

Cactus

4220 East Madison Street, Seattle. Phone 324-4140. Open Monday through Saturday for lunch, 11:30 A.M. to 2:30 P.M.; open Monday through Saturday for dinner, 5:30 to 10:00 P.M.; Sunday, 5:00 to 9:00 P.M.

Southwestern cuisine is a marriage of several culinary traditions: Native American, Spanish, and most especially those of Mexico and New Mexico. The result is a combination of ingredients and methods that trace their origins as far back as the arrival of the Spanish explorers of the 1500's. More currently, today's chefs are applying their own imagination to this rich heritage, and Cactus has brought together the traditional and contemporary in an intriguing and unique restaurant.

• •

Indian Fry Bread

4 cups flour
1/3 cup powdered milk
2 tablespoons baking powder
1 tablespoon salt
2 cups water

Combine and knead. Roll into balls. Roll into 3 inch diameter pancakes. Score with knife. Fry until brown in 350° oil.
Makes 3 pieces.

• •

Tapas (Eggplant with Cilantro Pesto)

1/2 cup good olive oil
1/8 cup red wine vinegar
1/8 cup balsamic vinegar
1 tablespoon oregano
1 tablespoon thyme
1 teaspoon white pepper
1 teaspoon kosher salt
2 teaspoons chopped garlic
2 teaspoons paprika
1 medium eggplant, sliced into
    1/2 inch circles (across
    eggplant)
Cilantro Pesto (recipe follows)

Whisk together the oil, vinegars, oregano, thyme, pepper, salt, garlic and paprika for 10 seconds to combine. Marinate eggplant in this mixture 10 minutes. Grill on barbecue over hot heat 2 minutes on each side, or until knife easily penetrates, basting occasionally with marinade. Serve with Cilantro Pesto.

Serves 2-4 as an appetizer.

CILANTRO PESTO:
1 bunch of cilantro
1/4 cup roasted pumpkin seeds
1/8 cup garlic
Pinch of salt and pepper
1 cup olive oil

Combine all ingredients except oil in food processor. Slowly drizzle in the olive oil.

Las Margaritas

13400 N.E. 175th, Woodinville. Phone 483-5656. Open Sunday through Thursday, 11:00 A.M. to 10:30 P.M.; Friday and Saturday, 11:00 A.M. to 11:00 P.M.

Fanciers of traditional Mexican food will be happy here, and for those seeking something different, there are some new tastes available as well: regional specialties that are unique, flavorful, and otherwise unavailable this side of the border. A fun and festive place, Las Margaritas has received excellent reviews and has several other locations in the Puget Sound area.

. . . .

Ceviche Blanco

2 pounds sierra or red snapper,
   cut into 1 inch x 2 inch pieces
1-1/2 cups cider or white wine
   vinegar or lime juice
1-1/4 cups water
Juice of 6 limes or bitter oranges
2 medium white onions, puréed
4 cloves of garlic, roasted and
   puréed
3 bay leaves
Sprig of thyme
Sprig of marjoram

Place fish in large glass bowl. Add remaining ingredients. Marinate in refrigerator for a minimum of 12 hours.

12 black peppercorns, crushed
2 tablespoons oregano
1/2 tablespoon thyme
5 fresh serrano chilies or 2
   fresh jalapeño peppers,
   washed and finely chopped
1/2 tablespoon coriander seed
4 cloves of garlic
1/2 tablespoon cumin seed
1/2 cinnamon stick

1-1/2 cups corn or olive oil
1 pound mushrooms, sliced
1-1/2 cups cilantro, finely
   chopped
1/2 cup Italian parsley, finely
   chopped
2 cups stuffed olives, finely
   chopped
3/4 cup capers
Salt and pepper, to taste
Cilantro, finely chopped
Olives, chopped

Place the first 9 ingredients in glass bowl. Mix well. Pour over fish. Add remaining ingredients three hours before serving. Refrigerate.

To serve, spoon into individual bowls, cocktail cups, or halved, seeded avocados. Garnish with chopped cilantro and olives. Serve with a variety of crackers.

Variation: Add 4 large ripe, finely chopped tomatoes or 2 large ripe, chopped avocados.

Serves 16.

. . . .

Bacalao a la Vizcaina
(Codfish with Potatoes, Olives and Chilies)

4 pounds dried codfish, soaked
  overnight in water changed
  3-4 times (fresh, poached,
  firm-fleshed white fish may
  be substituted; if so, do not
  soak)
12 cups milk
1 to 1-1/2 quarts olive oil
20 medium cloves of garlic
4-1/2 large white onions, finely
  chopped
15 large ripe tomatoes, roasted
1-1/2 medium white onions,
  quartered
6 cloves of garlic
Pinch of salt
2 cups parsley, finely chopped
1-1/2 pounds baby potatoes,
  boiled and peeled
2 cups olives, stuffed with
  pimiento
8 ounces pickled chilies gueros
  or canned jalapeños or
  other hot peppers
8 ounces canned red pimiento
8 ounces pickled chilies gueros
1 cup olives, stuffed with
  pimiento
3/4 cup parsley, finely chopped

After soaking fish in water, drain. Soak in milk about 2 hours. Remove fish and clean, discarding skin and bones. Finely shred fish. Set aside.

Heat oil in sauce pan. Brown 20 cloves of garlic in oil. Remove and set aside.

Add onion to oil and brown lightly.

In a food processor, place the tomatoes, raw white onion, 6 cloves of garlic and reserved fried garlic cloves. Purée well, then strain. Add strained mixture to hot oil (with browned onion). Simmer about 2 to 3-1/2 hours, or until it thickens and has a caramelized aroma. Rectify the seasoning, being careful not to over salt. Add parsley, shredded fish, boiled potatoes, olives and chilies gueros, with a little chili juice. Simmer 1 hour.

To serve, garnish with pimiento, chilies gueros, olives and parsley. This dish is even more delicious reheated.

Serves 8-12.

Casa U-Betcha

2212 - 1st Avenue, Seattle. Phone 441-1026. Open for lunch Monday through Friday, 11:30 A.M. to 2:30 P.M.; open for dinner every day, 5:00 to 10:00 P.M.

The recipient of numerous awards and great reviews, Casa U-Betcha quickly became a favorite hangout for Seattleites who favor lively, high-energy haunts. But wait! The food's great, too. Head chef (and, as her co-workers refer to her, "true soul mama") Lisa Esposito has brought creativity and flair to Casa's Mexican menu, with Caribbean, Spanish, and other influences spicing things up.

• •

Ceviche del Cabo

2 pounds fresh rock shrimp
2 cups plus 3 tablespoons fresh
    lime juice
1 cup Salsa Fresca (recipe
    follows)
1/4 cup tomato purée
1/2 cup minced, pickled
    jalapeño peppers
1 bunch of cilantro, chopped
1-1/2 tablespoons sugar
1/2 tablespoon salt
1/2 tablespoon black pepper
1/4 cup Quervo Gold tequila
Baby greens with pickled
    vegetables, Roma tomato
    slices and lots of fresh
    cilantro sprigs
Lime wedges

Marinate shrimp in 2 cups lime juice, stirring regularly to "cook" shrimp. After about 4 hours, or when shrimp are opaque, drain off the lime juice and discard. Set shrimp aside.

Combine remaining 3 tablespoons of lime juice, Salsa Fresca, tomato purée, jalapeños, cilantro, sugar, salt, pepper and tequila in large work bowl. Stir in the shrimp.

Serve immediately or chill until ready to use. Present on bed of mixed greens garnished with lime wedges, accompanied by fried flour tortilla chips.

Serves 6-8.

SALSA FRESCA:
6 Roma tomatoes, chopped
1/2 white onion, finely diced
1/2 bunch of cilantro, chopped
Juice of 2 limes
2 serrano chilies, minced
2 tablespoons salt
1 tablespoon olive oil

Combine all ingredients.

• •

Poblano Relleno en Nogada
(Savory Pork Stuffed Chilies in Walnut Sauce)

6 fresh poblano chilies, medium
    to large size
2 pounds ground pork
1/2 cup almonds
1 large white onion, diced
1 teaspoon ground cloves
6 allspice berries, ground
2 teaspoons salt
3 tablespoons sugar
1 tablespoon ground coriander
1 tablespoon ground cumin
1 teaspoon ground nutmeg
2/3 cup currants, plumped in
    hot water at least 20 minutes
1 cup Salsa Fresca (see
    Ceviche Del Cabo recipe
    above)
Flour
Batter (recipe follows)
Oil
Walnut Sauce (recipe follows)
Pomegranate seeds
Italian parsley

Roast chilies by putting them on a sheet pan and placing directly under the broiler. When black and blistering all over, place in a bowl and cover with a towel.

In a large sauce pan, cook pork on medium heat. As meat begins to cook, add almonds, onion and spices. Add the drained currants. Once the pork is cooked, remove from heat. Drain off fat. Add the Salsa Fresca. Allow to cool.

Take the chilies one at a time. Pull skin off, wetting hands to remove the skin. After skin is removed, very carefully make a small incision with a knife to remove the seeds from inside the chilies. Fill each chili with the pork stuffing, being careful not to split the chili open too much as this will make it more difficult to fry. When all chilies are stuffed, roll lightly in flour.

In a large skillet, heat enough oil to fill pan about 1 inch deep. Heat to medium low temperature. Place the chilies one at a time into the batter and then into the oil. Fry until golden brown, turning to cook all the batter. Remove and drain on paper towels.

To serve, place each chili on individual serving plate. Pour the Walnut Sauce across each chili so that the top and bottom are exposed under the sauce. Sprinkle with pomegranate seeds and arrange Italian parsley leaves around the chili.

Serves 6.

(recipe continued on next page)

Poblano Relleno en Nogada (continued)

WALNUT SAUCE:
4 cups walnuts
3 cups sliced almonds
14 ounces cream cheese
5 ounces goat cheese
3 ounces quesco cotija
2 cups heavy cream
1 cup half and half
2 cups milk
2 tablespoons chopped white
   onion
3/4 tablespoon ground
   cinnamon
1/2 cup brandy
1 tablespoon sugar
1 teaspoon salt

Grind walnuts and almonds in
food processor. Add remaining
ingredients. Transfer mixture,
which will be very thick, to a
blender. Blend to fine texture.
Refrigerate until ready to use.

BATTER:
2 cups beer, any generic beer
   will do
2 eggs
2-1/4 cups flour
1/2 tablespoon baking powder
1 tablespoon salt
1 tablespoon sugar
1 tablespoon chili powder

Combine wet and dry
ingredients separately. Add the
wet to the dry. Mix well.

• •

Mayas Restaurant

9447 Rainier Avenue South, Seattle.   Phone 725-5510.   Open Sunday through Wednesday, 11:00 A.M. to 10:00 P.M.; Thursday through Saturday, 11:00 A.M. to 11:00 P.M.

Mayas has earned a place on the list of Seattle's favorite Mexican restaurants. There is no pretense here; just good food from south of the border, at affordable prices.

• •

Fajitas

1 jalapeño pepper, minced
2 cloves of garlic, minced
1/2 cup olive oil
Juice of 3 limes
1/2 onion, minced
1/2 bunch of cilantro, minced
1/2 bottle of beer, optional
4 teaspoons soy sauce
1/2 teaspoon salt
1/2 teaspoon black pepper
1/4 teaspoon ground cumin
2 pounds beef skirt steak or
    chicken breast

Combine the first 11 ingredients in a blender and process until smooth. Pour over beef or chicken and marinate at least 4 hours or overnight if possible.

Drain and cook meat or poultry in favorite fajita style.

Serves 4.

• •

Cafe Vizcaya

2202 North 45th Street, Seattle. Phone 547-7772. Open Sunday through Thursday, 5:00 to 10:00 P.M.; Friday and Saturday, 5:00 to 11:00 P.M.

Cafe Vizcaya reflects its owner: authentic, Spanish and Cuban. Born in Cuba, Barbara Soltero lived in Spain before coming to this country and bringing with her skills in the cuisines of both. Cafe Vizcaya is unique and has received rave reviews since opening two years ago. On Fridays and Saturdays, traditionalists will find paella, a rice dish that is a standard in Spain.   Also offered is an extensive list of Spanish tapas: smaller, appetizer-sized portions, giving the diner an opportunity to sample many different flavors and textures. Cuban cuisine borrows from Spanish, French and African techniques, and various specialties are offered. Some have a unique twist, like the sweet potato fries, with a papaya and tomatillo salsa.

• •

Bacalo a la Vizcaya

2 cups heavy cream
Salt and pepper, to taste
1 teaspoon granulated garlic
1 medium onion, sliced
1 medium bell pepper, sliced
1 tablespoon capers
1 tablespoon minced cilantro
1 tablespoon minced garlic
1/2 cup olive oil
4 7-ounce black cod filets,
    marinated in lemon juice,
    salt and pepper
5 small red potatoes, sliced 1/4
    inch thick

Combine cream, salt, pepper and granulated garlic. Reduce sauce. In a separate pan, sauté onion, bell pepper, capers, cilantro, and minced garlic in olive oil. Add to cream sauce.

Bake cod at 350° for 20 minutes, or until done.

In a frying pan with olive oil, fry red potatoes until done, or light golden brown.

When ready to serve dinner, place cod over fried red potatoes. Pour cream sauce over the top. Serve with steamed white rice and black beans.

Serves 4.

• •

Pollo Romero

Juice of 4-6 lemons
1 teaspoon black pepper
6 tablespoons soy sauce
2 tablespoons fresh crushed
    garlic
1 tablespoon granulated garlic
1-2 tablespoons whole rosemary
2 tablespoons olive oil
4 7-ounce boneless, skinless
    chicken breasts

Combine lemon juice, pepper, soy sauce, garlic, rosemary and oil. Add chicken breasts. Marinate 1-2 hours.

Bake at 350° for 20-30 minutes, or until done and golden brown.

Serve with wild rice and red roasted potatotes.

Owner Soltero suggests that this marinade is also great with chicken wings for parties!

Serves 4.

Cafe Los Gatos

6411 Latona Avenue N.E., Seattle. Phone 527-9765. Open Tuesday through Thursday, 5:00 to 9:00 P.M.; Friday and Saturday, 5:00 to 10:00 P.M.; closed Sunday and Monday, and the first Tuesday of each month.

One thing that repeat customers can count on at Cafe Los Gatos is change: co-owners Yolanda Gradi and Peter Brickman change the menu monthly (the closure on the first Tuesday of the month is for that reason), so there is always something new and interesting to tempt you. The meals are home style, healthy and low fat (not always the case with Mexican restaurants), and the aromas and flavors are delightful.

• •

Pescado en Perejil
(Fish in Parsley Sauce)

2 tablespoons olive oil
1/2 medium onion, chopped
1 large clove of garlic, chopped
1 large bunch of parsley, leaves
    only, chopped
1 heaping teaspoon chopped,
    dried tarragon leaves
1/2 teaspoon cumin powder
1 small can chopped green chilies
1/2 cup chopped cilantro
1/2 teaspoon chopped green
    peppercorns
1/2-1 teaspoon chopped,
    pickled jalapeño pepper
Juice of 1 lemon
Grated zest of the lemon
1-1/2 cups white wine
Firm textured fish filets or
    chunks (rock fish,
    roughy, salmon - all are
    complemented by this sauce)
Sprigs of parsley
Lemon wedges

Heat oil and sauté the onion and garlic until soft.

Add all the remaining ingredients except the fish, parsley and lemon wedges. Simmer, covered, for 30-40 minutes. Add more wine or fish stock as needed. Cool enough to purée in food processor. Set aside.

Place fish in a glass baking dish. Cover with sauce and bake, adding butter if desired. Or, poach in the sauce until done. Or, drizzle the hot sauce over grilled fish. Or, place sautéed fish filets on a puddle of sauce on a hot plate.

Serve with rice and garnish with sprigs of parsley and lemon wedges.

Serves 4-6.

• •

Chancho Ado Bado

ONE DAY AHEAD (OR EARLY IN THE DAY):
2-3 pounds very lean pork butt
Black pepper
Paprika
Ground cumin
1-1/2 cups white wine
1/4 cup cider vinegar
2-3 sweet potatoes

Cube the pork. Place in a roasting pan and sprinkle liberally with black pepper, paprika and ground cumin. Roast at 500° 1/2 hour, or until meat is browned. Reduce heat to 375°. Add the wine and vinegar and cover tightly. Cook 1 hour. Remove meat from the liquid and cool. Cool the liquid and refrigerate. Remove all the fat that forms when the liquid is cold. Reserve liquid to make stock.

Peel and cube the sweet potatoes. Steam or boil until tender but not mushy. Cool and refrigerate.

ON THE DAY OF SERVING:
2 tablespoons olive oil
1 medium onion, chopped
3 cloves of garlic, chopped
1 small can frozen orange juice concentrate
1/4 cup lemon juice
1/2 cup cider vinegar
1 teaspoon ground annatto seeds
1 teaspoon ground cumin
1/2 teaspoon salt
Pinch of ground cloves
1-2 dashes habanera chili sauce, optional
2 teaspoons tapioca starch or arrowroot, dissolved in 1/4 cup water
Orange slices
Sprigs of cilantro

Heat oil and sauté the onion and garlic until soft. Add the reserved meat juices to the pan along with the orange juice concentrate, lemon juice, vinegar, annatto seeds, cumin, salt, cloves and chili sauce. Cover and simmer 1/2 hour. Add the tapioca starch and simmer until thickened.

Add the pork cubes and cook for 1/2 hour. Stir in the sweet potato chunks just before serving. Warm them in the sauce.

Serve with steamed rice and black beans.

Garnish with fresh orange slices and cilantro sprigs.

Note: Cafe Los Gatos suggests that this Peruvian recipe is well worth the time and effort spent to prepare it. If the meat and sweet potatoes are cooked the day before, it is actually very easy on the day of the dinner.

Serves 4.

Appendix

Glossary

A Brief Look At Some Words and Phrases

• •

AL DENTE
Translated, this Italian phrase means "to the tooth." When properly cooked, it is said that pasta should present a little resistance when bitten into; it should be chewy, not mushy.

ALL-PURPOSE FLOUR
This blend of hard wheats or soft wheats or both is generally enriched and is more coarsely milled than cake flour.

ALLSPICE
Also known as "Jamaican Pepper." Don't mistake these sun-dried, dark, reddish-brown seeds of the pimento tree for peppercorns. Their flavor is truly a sensuous blend of nutmeg, cinnamon and cloves, summing up the best of all three.

ANCHO CHILIES
These mild, richly-flavored dark chilies are often sold in a dried state.

ANCHOVY
This small silvery fish is first packed in salt for several months until the flesh is cured to a deep red, then packed in oil and canned, either as filets or in rolls or as paste.

ANDOUILLE SAUSAGES
Have a glass of water handy! This smoked pure-pork product with its grind of ham and pork is hot and spicy, with lingering tastes of chilies and cayenne pepper. These may be the most popular of Cajun sausages.

ANGELHAIR PASTA
Also known as "Capelli D'Angelo." This is the thinnest of pastas.

ANNATTO SEEDS
Also known as "Achiote." This native of the West Indies and the tropical Americas with orangey-red seeds offers color and a touch of pepperiness to fish dishes, stews and soups as well as cheeses.

ARBORIO RICE
This medium grain rice grows in Italy and is favored for making risotto because it cooks up firm to the bite.

ARROWROOT
Used as a thickening agent, this powder is made from the starchy root of a tropical plant with large leaves and white flowers.

ARUGULA
Also known as "Rocket." Add this aromatic salad item when looking for a peppery, piquant taste.

ASIAGO CHEESE
Semi-soft when young, this cheese becomes firmer and more aggressive in age. Recognize it by its light yellow color and slightly grainy texture.

ASIAN CHILI PASTE
This potent combination of hot peppers, salt and garlic with its enormous jolt of flavors will keep indefinitely in the refrigerator.

BALSAMIC VINEGAR
Time is the companion of the authentic balsamic vinegar. The boiled-down must of white Trebbiano grapes is aged, perhaps as long as decades, in a series of wooden barrels, until the vinegar is thick, velvety and highly aromatic.

BAMBOO SHOOTS
When the shoots of bamboo are about 8 inches high, they are cut and ready for use in cooking. The green outer part is removed and the inside is boiled in salted water. You'll discover this crunchy, creamy-colored vegetable either in cans or fresh.

BASIL
This strong, sweet-scented herb with a triumphant taste probably originated in India but today is closely linked with dishes from Italy, where it may be preserved in olive oil for export.

BASMATI RICE
A type of aromatic rice, the name of which means "Queen of Fragrance," this form of rice has a long, slender shape which elongates in cooking rather than expanding in width. The highest quality basmati rice will be aged up to 2 years, therefore reserving it for special occasion dishes.

BAY LEAVES
Although the plant bears yellow flowers in the spring and blue-black berries, it is the leaves that are cherished for their robust, full flavor. These strongly aromatic leaves are indispensable in many cuisines.

BEAN CURD
Also known as "Tofu." Made of puréed, high-protein soybeans and usually sold in a cake-like form, this item is characteristically smooth and creamy. Think of tofu as somewhat bland until prepared, when it passionately takes on the flavors of the other ingredients.

BELGIAN ENDIVE
This member of the escarole family possesses white, straight leaves which are closely bound together to form an oblong head. It offers a touch of bitterness to the dish.

BERBERE
This Ethiopian red pepper is not generally available in the United States. Your best bet is to purchase directly from Kokeb Restaurant which is able to import it from time to time.

BEURRE MANIE
In French cooking, this is butter that is kneaded with an equal quantity of flour, or (less frequently) potato starch or cornstarch, and used as a thickening agent. Be sure to blend into a smooth paste so that the mixture will be quickly absorbed into the sauce.

BLACK BEAN SAUCE

Fermented black beans, peppers, oil, salted mustard greens, prepared radish, soy sauce, sugar, garlic, and orange peel are some of the items you might find in this far from trivial sauce.

BLACK BEANS

Also known as "Turtle Beans." Soups, casseroles and purées are favorite uses for these small, kidney-shaped beans with a mealy texture and earthy tones.

BLACK FUNGUS

Also known as "Cloud Ears" and "Tree Ears." You'll easily spot these dark colored, meaty fungi for sale in their dried form.

BONITO

Bonito (a type of tuna) filets are slowly and thoroughly dried, taking on a slight tinge of green. The filets may be sold as is for the home chef to flake, or already formed into flakes (which curl and move when rehydrated, almost looking alive), or in a powder form for convenient use in soups and liquids.

BROCCOLI RABE

These green, ragged-edged leaves on green stems pack an intense flavor of broccoli with slightly hot tones.

BUCATINI PASTA

Yes, this pasta may look like spaghetti noodles at first glance, but examine it closer. There's a small diameter hole running through the middle of the noodles, top to bottom.

BULGUR

Also known as "Cracked Wheat." This treated grain, which includes the wheat germ, has been cooked, then dried, resulting in the cracking. Available in both fine and coarse grind, it lends a nutty-texture to the dish.

CAKE FLOUR

Selected soft wheats, milled so as to elicit a very fine powder, are reserved for this type of flour.

CALAMARI

Also known as "Calamary" and "Squid."

CAPERS

Tiny, olive-green buds of a bush native to the Mediterranean region are pickled in vinegar or preserved in a brine to provide a sour, but zesty flavored product. You'll encounter them in sauces, in meat dishes and as garnishes.

CARAWAY

With a sweet, fragrant flavor reminiscent of anise, these light to dark brown seeds are an important addition to many German, Austrian and eastern European cuisines, where the plant grows both wild and cultivated.

CARDAMOM

A perennial plant of the ginger family native to India, the plump, three-sided seed pods contain small, black or dark brown, very fragrant seeds. These seeds are a component of garam masala. Commercially ground cardamom can be less flavorful, as it may contain both the pod and the aromatic seeds.

CASCIOPPO SAUSAGE

Packaged in links, this non-fennel, mild, somewhat sweet sausage is spicier than American sausage but milder than many Italian sausages.

CAULDRON

This large, deep kettle or boiler was originally made of cast iron or copper with detachable handle and traditionally hung in the fireplace when soups and stews were to be made.

CAYENNE PEPPER

This is a blend of pungent small, fiery chilies and may differ from other chili powders due to its fine grind. Use care and restraint when indulging in this memorable seasoning.

CHAMPIGNON MUSHROOMS

Simply, "champignon" means "mushroom" in French. Feel free to use the usual white button mushroom so readily available, or indulge your food fantasies and substitute a more exotic species.

CHANTERELLE MUSHROOMS

An apricot aroma and a yellow, trumpet-shaped body distinguish this popular fungus found in conifer forests.

CHEDDAR CHEESE

This firm, buttery-textured cheese made from whole cow's milk has a nutty flavor and golden rich color.

CHEEHOU SAUCE

Blend sugar, vinegar, soybeans, garlic, sesame seeds and chilies, and you'll have the basis of this rich, brown sauce with its amalgam of flavors.

CHERVIL

Looking something like a cross between Italian and curly parsley, this annual has a dainty and fresh, although spicy, flavor. Some liken its properties to tarragon.

CHESTNUTS

The fruit of the majestic chestnut tree, prospering in southern Europe, north Africa and the Middle East, is available fresh in the winter months, encased in a heavy, hard, shiny brown shell, or all year long in its dried or canned state. Cooking renders the nut edible.

CHILI OIL

Use this authoritative oil towards the end of the cooking process and sparingly because it has been infused with hot chilies.

CHINESE PARSLEY
See Coriander.

CHINKIANG VINEGAR

Water, glutinous rice and salt synthesize to make this vinegar a standout.

CILANTRO
See Coriander.

CINNAMON STICKS
These are curled, paper-thin slices of the inner bark of a cultivated laurel-like tree. Although native to Sri Lanka and legendary as a spice, this item has become a staple of many cuisines, enhancing desserts, drinks, and meat dishes alike.

CLARIFIED BUTTER
To clarify butter is to remove the impurities. Butter is melted in a pan over very low heat. As foam forms on the surface, it is skimmed off. The resulting clear yellow liquid is then strained and used while the milky residue in the bottom of the cooking pan is discarded.

CLOVES
Starting out as the pink, unopened flower bud of an evergreen tropical tree, cloves turn a red-brown when dried. Save this strongly aromatic seasoning for sweet and savory dishes and sauces.

COCONUT MILK
This amenable liquid is made from the coconut flesh.

CODFISH
Also known as "Salt Cod." Soak this salt-cured fish before preparing in a dish.

CORIANDER
Also known as "Chinese Parsley." An annual native to the Mediterranean region and a member of the parsley family, its sweet seeds are a primary ingredient in pastas and spice powder mixtures, while its leaves are noteworthy for their clear, medium green color and flat, serrated leaves. The Spanish name for fresh coriander is "Cilantro."

COUSCOUS
There are many versions of this dish. Common to Algeria and Morocco, it's usually made with hard wheat semolina, less frequently with rice, corn or barley.

CREAM SHERRY
This smooth, sweet sherry is characterized by a sugar level of about 12-14% and an alcohol level of about 19%.

CRÈME FRAÎCHE
This French heavy cream, which is thicker than American cream, is formed from cow's milk. Lactic bacteria culture is added and allowed to mature so that the liquid develops a slightly nutty, distinctively sharp flavor without any residual bitterness.

CREOLE-STYLE SAUSAGES
See Andouille Sausages.

CRYSANTHEMUM LEAVES
These fingery leaves have a flowery, perfumey, slightly sweet and salty flavor with a tenderness similar to spinach.

CUMIN
The ground seeds of this member of the parsley family native to the Mediterranean region typically flavor Asian curry powders and spice blends. The warm, balsamic flavors are also found in Indian and Latin American dishes.

CURRANTS

Generally, these are small, blackish, seedless grapes that are grown primarily in Greece and dried for export. Less commonly, however, currants are the small, red, plump berries borne on a deciduous shrub.

CURRY

While curry blends vary greatly, this seasoning of Indian origins frequently embraces cumin, coriander, fenugreek, turmeric, ginger, pepper, dill, mace, cloves and cardamom. Different blends, of course, vastly impact the flavor and aroma of the resulting dish. Look for it in mild, hot and very hot versions.

CUTLET

From the French, the word commonly means a cross-sectional cut of meat or a similar shape of another item. Originally, it was reserved to mean a small slice from the neck.

DASHI

One of the basic ingredients of traditional Japanese cuisine, this all-purpose stock is prepared from dried bonito shavings and kelp, imparting a delicate smoky-sea undercurrent to foods.

DE-BEARDED

Prepare mussels by scraping off barnacles and scrubbing. Then, with a sharp knife, remove the "byssus" or beard clinging to the mussel.

DEGLAZE

This is the practice of adding wine, stock or other liquids to a cooking pan in order to create a sauce. The resulting liquid takes on both the color and the flavor of the original pan contents.

DEMI GLAZE

This French sauce often combines classical French sauce espagnole and French brown stock in equal portions. At times, Madeira, sherry or other wines may be introduced to lend additional undertones.

DIJON MUSTARD

Pale yellow in color, this commodity is traditionally made from husked and ground nigra seeds, then blended with wine, salt and spices to produce a sharp flavor which can vary from mild to hot.

ENOKI MUSHROOMS

These clusters of fungi, with off-white, slender, long stems topped with tiny caps, are often sold still clinging to the growing medium. You'll enjoy their surprising crunch and delicate flavor.

FENNEL

The seeds of this member of the parsley family populate Asian spice blends. The plant itself is noteworthy for its sweet, succulent flavors. Some consider this graceful perennial to be an appetite stimulant.

FENUGREEK

When separated from the pod, these small, yellowish-brown, very hard and pungent seeds are lightly roasted before becoming a basic ingredient in curries. Use moderately because fenugreek can quickly overwhelm the dish.

FETA CHEESE
This most commonly produced of Greek cheeses is traditionally made from goat's milk, although cow's milk is increasingly being employed. When fresh, the cheese has no rind and the paste is quite soft with occasional holes. A harder cheese is produced when it is allowed to mature 2-3 months. The name comes from the fact that it historically was cut into large blocks or slices and stored in barrels of brine.

FETTUCINE
This classical noodle, often associated with butter/cream sauces, is in the form of long, narrow ribbons, about 1/8 inch in width.

FILBERTS
See Hazelnuts.

FILLO DOUGH
These paper-thin sheets of rich dough are usually found in the frozen food case. Thaw completely before using and keep covered with a damp towel or clear plastic film during the preparation process so that the sheets will not dry out.

FINN POTATOES
The deepest colored of the yellow-fleshed potatoes, this variety is a good baker.

FISH SAUCE
Also known as "Southeast Asian Fish Sauce." Made from a mixture of salt and fresh shrimp or fish that is allowed to ferment up to 6 months, this thin, brown liquid claims to be the cornerstone of southeast Asian cooking, although the flavor may differ somewhat from region to region.

FISH STOCK
See Fumet.

FIVE-SPICE POWDER
Star anise, fennel, cinnamon, cloves and Szechwan pepper populate this essential, but very strong flavored, Chinese blend.

FRANGELICO
This Italian liqueur mesmerizes with its hazelnut flavors.

FRENCH-CUT
When the meat is scraped away from the end of the bones on a rack of lamb, it is referred to as a French-cut rack of lamb.

FUMET
Also known as "Fish Stock." Enlist this strong liquid to thicken and to flavor soups and sauces. It's the strained product of boiling together fish trimmings and seasonings in red or white wine or other liquids.

GALANGAL
Important in southeast Asian cooking, this root offers a ginger-like spiciness, but with the added bonus of a peppery imprint. Some compare its color and taste to saffron.

GARAM MASALA
This aromatic Indian blend of spices usually features black cardamom, cinnamon, black peppercorns, cumin and cloves. For best effect, add near the end of the cooking time or sprinkle a little on the dish just before serving for added panache.

GARBANZO BEANS
Also known as "Chickpeas." These rounded legumes are featured predominately in Mediterranean and Middle Eastern dishes.

GARLIC SAUCE
How convenient - garlic pounded and mashed and ready to use.

GHEE
This clarified butter-type product, typically used in Indian dishes, is made from butter or vegetable oils. It is said to have an advantage over other products because it neither burns nor browns during the cooking process. The most prized ghee is made from buffalo milk; perhaps one of the least desirable is from sesame oil. *See* Clarified Butter.

GINGER ROOT
This perennial, brown-colored rhizome has a rich, very pungent fragrance, characterized by a clean, hot aftertaste. It's available in many forms: sliced, minced, crushed, juiced. Select fresh young roots for a more delicate flavor and less fiber. Be sure to store in the refrigerator.

GORGONZOLA CHEESE
Named for a town outside of Milan, this semi-soft cow's milk Italian cheese is drier than blue cheese. Light tan in color on the outside, the cheese is yellow inside with marblings of blue-green mold. Its aroma and flavor vary from mellow to strong or sharp depending on maturity. Think of it as a classic dessert table cheese and as an appetizer cheese as well as a sauce seasoner.

GRANNY SMITH APPLE
Bright green and waxy with a firm, crisp, juicy flesh, this apple is sought out for eating as well as for cooking into jams and chutneys.

GRAPE LEAVES
You'll most often find the leaves of the grapevine packed in jars in brine. Or, pick your own leaves and freeze or can for future use.

GRAPPA
This strong brandy with its explosive taste is distilled from juices extracted from the skin and other residue which are left behind after the pressing of wine grapes.

GRATIN
The French meaning of this term is the crust formed on top of a food by the heat of an oven or broiler. Therefore, it is the name given to dishes prepared in this manner, such as gratin of potatoes.

GREEK OREGANO
Delicate in fragrance and in taste but certainly not soulless, this perennial member of the mint family is a native to the Mediterranean region, growing as a shrub on hillsides.

GREEN PEPPERCORNS
These immature berries of a tropical vine native to India are mild tasting. Packaged freeze-dried, they are almost hollow with a brittle shell. Canned in brine, they are tender to the bite.

HABANERA CHILI SAUCE
Don't be caught napping with this tangy sauce! It's based on habanera chilies, considered the hottest of them all. When fully ripe, they have turned a golden shade of orange and are wrinkled in appearance. They are slightly smaller than a jalapeño pepper in size.

HAZELNUTS
Also known as "Filbert," which is a variety of large cultivated hazelnut. There are many varieties of the trees growing these nuts, ranging from the Middle East to North America. The nuts enliven preparations as varied as desserts to meat dishes and sauces.

HERBS DE PROVINCE
This fragrant blend is commonly a swirling of basil, oregano, marjoram, tarragon, thyme, savory, bay, fennel, sage, and rosemary.

HOISIN SAUCE
A combination of soybeans, garlic, chili peppers and several spices, this congenial Chinese sauce is deep reddish-brown in color and has a medium thick texture.

HUNGARIAN PAPRIKA
See Paprika.

ITALIAN HERB BLEND
Buy packaged off the grocery shelf or make your own by combining such representative Italian seasonings as marjoram, thyme, rosemary, savory, sage, oregano and basil.

ITALIAN PARSLEY
This flat-leafed parsley is considered to be superior to the more decorative curly variety of parsley, being distinguished by a more full-bodied, sweeter and yet more delicate flavor.

ITALIAN SAUSAGE
Coriander seeds, fennel seeds, garlic, salt and pepper traditionally flavor this dependable variety of sausage.

JACK CHEESE
Also known as "Monterey Cheese." This semi-hard cheese made from cow's milk has a thin rind, creamy yellow interior and can be portrayed as somewhat bland and buttery.

JALAPEÑO PEPPERS
These thick-fleshed, cylindrical, medium-hot peppers are marked by a dark green flesh, which is sometimes highlighted with tinges of orange.

KAFFIR LIME
The very aromatic leaves of this citrus family member are a common ingredient in Thai soups and dishes.

KAHLUA
This Mexican liqueur presents a sweet, voluminous coffee flavor.

KALAMATA OLIVES
Also known as "Greek Olives" and "Calamata Olives." These olives, sharing the name of a Greek town, are brine-cured.

KILO
This European measure (short for "kilogram" and abbreviated "kg" or "k") converts to 2 pounds and 2 ounces.

KOSHER SALT
This pure product, produced under rabbinical supervision, is recognized for its large, coarse, flaky crystals that dissolve less readily than common table salt.

KUMQUATS
About the size of a large olive, this tiny, bite-sized citrus fruit can be comfortably eaten, rind and all, thanks to its pleasantly snappy flavor. The sweet rind and tart flesh mingle to suggest an orange-like sensation on the tongue.

LEEKS
A more controlled flavor sets the leek apart from the onion. It is best described as having a bulbous bottom and stem which is clothed in leaves to form a cylindrical shaft. Wash this vegetable carefully for dirt tends to hide in its firm leaves.

LEMON GRASS
The bottom of the stalk of this tall plant is oftentimes called upon to impart a strong lemon flavor to Asian spice blends and dishes.

LENTILS
These are the small, rounded, flat seeds from a pod growing on a small annual plant. Considered to be a staple in Middle Eastern and Asian areas, this very nutritious legume, with its 24% protein content, comes in many varieties.

LILY BUDS
Also known as "Golden Needles." Soak these dried, pale golden-brown strips in warm water and cut off the tough ends before using. Usually about 2 inches in length, they are most evident in Chinese dishes.

LINGUINI
You can easily describe this pasta by noting its thin, flat shape and eggless formula.

LONG GRAIN RICE
This form of rice is 3 or more times as long as it is wide and is higher in starch than the short or medium grain rices. It's distinguished by grains that have cooked up separately and fluffy.

LONGAN
Also known as "Dragon's Eye." Native to India, enjoy the transparent flesh tucked inside a smooth brown shell as you might a litchi, although the flavor is less pronounced than the litchi. The season is short, usually fruiting during the months of July and August.

LOX
Salmon is cured in brown sugar and salt for several days, then placed in a strong brine solution for several more days, then soaked and rinsed in cold water, and finally smoked for a couple of days to produce a moist, rich and distinctive-tasting product, deep red in color.

MACE
The outer coating of the nutmeg, a peach-like fruit, this spice has a seductive sweetness with a little more bloom than nutmeg.

MAGGI
Use a moderate touch with this concentrated thin brown liquid seasoning, which offers both a gentle color and saltiness to preparations.

MALT SYRUP
To manufacture this item, powdered malt is soaked in water, filtered and then finally evaporated into a brown, sticky syrup.

MANGO
This elliptical-shaped fruit may be as common in the tropics as the apple is in more temperate climates. The flesh is juicy with a peach-like, intense flavor accompanied by resinous overtones and tender fibers that embrace a single flat pit. The skin color varies from red-green to yellow-green.

MANILA CLAMS
Also known as "Asari" and "Japanese littleneck." Considered to be the most tender of the Western clams, many enjoy this seafood on the half shell.

MARJORAM
A perennial member of the mint family, this understated herb is native to Portugal and brings an aromatic, mellow quality to many dishes.

MARSALA
This brownish colored, fortified dessert wine originated in Sicily. Look for this full-flavored beverage in dry to sweet renditions.

MASCARPONE CHEESE
This Italian version of cream cheese is both delicately rich and faintly tart.

MATZOH MEAL
Matzoh is the Jewish unleavened square cracker that is eaten during Passover instead of bread. Matzoh meal is like bread crumbs, only made from matzoh.

MEDALLIONS
Also known as "Tournedos." This word, borrowed from the French language, means that something is cut into a round or oval shape. It's a scallop, usually of meat.

MEDIUM GRAIN RICE
These grains are 2 times as long as they are wide, and they cook up moist and tender with a slight stickiness.

MINT
Variety characterizes this family, which includes apple mint, peppermint, pineapple mint, among others - all of which lend a fresh and clean quality to a preparation. Vietnamese mint is an aromatic herb with long dark green leaves and a particularly biting taste. Spearmint appears to be the popular choice for most cooked dishes.

MIRIN

Also known as "Rice Wine." Eight percent alcohol by volume, super sweet mirin does not need to be refrigerated. Try substituting sweet sherry if this Japanese rice wine is unavailable.

MISO

Cooked, fermented soybeans constitute this Japanese paste. There are many adaptations, running the spectrum from mild to pungent, light to dark in color, and in varying degrees of saltiness.

MONTRACHET CHEESE

This log-shaped, creamy French goat cheese is made in Burgundy and is sometimes dusted with vine or wood ashes.

MOZZARELLA CHEESE

This semi-soft, chewy cheese hails from Italy where it may be made from water buffalo milk. Recognize it by its creamy white color, rectangular or spherical shape, and mild, delicate flavor.

MSG

Monosodium glutamate is the full name of this flavor enhancer. Although it occurs naturally in foods, MSG is said to cause headaches and other adverse reactions in some individuals. Use judiciously.

MUSHROOM SAUCE

Rich, medium thick and brown, this efficient sauce is a perfect addition when a touch of mushroom seasoning is required.

NAM PIK PAO

Also known as "Chilies in Oil." Chilies, onions, garlic, shrimp and sugar make up this very deep colored sauce with its uncompromising flavors.

NAPPA CABBAGE

This cabbage has a compact barrel-shaped head and pale green crinkled leaves that reveal broad, thick white ribs. Appreciate it for its mild and sweet flavors and its juicy, crisp texture.

NITER KIBBEH

This Ethiopian herb butter marries garlic, ginger, fenugreek, and other seasonings, some of which are not generally available in the United States. Contact Kokeb Restaurant if you would like to purchase some butter for home use.

NOVA COLD SMOKED SALMON

Also known as "Nova Scotia-style." This cured fish is commonly understood to be a mildly flavored, less salty type of lox with a light smoke.

NUTMEG

The brown kernel enclosed in a shiny brown seed coat, this exotic spice may be acquired either in its whole form or ground. Savor it for its sweet, nutty flavor and woody scent.

OKONOMIYAKI SAUCE

This medium thick, brown sauce combines onions, carrots, celery, tomatoes, apples, plums, sugar, vinegar and similar seasonings to bring about the perfect accompaniment to Japanese "pancakes" and other foods.

OLIVE OIL

There are many variations in the flavor and color of olive oil. **Extra Virgin** oil is the first cold pressing of the ripe olives and produces a pale yellow oil of very delicate flavor. **Virgin** oil is slightly more acid than extra virgin oil. **Refined** oil is made from pressings done under heat and then refined to remove any unpleasant taste or acidity. **Pure** oil is typically a blend of **Refined** and **Virgin**.

OREGANO

The leaves and tops of this flowering shrub add essential flavorings to Mediterranean and Mexican dishes, varying from full and robust with a bitter pungency when grown in hot, southern climates, to a more delicate flavor when grown as an annual in milder, more northerly locales.

OYSTER MUSHROOMS

This popular fungus is oyster-shaped and ranges from cream to pale gray in color. Discover it in clusters on deciduous trees and stumps throughout the year. Appreciate it for its firm flesh and delicate flavors.

OYSTER SAUCE

Oysters cooked in soy sauce and brine produce this rich, thick gray-brown Chinese sauce, noteworthy for seasoning meats, poultry and seafoods.

PANCETTA

You'll discover that this Italian bacon has a distinctive flavor all its own. Unlike American bacon, pancetta is cured in spices and in salt, never smoked, and is aged a few months before being sold.

PANKO

This Japanese version of bread crumbs offers a light, delicate and especially crunchy coating to fried and breaded foods. It is often formed from wheat flour, sugar, paprika and annetto extract.

PAPAYA

Several strains are available and all are filled with small, peppery flavored black seeds. Solo papaya is distinguished by its somewhat rounded pear shape, tender green to yellow skin which, at times, is mottled with green. Mexican papaya, a seemingly elongated version of the solo papaya, possesses a thicker bright green skin, mottled with yellow. Some consider the Mexican papaya to be the more watery and less flavorful of the two.

PAPRIKA

This ideal food enhancer is made from the dried pods of red bonnet peppers which grow throughout Europe, the best and the sweetest of which are said to grow in Hungary.

PARBOIL

Also known as "Blanch." Simply, this cooking method dictates that the item is dropped into boiling water then plunged into cold water to stop the cooking process. At times, parboiling is done to firm up the food; at other times to set color; and at still other times to aid in peeling off the skin.

PARMESAN CHEESE

A hard grating, granular, brittle body marks this Italian cheese. It is characterized by a light yellow color with black or brown coating, cylindrical shape and a sharp, piquant flavor.

PARMIGIANO REGGIANO
This is probably the most famous of the grana (grainy) cheeses, produced only in a small area of northern Italy and, by law, aged at least one year.

PENNE PASTA
This quill-shaped pasta is actually tubes that have been cut on the diagonal.

PEPPERONCINI
Look for these small red or golden chili peppers with their quick, hot bite packed uncompromisingly in vinegar.

PERNOD
Licorice flavor, the gift of aniseeds, permeates this French liqueur, once thought to be addictive.

PESTO
The Italian word for ground or pounded, pesto originated as a northern Italian sauce comprised of olive oil, garlic, basil, cheese and pine nuts, although today there are as many variations on this formula as there are cooks. Consider using it with pasta, in soups and on vegetables.

PICKLED CHILIES GUEROS
These medium hot yellow chilies with their waxy appearance are often sold in a pickled version.

PICKLED RED GINGER
Also known as "Amasu Shoga." Thinly sliced ginger root is processed in vinegar, sugar, salt and red food coloring to produce a refreshing and purifying taste on the tongue. It is used in Japan to cleanse the palate between courses of sushi, for example.

PINE NUTS
Closely linked to Italian cuisine, these whitish-cream, oblong-shaped nuts hold a hint of pine flavoring, for they are actually removed from between the scales of cones of the Mediterranean stone pine tree.

PINK PEPPERCORNS
Available in both a dried and a pickled form, these peppercorns can be mashed to release their aromatic resinous flavor. Appreciate them for their mild heat and sweet-hot flowery flavor.

POBLANO CHILIES
You'll probably rate these suave dark green chilies between 1 and 5 on a hotness scale of 10 and frequently find them being stuffed due to their elongated bell pepper shape.

POIRE (EAU-DE-VIE)
Literally from the French word for "pear," look for this sensuous pear brandy being sold under the label of the Oregon distillery, Clear Creek.

POLENTA
This coarse ground Italian cornmeal may be thick and porridge-like or molded and sliced. It is a staple of certain northern areas of Italy, especially around Florence and Venice, and was traditionally made with water in a copper pot and stirred with a wooden spoon.

POMEGRANATE SEEDS
The sweet-sour tones of these pinkish seeds of a Mediterranean plant show up in items as diverse as beverages, salads and fritters.

PONZU SAUCE
Basically, add a citrus flavor to soy sauce, and it becomes ponzu sauce.

PORT
This fortified dessert wine from Portugal is most noticeable in England as a beverage and in English cooking where it is valued for its mellow tones.

PORTOBELLO MUSHROOMS
This cultivated, large capped, brown agaricus mushroom with dark gills and white, meaty flesh which bruises pinkish-beige, is usually available fresh. Look for the more mature specimens, which are considered more flavorful.

PRESERVED BLACK BEANS
Also known as "Black Beans" and "Salted Black Beans." Pound for pound these salty soybeans pack an unbeatable flavor punch into fish and pork dishes.

PROSCIUTTO
You'll discover a delicate sweet flavor in this dry, very firm, salt-cured ham from Italy.

PURÉE
When the goal is to have a creamy preparation, purée the cooked items either by pressing and sieving or by using a blender or food processor.

QUESCO COTIJA
This Mexican cheese, which looks and handles much like feta cheese but lacks feta's tangy or tart taste, is made from cow's milk.

RADIATORE PASTA
Literally translated from the Italian, this is the word for "radiator," which the pasta shape resembles. It is stubby, only about 1 inch in length, and tightly spiraled.

RADICCHIO
A bitter, peppery taste marks this variety of endive, which reminds one of a small purple cabbage with white vined leaves. Add to salads for extra pizzazz.

RASPBERRY VINEGAR
Fruit-flavored vinegars are typically combinations of white wine vinegar, fruit and sugar and are best stored in the refrigerator until invited to dress greens and fruits or to unite in marinades.

RED CURRY PASTE
Red chilies, salt, onions, shrimp paste, and lemon juice or lime juice or vinegar - all are pounded together to produce this memorable seasoning.

RED GINGER
This is thinly sliced ginger root which has been packed in a sugar syrup and red food coloring.

RICE NOODLES

These noodles are made from rice and work well with dishes as diverse as soups, salads and stir-fries. There are several variations, ranging from Chinese fresh noodles (sold in square sheets) to Vietnamese bun (puff up dramatically when fried) to Thai sen mee (thin noodles sold in skeins).

RICE PADDY HERB

Also known as "Ngo Om." A light citrus, almost minty flavor permeates these serrated, medium green colored leaves growing on a light green stalk punctuated with tiny purple blossoms.

RICE VINEGAR

The mildest of vinegars, this fragrant, slightly sweet Asian product is made from pressings of fermented rice. Keep it handy for salad dressings or whenever a distinctive vinegar will be appreciated.

RICE WINE

See Mirin and Sake.

RICOTTA CHEESE

Italian in origin, this soft white cheese can be moist and grainy or dry. It is often said to be similar to cream cheese in texture with a bland, but semi-sweet flavor.

RIGATONI PASTA

You'll find this pasta to be flat, ridged macaroni tubes.

RISOTTO

This Italian dish is often characterized by a broth-cooked rice, butter, cheese and bits of meats and/or vegetables. The texture of the rice should be creamy with a flowing consistency.

ROMANO CHEESE

This Italian cheese is hard and granular, with yellowish white interior and greenish black outside. Its flavor is described as sharper and more piquant than Parmesan.

ROQUEFORT CHEESE

Named after a hilly region in the southern part of France, this cheese ripens into a cream-white, rich and buttery paste with even greenish-bluish veins. Connoisseurs consider the inimitable taste of this cheese to be pronounced, but subtle, and with a slight tang.

ROSEMARY

This native of the Mediterranean area brings bold, pungent tones to dishes. The evergreen leaves can be used dried or fresh, and the flowers can be employed as garnishes or crystallized.

ROUX

This mixture of flour and butter, usually in equal proportions, performs as a thickener. A brown roux, which is used in brown sauces, is simply cooked longer than a white roux, which is considered more appropriate for white sauces.

SAFFRON

The dried yellow stigma of a fall-flowering, violet-colored crocus, this spice is reputed to be the world's costliest, with over 200,000 stigmas constituting a pound. Be aware - powdered saffron may be of inferior quality or adulterated. Be conservative - too much saffron may give a rather unpleasant, medicinal flavor to foods.

SAGE

An ancient herb valued for its medicinal and cooking properties, the grayish-green leaves of sage lend a slightly musty and bitter touch to foods. Use with discretion.

SAKE

This Japanese dry rice wine tenderizes meats and fishes and is said to help remove strong odors. Distilled from steamed rice, it ranges from dry to sweet in flavor and sometimes haunts with a bitter aftertaste.

SAKE KASU

The residue from the sake-making process is the basis of this surprisingly powerful paste which can be used as a marinade for fish or added to soups as a seasoning.

SATAY SAUCE

Chilies and peanuts ground into a paste blended with lemon grass, dried shrimp, coconut milk, lemon, sugar and salt form this Indonesian accompaniment to the famous skewered meat grilled over charcoal, saté.

SATÉ CHILI SAUCE PASTE

Here, an additional touch of chilies is added to the traditional formula.

SAUTÉ

This style of cooking insists that the food be cooked in fat or oil in a frying pan or heavy sauce pan until brown.

SCALOPPINE

This is a popular Italian technique of preparing items by trimming, pounding and then quickly cooking for the maximum flavor.

SCHMALTZ

This Jewish item is the rendered fat from a chicken or goose, sometimes used instead of butter or oil in cooking.

SCOTCH BONNET CHILI

This is a local Jamaican chili of potent fieriness and distinctive aroma. Keep an antidote handy!

SEA URCHIN ROE

Typically, 6 to 12 urchins will provide one serving of this 5-branched roe. The female ovaries are generally more egg-like while the male gonad has a finer texture.

SECKEL PEARS

These early to mid-season pears are a very small, very sweet and aromatic variety. The flesh is granular; the shape is roundish to pear-shaped with a yellow-brown appearance.

SERRANO CHILIES

One of the hottest of the peppers, these are dark green in appearance, often being tinged with orange in age, and shorter and thinner than jalapeño peppers. Save these for sauces wielding enormous power!

SESAME OIL

A darker, more aromatic, more flavorful oil than most, made from black or toasted white sesame seeds, it imparts a nut-like taste and tantalizing flavor to a wide range of dishes.

SESAME SEEDS
Available in creamy white, red, brown or black colors, these tiny flat seeds show up in many different cuisines lending a sweet, nutty quality and visual interest to a wide range of dishes.

SHALLOTS
Known for their concentrated onion flavor, but without the bitterness, these highly prized vegetables are grown from bulbs and are available in a variety of sizes and shapes.

SHERRY
Rich and nut-like in flavor with a delicate bouquet, this fortified Spanish wine ranges from dry to sweet, pale to dark amber.

SHIRATAKE NOODLES
See Yam Noodles.

SHITAKE MUSHROOMS
Spot this fungus by looking for its large, bark-colored caps that can be either smooth or bumpy with lighter colored striations. They are favored for their aromatic qualities; their smoky pepperiness is legendary. Be sure to soak dried shitake 30 minutes to 1 hour in warm water before using.

SHORT GRAIN RICE
With the length of these grains less than 2 times the width, they cook up softer and stickier than medium grain rice.

SOFT SHELL CRAB
Also known as "Blue Crab." Although several species can be encountered in this stage, you'll happily discover that the blue crab is sufficiently meaty to be consumed, although it is more commonly chosen as a seasoner and then discarded.

SORREL
The fleshy leaves of this plant lend an unmistakable tart taste to preparations that vary from soups to salads. There are several varieties, ranging from large to small and from dark to pale green leaves.

SOY SAUCE
Fermented soybeans are the basic ingredient in this savory, salty liquid that touches so many Asian recipes. Rich in vitamins, dark brown or light-colored, it comes in a number of versions, including mushroom. Japanese soy sauce is much lighter than the Chinese product and sweet soy sauce is really very sweet, dark and thick. Choose the kind needed to enhance the flavor and to color your special dishes.

SPANISH-ONIONS
These rather sweet onions are considered to be relatively mild, yet full-bodied with a flavor that tends not to overwhelm their preparation.

SPÄTZLE
These small dumplings (made of flour, egg and cream and poached in boiling water) are characteristic of southern German cuisine and are found both as an entrée and as a garnish. The name comes from a word meaning 'little sparrows'.

SPECK
This Italian smoked ham is from Alto Adige.

STAR ANISE
Borne on a tree from the magnolia family, these seed pods (picked before they are ripe) are shaped like an 8-pointed star, with segmented sepals, each containing long, shiny brown seeds. Star anise is often found in Chinese marinades and in Five-Spice Powder.

STINGING NETTLES
This weed can be annoying due to its stinging qualities, but the leaves, picked when the plant is about a foot tall, can make tasty cooked greens or an interesting addition to soups. Be sure to wear gloves when foraging for stinging nettles!

STIR-FRIED
This method originated in China and prompts the chef to cook the ingredients using a very little hot oil in a wok or pan. The items are continuously stirred, allowing them to maintain their shape and crisp texture, in a process not unlike sautéing.

SUN-DRIED TOMATOES
Harvested tomatoes are allowed to slowly dry in the sun, resulting in an intense concentration of fragrance. You'll frequently find them packed in olive oil.

SZECHWAN PEPPERCORNS
These dried berries of an Asian shrub hand over a delicate heat and marked perfume to any dish in which they are involved.

SZECHWAN PICKLED MUSTARD GREENS
Predominately seasoned by a blend of soy sauce, aromatic peppercorns, vinegar and sugar, this item is slightly sweet-tart and an interesting choice to lend character to a dish.

TABASCO SAUCE
Distinctive Louisiana chilies form the backbone of this memorable mix of spirit vinegar and salt. This red liquid is a motherlode of hot! Use it sparingly.

TAHINA
Also known as "Tahineh" and "Tahini." Store this creamy-gray, thin paste of ground sesame seeds in the refrigerator.

TAMARIND
A blend of sweet and sour flavors come from this dark brown fruit of a tropical evergreen. You'll find its distinctive gifts in curries, in chutneys and jams, in drinks, and in various sauces.

TANDOOR
This charcoal-fired clay, cylindrical oven cooks tandoori, a style particular to northern India and Pakistan, which embraces a variety of foods including chicken, fish, and bread.

TARO
The root of this perennial plant is an important staple with a nutty, potato-like texture, shape and flavor while the leaves add color and substance to soups.

TARRAGON

In spite of a name meaning "little dragon" in Latin, this seasoning with its long, thin leaves is valued for its delicate flavors. It combines with other ingredients in a pleasant union.

THAI CHILI PEPPERS

About 1 to 1-1/2 inches in length and thin, these chilies range from a deep, true green in color to red and orange. They are considered to be even hotter than the serrano chilies. Use caution!

THYME

This herb, with its tiny rounded gray-green leaves, lends a sharp, aromatic touch to dishes. It's a basic ingredient of bouquet garni and is a noteworthy addition to oils and vinegars as well as meat and vegetable dishes.

TOFU

See Bean Curd.

TOM YUM PASTE

An instant sour shrimp paste, this item combines chilies, galanga, lemon grass, citrus, oil, salt and sugar to make a unique contribution to both the Asian grocery shelf and the home kitchen.

TONKATSU SAUCE

This rich brown mixture of various vegetables and fruits (apples, carrots, tomatoes, onions, etc.) is mellowed with the addition of sugar, vinegar and other seasonings to bring out the best in Japanese "pancakes" and cutlets.

TORTELLINI

Meat, cheese and/or vegetable fillings define these rings of thinly rolled pasta.

TOURNEDOS

See Medallions.

TUACA

This golden amber Italian liqueur is remarkable for its luxurious hints of orange and vanilla.

TURMERIC

This root belongs to the ginger family. With its brown skin and bright yellow interior, it brings color and flavor to many Indian and Asian dishes, including curries and pickles. Some consider it to have digestive and antiseptic qualities, although you'll want to use it with restraint due to its somewhat medicinal aroma.

TURNIPS

This dried item is actually cut-up turnips that have been preserved with salt. Before using in a dish, separate the turnips, rinse well and soak in warm water about 45 minutes.

UDON NOODLES

These broad, chewy Japanese noodles are made from wheat and often have square edges. While the fresh noodles may be up to 3/16 inch thick, the dried ones may more closely resemble fettucine noodles.

VERMOUTH

An infusion of spices and roots into white wine produces this special beverage which adds an herbal fragrance and rich, smooth taste to various sauces and dishes. It is available in sweet (reddish-brown colored) and dry (clear) versions.

WALLA WALLA SWEET ONIONS

One of a number of the sweeter, milder onion varieties possessing more sugars and less sulfur-containing compounds than other onions, Walla Walla sweets are usually available only from late spring through August. Store these delicate onions in the refrigerator.

WHIDBEY'S LIQUEUR

Whidbey Island loganberries contribute their flavorful juices and deep red tones to this sweet liqueur made in limited quantities in Washington state.

WORCESTERSHIRE SAUCE

Beloved by the British, this thin, dark colored, essential condiment traditionally combines chilies, shallots, cinnamon, cloves, garlic, nutmeg, cardamom, soy sauce, ketchup and vinegar.

YAM NOODLES

This thin, gelatinous, white noodle-like substance is formed from mountain potato flour and is sold fresh or in cans for use in soups and stir-fries.

YOGURT

Milk is first heated, then cooled and combined with a starter culture to produce a homogenous, velvety texture with no whey separation. The taste is fresh with a mildly acidic quality and delicate aroma.

• •

Guide to Sources
of Ethnic Ingredients

• •

Asia Spices   15920 N.E. 8th, Bellevue   643-0366
Indian and Pakistani ingredients.

Carso's Pasta Co.   2808 - 15th Avenue West, Seattle   283-8227
High quality fresh pasta, all fresh ingredients, organically grown when possible.
Primarily a wholesaler, selling through high quality retail outlets such as QFC
Stores, but happy to refer retail customers to nearest outlet and will, under certain
circumstances, sell direct to the public.

Cerbone's   31229 Pacific Highway S., Federal Way   941-0937
High quality and great variety of produce, often at bargain prices.

Cibo   823 Yale North, Seattle   622-1016
Cheese and pesto specialties.

DeLaurenti's   1435 First Avenue, Seattle   622-0141
            (in the Pike Place Market; also Bellevue)
Wide variety of Italian and French items, as well as excellent cheeses.

Frank & Guy's Meat Market   31205-C Pacific Highway S., Federal Way   839-0722
Excellent source for custom meats and specialty sausages.

Gan-Shan Company   417 - 7th Avenue South, Seattle   682-4466
Asian produce.

Hans' Sausage and Deli   717 S.W. 148th Street, Burien   244-4978
Homemade German sausage, German wines, chocolates; other European specialties.

Harvest Produce Corp.   3519 S.W. 100th Street, Seattle   935-0288
Wild mushrooms, fresh herbs, edible flowers.

Hess's Delicatessen   6108 Mt. Tacoma Drive S.W., Tacoma   584-1451
Good source for German ingredients and spices.

Kokeb Ethiopian Restaurant   926 - 12th Avenue, Seattle   322-0485
Ethiopian specialty ingredients.

La Mexicana Foods   1914 Pike Place, Seattle   441-1147
            (in the Pike Place Market)
All Mexican ingredients, tortillas, tomato products.

Larry's Markets   3725 S. 144th Street, Seattle (just off   246-3663
            Pacific Highway); 6 other area locations
Wide variety of high quality ethnic items.

Pacific Food Importers   1001 - 6th Avenue South, Seattle   682-2002
Like an "outlet store" of ethnic foods - wide selection at very reasonable prices.

Pike Place Market   First and Pike, Seattle   no phone
Produce - especially the small, low stalls, such as Lombrici's and Verdi's.

Puget Consumers Co-op   6504 - 20th N.E., Seattle (and many   525-1450
other locations throughout Seattle area)
A good source for grains, legumes and flours, natural and organic foods.

R & M Spices   5501 University Way N.E., Seattle   526-1973
Indian and Pakistani ingredients.

Star Tofu Mfg. Company   608 S. Weller Street, Seattle   622-6217
Tofu.

The Cake House   620 S. Weller Street, Seattle   223-2766
Asian bakery: buns, tarts, cakes, etc.

The Souk   1916 Pike Place, Seattle   441-1666
(in the Pike Place Market; also Northgate)
Middle Eastern and Indian ingredients; meats and chicken.

Tsue Chong Noodle Co. Store   801 S. King Street, Seattle   623-0801
Chinese noodles, egg roll and wonton wrappers, fortune cookies.

Uwajimaya   6th Ave. So. and S. King St., Seattle;   624-6248
also Bellevue
Perhaps the best known of any Asian foods source, with a wide variety. Japanese
foods, of course, but all other Asian origins as well. Very large selection of
fresh seafoods, produce and meats.

Viet Hoa Market   676 S. Jackson Street, Seattle   621-8499
Southeast Asian foods, good produce section.

Viet Wah Supermarket   1035 S. Jackson Street, Seattle   329-1399
Very large variety of Asian food items, especially fresh fish and produce.
Manager Dien K. Vuu has been especially helpful on our visits there.

Wa Sang   663 S. King Street, Seattle   622-2032
Good variety of Asian ingredients.

Wah Young   719 S. King Street, Seattle   622-2416
Chinese ingredients - dry and packaged goods, rice, spices; primarily a supplier
to restaurants, but also sells retail.

Welcome Supermarket   1200 S. Jackson, Seattle   329-7044
Chinese, Thai and Vietnamese meat, produce, packaged goods, some imported
frozen fish.

Yanni's Lakeside Cafe   7419 Greenwood Avenue N., Seattle   783-6945
Caesar salad dressing.

INDEX

Lines in **boldface** are names of recipes.
Lines in CAPITAL letters are names of restaurants.

• •

Help!

Much of the fun we've had in compiling and writing this book has been derived from the many fascinating people whose paths we've crossed along the way. We've learned from all of them, and couldn't have done it without their help. You can help, too! We'd appreciate any comments you might have regarding *Dining Ethnic Around Puget Sound*, particularly ways in which future editions could be improved. We're looking forward to hearing from you!

Steven and Mary Taylor

• •

Sure, these are great restaurants, but here's a personal favorite of mine:

_____
_____
_____

In the next edition, I'd like to see this book change in the following way(s):

_____
_____
_____
_____

I know someone who'd enjoy a copy of *Dining Ethnic Around Puget Sound*. Here's my check for $19.00 (includes postage, handling and Washington state sales tax). Please mail *Dining Ethnic* to them as soon as possible, and include a gift card reading:

_____
_____

Their name and address is: _____

_____
_____

My name and address is: _____

_____
_____

Please return to:
Poverty Bay Publishing Co.
529 S.W. 294th Street
Federal Way, WA 98023

Thanks!

To Steve and Mary Taylor for attaching their generosity to this fine project. To John Hinterberger and Fred Ferretti for their good words. To Greg Walters for doing his excellent graphic design yet another time, helping Northwest Harvest.

To all who read this book and will have contributed thereby to the provision of food for families, individuals... and especially the children... for whom the life of poverty is not only painful but an injustice that ought not be.

Northwest Harvest charges no fees, requests no tax dollars, and is supported solely by a generous community consisting of individuals, churches, temples, organizations, corporations and foundations. Northwest Harvest would simply not exist were it not for caring people such as you.

Thanks!

NORTHWEST HARVEST / E.M.M.
P. O. Box 12272, Seattle, WA 98102-0272
(206) 625-0755
Toll-Free Statewide outside King County: 1-800-722-6924
FAX; (206) 625-7518